The Women

Archana Garodia Gupta is from New Delhi and holds an MBA from IIM, Ahmedabad. She is an established national quizzer, a 'Champion of Champions' at BBC's *Mastermind India*, and regularly writes articles on history and business for various magazines. She was, until recently, the national president of the FICCI Ladies Organization (FLO), where she set up programmes for the empowerment of Indian women. She is the co-author of *The History of India for Children*, which has been published in two volumes by Hachette India.

The Woman Who Ruled India

[illegible]

the WOMEN WHO RULED INDIA

LEADERS. WARRIORS. ICONS.

ARCHANA GARODIA GUPTA

hachette INDIA

First published in 2019 by Hachette India
(Registered name: Hachette Book Publishing India Pvt. Ltd)
An Hachette UK company
www.hachetteindia.com

2

ISBN 978-93-5195-152-0

Hachette Book Publishing India Pvt. Ltd
4th & 5th Floors, Corporate Centre,
Plot No. 94, Sector 44, Gurugram – 122003, India

Typeset in Chaparral Pro 11/15.5
by Inosoft Systems, Noida

Printed and bound in India by
Manipal Technologies Limited, Manipal

To my mother, Chandra Garodia, and my father,
Balkrishna Garodia, who never imposed roles

Contents

Introduction

Women rulers have been few and far between in Indian history, as also in world history – but that still leaves hundreds of women who have ruled, and whose stories can be told.

I have selected but a few among them to write about. These women have all ruled independently, either as regents or titled rulers. History is replete with tales of women who influenced their husbands or sons, and have been immensely powerful, but I have included only women who ruled directly, and not through agency, with the sole exception of Nur Jahan.

Some of these women are national heroines, and there are innumerable books and legends about them. Some are lesser known, but are celebrated in the folk memory of their region. Records on many are quite sparse. I have used as many disparate sources as possible: contemporary texts, accounts of foreign travellers as well as secondary sources. I have also used legends and folk tales, which, while difficult to verify, offer nuggets of information and help flesh out the person. It has been quite a task to separate the wheat from the chaff.

These portraits are painted 'warts and all'. They are not hagiographies – because these women were not saints. They often made wrong decisions and took on wrong advisors, and sometimes lied and cheated in their quest for power. But they were invariably courageous and intelligent. Above all, they were leaders. We will not hold women leaders up to impossible standards, different from the measures we use for men.

There is a famous (and spectacularly sexist) quote by Samuel Johnson, on the subject of a woman preaching: 'Sir, a woman's preaching is like a dog walking on his hind legs. It is not done well; but you are surprised to find it done at all.' Au contraire, these women are worth knowing and writing about not only because they ruled, but also because they ruled well, in any case at levels comparable to male rulers in a particular period. Ahilya Bai's Indore, for instance, was considered the best governed state in India in the 18th century.

To those who know their stories it will seem amazing that these women actually became rulers – there was no precedent or pathway for them. Women were not given the appropriate education, and their movements and interaction with men was restricted; many were veiled. Even after gaining the throne, they invariably faced stiff resistance internally from their nobles, who could not stomach the thought of being ruled by a woman, and from external rulers, who thought them weak and easy to conquer. Nevertheless, rule they did, with grit and punk.

The women rulers in this book span most of India's ages and regions. A notable exception is ancient India; while there were many women rulers at the time, there is unfortunately very little information available on them. We know about Prabhavati Gupta, the daughter of Chandragupta II Vikramaditya, who ruled the Vakatakas for 20 years in the fourth century only through a couple of copperplates, and about the Indo-Greek queen Agathocleia who ruled in the second century BCE from coins that have been found.

The histories of many more women rulers wait to be told.

The Mahadevis of Odisha

The Bhaumakara Queens

Tribhuvanamahadevi has ascended the lion-seat, like Katyayini
Her lotus-like feet are kissed by the heads of feudatory chiefs, bowed down with devoted loyalty,
She resembles the goddess of fortune,
She delights the people with light taxation, resembling the moon that delights the people with soft rays.
She resembles the lotus-tank, appointing officers with clean hands and pure natures like lotuses.

From the Dhenkanal copperplate
on Tribhuvana Mahadevi I

The tale of the queens of the Bhaumakara dynasty is a remarkable chapter in Indian history. There are few references to them in ancient works of history or literature, except for a brief mention in an Arabic book on world geography, the Hudud-al-Alam. *However, a number of copperplates bearing inscriptions about them have been found during archaeological excavations in Odisha, which have helped reconstruct their fantastic and little-known story. The Bhaumakara dynasty ruled for 200 years, between the eighth and 10th centuries* CE, *mostly in the region of present-day Odisha, and of the more than eighteen rulers of the region who belonged to the dynasty we know that at least six were women.*

The region of Odisha had well-established kingdoms like Kalinga since ancient times, which found mention even in the Mahabharata. In the larger Indian context, it has always been famed for its elephants. The *Hudud-al-Alam* mentions that 'extremely large' and 'the tallest elephants in the country' were found in the region. These were sent to different Indian states by land and water, as well as exported to Sri Lanka in ships. In fact, Odisha had an interesting relationship with Sri Lanka: according to legend, the founder of the Sinhala kingdom, Vijay Singh, migrated from this region to Sri Lanka in around 500 BCE.

Odisha was fragmented into the smaller, independent kingdoms of Odra, Utkala, Kalinga and Toshali, among others, but at certain points in history, the kingdoms would be united under a powerful king, or briefly become part of a Greater Indian empire, like that of Ashoka or Harsha. Odisha's conquest by Ashoka in the third century BCE is immortalized in Buddhist history; tortured by guilt at the death and destruction he had caused, Ashoka went on to promote Buddhism worldwide as a religion of peace and non-violence. For most of its later history Odisha stayed independent, before being conquered by the Mughals in the 16th century.

The region became a major centre of Buddhism. Many large monasteries came up, especially the *mahavihara* (great monastery) in Ratnagiri. The Chinese Buddhist scholar Xuanzang, or Hiuen Tsang, who roamed the length and breadth of India in the seventh century CE, mentions in his travel account that there were about 10,000 monasteries inhabited by as many as 10,000 monks each in the kingdom. According to Sri Lankan legend, one of the Buddha's teeth was enshrined in Odisha as a relic, in a monastery in Dantapuri (modern-day Puri, according to certain scholars). When the kingdom of Kalinga came under attack from the neighbouring king Ksheeradara's sons in the fourth century CE, Kalinga's King Guhashiva sent the tooth away for safekeeping, hidden in his daughter Hemamala's hair. Along with her husband Dantakumar (or 'tooth prince' – clearly eponymous!), she took a ship from Tamralipti to Sri Lanka, where the couple presented the tooth to the overjoyed king of Anuradhapura, Kirti Sri Megavanna. The tooth is now enshrined in Kandy.

In 700 CE, a potpourri of religions thrived in the region: Buddhism in all its variants of Mahayana, Hinayana and Vajrayana, and Hinduism in its own forms, Vaishnavism, Shaktism and Shaivism. Interestingly, it has been documented that different dynasties, kings of the same dynasty, and even husbands and wives, patronized different religions without much conflict. For instance, Subhakara I (c. 790 CE) was a Buddhist while his wife Madhava Devi was a Shaivite.

In the seventh century CE, Harsha of Kannauj conquered Odisha. There is an interesting anecdote from this time that highlights the freedom of expression and the freedom to dissent that was often seen in ancient India. Xuanzang says that when Harsha, who supported the Mahayana sect, visited Odisha, he was greeted by belligerent Hinayana monks who proclaimed, 'We hear that the king has built by the side of the Nalanda University a vihara of brass, a work magnificent and admirable. But why did not Your Majesty construct a Kapalika temple or some other building of that sort?' When asked to clarify what they meant, they said that the Nalanda priests advocating the Mahayana 'sky flower' doctrine were no better than the reviled Kapalika sect! The all-powerful conqueror Harsha, instead of punishing the monks for their *lèse-majesté*, spent time and effort to reason with them; he even asked the head of Nalanda, the most important Buddhist university in India at the time, to send four scholars (including Xuanzang) to debate with the Hinayana monks!

After Harsha's death in 647 CE, Odisha was once again divided into small kingdoms ruled by local dynasties, the Shailodbhava dynasty being the most prominent of them. In the eighth century, Odisha was invaded by Shri Harshadeva, the king of Kamarupa (Assam), leaving it in disarray. The Tibetan historian Taranatha, in his *History of Buddhism in India*, wrote about the chaos that ensued in Odisha as well as Bengal in the early part of the eighth century, saying, 'In Odisha, in Bhengala, each Ksatriya, Brahmana, and Vaisya constituted himself the king of his surroundings, but there was no king ruling the country'. It was during the power vacuum following this invasion that the Bhaumakara dynasty rose to prominence.

At its maximum extent, the Bhaumakara kingdom included the districts of Cuttack, Puri, Ganjam and Balasore in today's Odisha, as well as Midnapur in present-day southern Bengal. What we know of the Bhaumakara rulers is largely drawn from the numerous copperplates detailing the grants given by them, which have been found all over their kingdom. In view of the very scarce information available, it is very difficult to estimate the regnal dates and duration of each ruler. The copperplates are highly laudatory, as they were commissioned by the rulers themselves or their descendants, and their contents can be exaggerated at times. However, we can draw some conclusions from what they reveal – if a queen managed to rule for 20 years, for instance, then she must have been effective, if not as wondrous as the copperplate makes her out to be. The copperplates are dated using the Bhauma era, of which the zero point is thought to be 736 CE.

It is estimated that a king named Kshemankara founded the Bhaumakara dynasty in 736 CE. There is much debate about the origins of the dynasty. While it has been established that the dynasty was non-Aryan, till date historians have not been able to agree on whether its people were of local extraction or from Assam. The proudly *mlechcha* (non-Aryan) dynasty of Assam, which had just invaded Odisha, claimed descent from Bhaumasur (the mythical son of the Varaha avatar of Vishnu and Bhumi, the Earth goddess), and his son Bhagadatta, king of Pragjyotisha, who, as per the Mahabharata, had died during the great battle at Kurukshetra leading a troop of elephants on the Kaurava side. The Bhaumakaras also claimed descent from Bhaumasur. However, the kings of Assam were staunchly Hindu, while Kshemankara was a Mahayana Buddhist. Surprisingly, for a follower of the anti-caste Buddha, he is praised in the Neulpur inscriptions for having re-established the distinction between the four castes, which had, as the inscription says, 'unfortunately' been ignoring their respective duties before his advent. The maintenance of the 'Varnashram dharma' is, after all, stated to be one of the prime duties of a king in traditional texts like the Arthashastra.

The Bhaumakara kings consolidated their power from their base in Toshali, slowly converting all the independent kingdoms of Odisha into feudatories. The original rulers of the *mandalas*, or provinces of Svetaka, Kodalaka, Yamagartta, Airavata and Khinjali continued to govern their territories, while now sending tribute and troops to the Bhaumakaras, their feudal overlords. The Bhaumakaras enjoyed great loyalty from their feudatories and witnessed very few rebellions.

Like many independent kings of the time, the Bhaumakara kings too soon assumed the full-fledged imperial titles of *maharajadhiraja* (King of Kings), *paramabhattaraka* (Most Venerable) and *paramesvara* (Great Lord). The first few kings of the dynasty were staunch Buddhists, and titles such as *paramtathagata*, *paramsaugata* and *paramopasaka* signified their allegiance to the Buddha. These kings patronized Buddhist scholars and built important Buddhist monuments in their capital Guhadevapataka or Guhesvarapataka or Viraj (present-day Jajpur), as well as at many other locations like Ratnagiri, Udaygiri and Lalitagiri.

To quote from the various copperplates, these were kings 'who used up their treasuries for religious purposes to enlighten their people, who adorned the earth by building mathas and monasteries in an unbroken line'. Their capital 'shone white, with buildings that touched the sky, just like the fame of the king, crowned with waving Chamaras. The white city walls were washed with the foam of moats, which resembled the sea.'

Unfortunately, very little survives of these buildings as they were destroyed during the invasions in the 16th century CE by Kalapahad, a general of the sultan of Bengal.

During the reign of the Bhauma kings and many centuries thereafter, Odisha's sea-trade links with South East Asia led to profuse cultural exchanges. The Indonesian and Malay word for 'Indian' is still 'Kling', derived from Kalinga. The temple architecture of Odisha strongly influenced temple styles in Indonesia and Cambodia. Many thousands of merchants, Buddhist monks and Hindu priests went to South East Asia and China from Odisha via the sea route. The main port for these voyagers was Tamralipti (present-day Tamluk) in West Bengal, although Puri was also an important port. Fa Hien, the Chinese Buddhist monk, is known to have sailed for China from Tamralipti.

Kshemankara's son King Shivakara I Unmattsimha greatly extended the empire, conquering Radha, or south Bengal of the time. There is a Chinese record of one of his emissaries carrying Buddhist texts being received by the Tang dynasty king Te-Tsong in 788 CE. This emissary was the important monk Prajnya, who then stayed on in China. To give an idea of the spread and influence of the Buddhist world, Prajnya had been born in Kapisa (Kabul in Afghanistan), had studied for 18 years in various universities, including Nalanda in Bihar, and had then moved to the Ratnagiri monastery in Odisha. He later became an influential preacher of the religion in China and Japan, translating many books into Chinese, and teaching Japanese scholars.

Surprisingly, although Odisha was very prosperous, particularly due to its trade with the Suvarnadvipa ('golden islands', as South East Asia was then known), and had a wealth of the coveted tall, dark and handsome elephants, it suffered very few invasions between the seventh and 13th centuries. Three major powers reigned in India during this period: the Rashtrakutas in the south, the Gurjara Pratiharas in the north-west and the Palas in Bengal, who were busy warring with each other. While Rashtrakuta inscriptions mention their conquest of Kalinga in the ninth century, there is no record or evidence of a permanent occupation. The Palas of Bengal invaded Odisha in the ninth century and as per their inscriptions, 'the lord of Gauda (Devapala), exterminated the race of the Utkalas.' The Tibetan historian Taranatha says that Devapala raised a big army and 'conquered the whole of Odisha'.

By this time the Bhaumakara dynasty had ruled for nearly a century. This is when Tribhuvana Mahadevi, the first Bhaumakara queen, entered the scene. She was the daughter of Rajamalla I, the king of Mysore from the Western Ganga dynasty. Her father helped her husband Lalitahara, a Bhaumakara prince, re-establish his kingdom after the Pala invasions, and possibly usurp it from his elder brother Shivakaradeva II.

To quote from a copperplate: '[When] the [Bhauma] Kara family had nothing left to depend upon but their past glory, Sri Lalitaharadeva, received the hand of the daughter of Rajamalladeva, the tilak of the southern region, who pulverized the mountain-like enemies with his thunder-like arms.'

In the plates, Tribhuvana Mahadevi is described thus: 'She had hundreds of auspicious signs on her body, signifying sovereignty over the entire world. She was the seat of all the kalas [fine arts], the embodiment of magnanimity, the flower of the tree of courtesy. She was like a shoot emerging from the root of beauty for the conquest of the world.'

Her husband has also been described as a paragon of virtues:

> Sri Lalitaharadeva, the best of men
> Shone like the moon lighting up the Lotus pond of the Kara family
> His lotus-like lips, blessed by Saraswati, spoke the truth
> He granted as much wealth as supplicants desired, like the Paras [the Philosopher's stone]
> His hands were perfumed by the flowers in the hair of his enemies' wives, whom he dragged [by the hair!]
> His footstool shone with the gems adorning the heads of defeated kings.

Lalitaharadeva (also known as Gayada) died young, however, and their son Kusumahara ascended the throne in 839 CE. But he too died young, leaving his infant son as heir. On the request of the nobles, Tribhuvana Mahadevi (also known as Gosvamini) ascended the throne in 846 CE.

Tribhuvana Mahadevi reigned for 20 years. Her rule is documented through the accounts of her descendants, and various copperplates dating back to this period. She managed to keep her vassals well under control, and her administrative abilities were legendary. She kept taxes low and appointed honest officials. One of the copperplates describing the queen Tribhuvana Mahadevi I found at Dhenkanal likens her to the moon for her benevolence and virtuous rule. They say, 'She took upon herself the burden of the entire kingdom and shone like Shesha, holding up the entire earth on her hoods... During her rule the country advanced in three branches [of administration], foes were extirpated, her glory spread abroad, and there was harmony among the people.'

'Tribhuvana Mahadevi I made her three Shaktis shine perpetually,' says another copperplate – the three shaktis being *prabhushakti* (personal power), *mantrashakti* (advice of the ministers) and *utsahashakti* (enthusiasm or the army). Yet another claims that she was proud of the *mridu kara* (low rate of taxes) that her subjects had to pay. Unlike the previous rulers, who were Buddhist, Tribhuvana Mahadevi has been described as a *Vaishnava* in various inscriptions, but has also been compared to Katyayini, the avatar of Durga worshipped in Odisha.

The *Hudud-al-Alam* mentions that the royal power in Ursin (Odisha) belonged to a woman called *rayina* (rani). It further says that 'Dahuma [Bhauma] does not consider any one superior to itself and is said to have an army of 3,00,000 men.' At the time, a kingdom with noblemen and, indeed, a populace who would readily accept female rulers was extremely rare. Tribhuvana Mahadevi's excellent rule made the nobles more receptive to future women rulers. However, this led to unforeseen complications. Kings who had married their daughters into the Bhaumakara family started conspiring to have their daughters declared the ruler, instead of the usual attempts to have their daughters' sons ascend the throne.

Tribhuvana Mahadevi abdicated the throne in favour of her grandson Shantikara II after two decades. A few decades later, Tribhuvana Mahadevi I's great grandson, Subhakara IV, was married to Prithvi Mahadevi, the daughter of Janamejaya, the Somavanshi king of Kosala. (The Somavanshis claimed to have descended from the moon, and named their heirs after ancestors they claimed from the Mahabharata. Curiously, they chose names of ancestors with controversial and frankly unsavoury stories, such as Nahush, Yayati and Janamejaya, instead of the more traditional names such as Rama and Krishna.) Subhakara IV was considered a scholarly and virtuous ruler, though a little weak, perhaps as he was under constant pressure from the aggressive Somavanshis.

When Subhakara IV died, the Somavanshis seized power and had Prithvi Mahadevi crowned the queen, overruling the claims of Subhakara's brothers' sons. An inscription in Brahmeswara says that Janamejaya, the Somavanshi king, killed 'the king of Odra', presumably Subhakara IV, with a lance. Prithvi Mahadevi took the regnal name of Tribhuvana Mahadevi II, to increase her acceptance among the nobles. This ploy, however, did not work for long; she was soon dethroned by nobles who were worried about Somavanshi power being on the rise, and replaced by her nephews-in-law, who ruled sequentially as Shantikara III and Subhakara V.

After the death of Subhakara V, the last known male member of the Bhaumakara family, the throne was occupied by four queens in succession.

The first to rule was Gauri Mahadevi, the wife of Subhakara V, who was probably the regent for Dandi Mahadevi, her daughter. She was able to maintain order. One account states, 'at her lotus-like feet was prostrate the entire population [of the kingdom].'

Dandi Mahadevi took the throne thereafter in 916 CE and ruled successfully for 20 years. The maximum number of grants made by a Bhaumakara ruler to the people have been found belonging to this period. The grants eulogistically say she secured the borders of her kingdom from 'formidable and hostile kings' who were 'humbled by her prowess'. The prosperity of her kingdom is evident from the description of pearls and gems on the copperplates of the time. Dandi Mahadevi was a devout Shaivite, as evidenced by her adoption of the title Paramamaheshvari (Great Follower of Lord Shiva) in her records.

After her death, the two queens who followed had short reigns and were the last of the Bhaumakara dynasty. Dandi Mahadevi's stepmother, Vakuladevi, who was born into the Bhanja dynasty, came to power first. The ascendancy of the Bhanjas created conflicts among the vassals. After her, Vakuladevi's sister-in-law, the widow of Shantikara III, Dharma Mahadevi, ruled for a while. She is the last known ruler of the

Bhaumakara dynasty, and nothing more is known about them after about 940 CE. The kingdom was conquered by Yayati, the Somavanshi king and brother of Prithvi Mahadevi. The Somavanshis went on to rule till the 12th century.

It is interesting to note that most of the Bhaumakara copperplates record grants to Brahmins in the north, especially from the Kannauj region. Kannauj was the most important city in the north for nearly 500 years after Harsha. Many Brahmins were migrating to Odisha from the north at this time, because of the shift to Hinduism from Buddhism in Odisha; Yayati is supposed to have brought in 10,000 Brahmins from Kannauj.

We also see a love for elaborate poetic expression, which was common among the Sanskrit writers of the time. Even in an official document, instead of simply saying that the grant is in perpetuity, the writer says:

> as long as the sun, the moon and the earth endure.
>
> ...continue as long as the heavenly stream [the Ganges], which shines like the festoon of Malati flowers, flows on the head of enemy of the love-god [Shiva who destroyed Kamadeva],
>
> as long as the tremulous shore of the sea, encircling the earth, continues to be agitated and
>
> as long as the stars, adorning the pavement of sky like jewels, shine.

Between the successful reigns of Tribhuvana Mahadevi I and Dandi Mahadevi, and the debacle that was the rule of Prithvi Mahadevi, we see nearly a hundred years of women's rule in

Odisha – good, bad and unremarkable, but well-accepted by the nobles and subjects alike. It is interesting to note that none of the queens adopted a son to bolster their legitimacy, which was the age-old practice in India. The later queens of the dynasty ruled directly, and not as regents, and to the exclusion of existing male heirs, sons of brothers and cousins, which was practically unheard of in India even during the many centuries that followed. In this, the Bhaumakara dynasty's record is unequalled.

The Curious Case of the Calendar

A little note on Indian calendars. Indian kings had the habit of declaring the beginning of a new era starting with the founding of their dynasty. This new zero-point date would be followed in their kingdom and by their feudatories, until they were replaced by another dynasty, at which point a new calendar would be inaugurated. Hundreds of such calendars were created over the centuries, including those of the Gupta era beginning in 319 CE, and the Harsha era beginning in 606 CE. Oddly, there is much confusion about the origins of the two calendars in common use today: the Vikrama Samvat with a zero point of 56 BCE and the Saka Samvat with a zero point of 78 CE. The Vikrama era is supposed to have been founded by the legendary King Vikramaditya in Ujjain, but we have no historical records of such a king in that period. The Saka era is variously supposed to have been founded by the Saka king Azes, or the Kushan king Kanishka or even by Shalivahan the Satavahana. It is quite amazing that a billion people follow calendars with zero-point dates of unknown origin – why these two calendars with no major significance should have survived is a mystery. In other world calendars, zero points are considered extremely important dates for those cultures: the Christian era begins with the birth of Christ, the ancient Roman calendar with the foundation of Rome.

The Controversial Queen of Kashmir

Didda

> The statesmanlike instinct and political ability which we must ascribe to Didda in spite of all the defects of her character, are attested by the fact that she remained to the last in peaceful possession of the Kashmir throne, and was able to bequeath it to her family in undisputed possession.
>
> Sir Marc Aurel Stein, in his translation of Kalhana's *Rajatarangini*

Rani Didda's (r. 958–1003 CE*) rule represents the peak of women's power in Kashmir, which, unusually, had many women rulers both before and after her. She is sometimes called 'Catherine of Kashmir', a reference to the ruthless Catherine the Great of Russia, who ruled long and well with the help of her lovers and favourites, whom she periodically purged. In spite of her physical handicap and her gender, Didda was able to rule Kashmir with an iron hand for 50 years.*

Unlike many other periods in ancient India, the history of Kashmir has been passed down to us in great detail thanks to the 12th-century chronicler, Kalhana, who describes it exhaustively in his work, *Rajatarangini*, written in 1149 CE. It is generally considered to be the oldest written history in

India. It is brutally frank in its tales of blood and betrayal, and of kings of all castes – a clear indicator that it was not commissioned by the rulers themselves, who would have otherwise insisted on being mentioned as having appropriately glorious ancestors. To quote the historian R.S. Srivastava, 'In his history there are no heroes or heroines... Indeed, whether we love them or not for their virtues, it is their vices which make them unforgettable.'

At a time when rule by women was not supported either in Hindu or Buddhist scripture (in the Udyogparva in the Mahabharata Vidura goes so far as to say, 'The country where a woman, a child or a gambler rules, sinks helplessly as a stone raft in a river'), Kalhana mentions two queens who ruled before Didda. One was the mythical Kashmiri queen Yashovati, who was crowned with the support of Lord Krishna. Kalhana's comment on her saintly rule is this: 'The eyes of men which viewed womenkind with scant courtesy, considering it as one of the objects of their pleasure, looked upon this mother of her subjects as if she were a goddess.' The other woman ruler, Sugandhadevi, is known to have been in power just 50 years before Didda. She ruled at the beginning of the 10th century, first as a regent and then directly, though as the latter only for two years. Coins minted during her reign mention her as 'Sri Sugandhadeva' rather than 'devi'. Kalhana writes that she was overthrown and executed by her own courtiers.

At the beginning of the first millennium, Kashmir was a major intellectual centre for Buddhism, especially under Kanishka, the emperor of the Kushan dynasty. In the fourth and fifth centuries CE, hundreds of Kashmiri missionaries, among them the venerated Kumarajiva, travelled up the Karakoram Silk Route to spread the message of Buddhism to China. However, by the sixth century, Kashmir had been devastated by the invasion of the Hun ruler Mihirakula, who persecuted Buddhists and encouraged Shaivism. Kashmir, which had been the nursery of Buddhist scholars for hundreds of years, was now strongly Hindu. In the seventh and eighth centuries, the Karkota dynasty came to power in Kashmir. Its most powerful ruler, Lalitaditya Muktapida, created a brief Greater Indian empire when his troops raided lands as far as Assam, Afghanistan, Tibet, the Vindhyas, Gujarat and Sindh. He even had diplomatic relations with the Chinese emperor and offered to host 2,00,000 Chinese troops in Kashmir to fight their common enemy, the Tibetans. Fortunately, no Chinese troops showed up in Kashmir until the 20th century!

The Karkota dynasty was followed by the Utpala dynasty in the ninth century, which, after a brief moment of glory under King Avantivarman, became embroiled in civil war. The kingdom of Kashmir, which was now restricted to the Jhelum valley, was going through turmoil. The *damara*s (feudal landlords) and the *tantrins* (hired soldiers) frequently changed allegiance and constantly rebelled. Kings lasted but a few years and the people were left to the mercy of the government officials. Kalhana wrote, 'Truly, government servants are a plague to the people and harass them like cholera or dysentery.'

Parvagupta, a former minister of Kashmir, crowned himself king in 949 CE, killing the boy king Sangramadeva and throwing his body, weighed down with a stone, into the Jhelum. He, however, died painfully of dropsy (oedema) in just a year, leaving the throne to his son Kshemagupta. Kshemagupta was pleasure-loving and dissolute. He was addicted to women, gambling, and especially to hunting jackals in the woods, in a Kashmiri version of the British fox hunt.

It was during Kshemagupta's reign that Didda made an appearance. Didda's lineage can be traced back to the ancient and powerful Hindu Shahi dynasty who ruled Kapisa (now in Afghanistan) and Gandhara (which is in modern-day Pakistan) after the decline of the Kushan Empire, from the third to the 11th century CE. Her mother, daughter of King Bhima Shahi, was married to Simharaja, the king of Lohara (currently Lohrin in Poonch), a small kingdom adjacent to Kashmir.

Didda (b. 924 CE), the daughter of Simharaja, was beautiful but lame. She is often referred to as *charan-hina* (footless) in the *Rajatarangini*. Though she could walk, a woman called Valga would carry her around – even in running competitions. Didda would, of course, always win, as nobody dared to defeat the queen! In gratitude, Didda later built a *math* (temple) for her aide called Valgamath. Didda was still unmarried at twenty-six, very much over the marriageable age by the norms of the era, when Kshemagupta, looking for political legitimacy for his rule, offered to marry her, as she possessed the singular qualification of being the granddaughter of the mighty Shahis.

The wedding took place in 950 CE and Didda came to Srinagar as a bride. Soon her husband came under her spell so visibly that he started being taunted by the populace as 'Diddakshema'. Such was his infatuation that Kshemagupta had coins minted with 'Di(dda) Kshemagupta Deva' inscribed on them. Didda's influence over the king, however, created many enemies for her, among them the well-entrenched prime minister Phalguna, whose daughter Chandralekha was also married to Kshemagupta. Didda gave birth to a son, who was named Abhimanyu. When her grandfather, the powerful Bhima Shahi, visited Kashmir to see his great grandson he ordered the building of the temple known as Bhimakeshava near Martanda.

In 958 CE, Kshemagupta contracted a violent fever during one of his beloved jackal hunts. He was taken to the Kshemamath in Varahamula (now Baramulla) and died there. Panicking at the thought of what was to be her fate, Didda immediately secreted away her son, fearing he might be killed. She was now on her own, surrounded by threats to her son's life as well as her own. The first challenge came when the courtiers gathered for the king's funeral and, as per the prevailing royal custom, exerted pressure on Didda to commit sati along with the other queens, including Chandralekha, Phalguna's daughter. Didda staged a great show of preparing for sati, and at the last moment desisted on entreaties by some ministers to live on as her son was a minor. Her son Abhimanyu was then duly crowned and she became the regent. The prime minister, Phalguna, fearing for his life under Didda's rule, fled to Poonch.

Now set to rule the kingdom on behalf of her son, Didda was suspicious of everybody. The first direct challenge she faced was from Kshemagupta's nephews, Mahiman and Patala. They gathered many allies, especially powerful Brahmins from Lalitadityapur, and surrounded her while she was visiting the Padmasvamin temple. She managed to get her son away to a *math* and then asked for negotiations to commence. During the talks, she managed to ward off some of the allies with bribes and placate others. Her faithful minister, Naravahana, then won a victory in battle over the rest. She ruthlessly ordered the killing of many of the rebels, including her husband's nephews, but forgave some she thought would be of use to her. One of them was the warrior Yashodhara, whom she designated commander-in-chief, and sent off to subdue Thakkana, a king of Shahi descent who ruled a neighbouring kingdom. Yashodhara won, but let Thakkana retain his kingdom. When he came back, expecting a hero's welcome, Didda made an attempt to arrest him, possibly because the sight of a victorious army marching to the capital made her insecure about her throne, as it would any ruler, especially when the commander is known to have previously rebelled against the king. Many regime changes have been thus effected by victorious generals the world over, especially in Ancient Rome, the prime example being that of Julius Caesar. The attempted arrest, however, was botched up and Yashodhara immediately revolted, joined now by many nobles. This was perhaps the toughest revolt Didda ever faced, but she managed to suppress it with the help of her ministers,

Naravahana and Rakka. Again, the rebels and their relatives were brutally killed.

Kalhana says of the crushing of the rebellion: 'The Lame Queen whom no one had thought capable of stepping over a cow's footprint got over the ocean-like host of her enemies just as Hanuman got over the ocean.'

Naravahana now became the most important man in the kingdom. Didda, increasingly nervous of his power, became aloof and started favouring others. Heartbroken, Naravahana committed suicide. In a little while Rakka too died. Didda, left alone again, could see the *damaras* uniting against her, and recalled Phalguna, who was living in retirement in Poonch, who then effectively subdued the *damaras*.

Meanwhile Abhimanyu was growing up and it seems was quite disturbed by his mother's shenanigans. As Kalhana put it, 'He was learned, his eyes had the beauty of lotuses, he was honoured by the sons of savants, he had studied the Vedas. He was asparkle with scholarship and youth. To one of such a very pure temperament co-operation with vile conduct proved withering, like the heat of the sun to the Sirisha flower.'

In 972 CE Abhimanyu died of consumption. His minor son Nandigupta was crowned king after him and Didda continued to rule as regent. For a year, a grief-stricken Didda immersed herself in constructing buildings in memory of her son. She built the Abhimanyusvamin temple and a town she named Abhimanyupura, as well as the Diddasvamin temple, Diddapura town and Diddamath, in a part of Srinagar now called the Diddmar area. She is credited with laying the foundations of 64 buildings in her lifetime.

Her run of bad luck continued through this time. Nandigupta fell sick and died within a year of ascending the throne, followed by the death of her next grandson, Tribhuvangupta, who had been crowned king the very same year. Many accused the queen regent of witchcraft and held her responsible for bringing about their deaths, though it seems quite unlikely, as she had no advantage in doing so. Undeterred, Didda now crowned Bhimagupta, her third grandson, the ruler of Kashmir in 975 CE. Phalguna, whom she had made her chief minister, died during Bhimagupta's reign.

Now began a new chapter in Didda's life, brought in by a young man called Tunga. Tunga was a Khasa buffalo herdsman from Poonch, who had come to Kashmir with his brothers and was employed as a letter carrier in Didda's administration. Impressed by his capabilities, she started promoting him to senior administrative posts, until he finally became prime minister and the commander of her armies. He continued to capably hold these posts for nearly forty years, even after her death. He was widely considered to be her lover, although she was over fifty years old by the time she met him.

Meanwhile, Bhimagupta was close to attaining adulthood and started showing interest in administration and reform. However, he died under mysterious circumstances in 981 CE, many say after being imprisoned and tortured by Didda. After his death, Didda ascended the throne in her own name and issued coins in the name of 'Sri Didda', which are widely available even today.

Didda ruled for the next 22 years with absolute power, quashing periodic rebellions by using her standard combination of bribes, placation and ferocious reprisal, until she died in 1003 CE at the age of 79. There is a story in Roman history about King Tarquin, who when asked by his son for advice on how to rule, goes to the garden and scythes off the heads of the tallest poppies. Didda did just this, with the faithful Tunga by her side, until there was no opposition left. She put down a major revolt spearheaded by her nephew Vigraharaja. Tunga and his brothers also won a major victory over Prithvipal, the king of Rajapuri (Rajouri).

Kalhana says of Didda, 'Those treacherous ministers who for sixty years... had robbed sixteen kings, from King Gopala to Abhimanyu, of their dignity, lives and riches, were quickly exterminated by the energy of Queen Didda.'

There is a quaint story about how Didda chose an heir. She called for many boys from her maternal family and placed a heap of fruits in front of them, challenging them to pick up the maximum number. The boys started grabbing the fruits and fighting with each other. In the end her brother's son, Samgramaraja, had the maximum number of fruits without actually engaging in any physical fighting. He had managed to incite the other boys to fight with each other while he calmly gathered up fruits. Impressed by his political acumen, Didda declared him her heir. She made Samgramaraja and Tunga swear a holy oath that they would work with each other, which created great stability in the kingdom for the next two decades.

Thus, Didda's maternal dynasty, the Loharas, established power in Kashmir, although according to the prevalent patriarchal norms, her heir should have been a blood relation of her husband rather than of her. When Mahmud of Ghazni attacked Kashmir, first in 1015 CE and then again in 1023 CE, Samgramaraja was one of the few kings in India to resist him successfully, in part because of the strong army and administration created by Didda, and partly because of the onset of winter.

The rule of the Lohara dynasty in Kashmir finally came to an end in 1320 CE with the savage attack of the Mongol chief Dulacha on Kashmir. The kingdom was devastated and plundered over eight months. However, while leaving with their loot, the Mongol army was destroyed to a man at the modern-day Banihal Pass by a fierce blizzard. Just like for Russia, winter proved an able general for the Kashmiris.

A new dynasty was then founded by Rinchan, a Buddhist from Ladakh, who later converted to Islam and took the name Sultan Sadruddin, becoming the first Muslim ruler of Kashmir.

Didda is a controversial ruler, who is difficult to slot into easy categories. All sources on her life and reign agree about her tremendous survival skills, her ruthless application of the maxims of the *Arthashastra*, her ability to rule and to select able lieutenants, and her success in achieving stability for the fractious kingdom she had inherited. However, her visible lust for power and snidely attributed obsession with the opposite sex, both considered admirable in men, were seen as failings and as an evil streak in a woman of her time. The innumerable lovers ascribed to her could well be due to gender bias by historians – after all, how else could a woman succeed in securing the loyalty of her ministers? Unless, of course, by witchcraft, which she was also accused of.

Immigrant Fruit

There is a charming story about the much-loved fruits of Kashmir like peaches, apricots, pears, etc.

In the first century CE, Kanishka consolidated Kushan power across large portions of north India, central Asia and some parts of China. The most striking of his victories were his conquest of parts of modern-day China, that of Kashgar, Yarkand and Khotan. In doing this, he not only freed himself of the obligation of paying a regular tribute to Chinese rulers, but also took some of them hostage. One of these included a Chinese prince, who was held captive in various locations including Punjab and Kashmir. When the traveller Xuanzang visited Punjab some centuries later, he was taken aback to find paintings of a Chinese prince and his companions dressed in traditional Chinese garb, and whom the resident monks still honoured as their benefactor.

Incidentally, this Chinese prince was very fond of some fruits unknown in India, so they were imported from China to be cultivated for him. And thus the *chinani* (the pear) and the *chinarajputra* (the peach) were introduced to India.

The Tragic Sultan of Delhi

Raziya Sultan

> Sultán Raziya was a great sovereign, sagacious, just, beneficent, the patron of the learned, a dispenser of justice, the cherisher of her subjects and of warlike talent, and was endowed with all the admirable attributes and qualifications necessary for kings. She was endowed with all the qualities befitting a king, but she was not born of the right sex and so in the estimation of men all these virtues were worthless. (May God have mercy on her!)
>
> Minhaj-i-Siraj, contemporary historian

Raziya Sultan (r. 1236–40 CE) was the only woman sultan of Delhi, universally acknowledged as possessing all the virtues of a good king. She ruled during the initial period of the Islamic conquest of India. In an extremely complex and violent world, she managed to hold on to her kingdom for just four years, and died tragically young.

When Shamsuddin Iltutmish became the sultan of Delhi in 1211 CE, the rule of the Slave dynasty was fairly new in India, having been established in 1206 by Qutubuddin Aibak, a *mamluk*, or slave, who served Muhammad Ghori and was appointed by Ghori as the viceroy of India after the Turks defeated Prithviraj Chauhan, the Rajput ruler of Delhi in

1192 in the second Battle of Tarain. Iltutmish, who ruled for 26 years, until 1236, can be considered the true founder of the Delhi Sultanate. His decision to move the capital of his empire to Delhi from Lahore changed the status of Delhi from the farthermost outpost of the Ghorid Empire to the centre of the new Islamic kingdom in India.

India was a little different from other Islamic kingdoms, since the vast majority of the people were non-Muslim and remained so. Ziauddin Barani, a historian of the Delhi Sultanate era, says that early in Iltutmish's reign, a party of theologians approached him with the plea that the 'infidel Hindus' be forced, in accordance with Islamic law, to accept Islam or face death. Iltutmish told them that this was totally impractical, since in India Muslims were 'as few as grains of salt in flour'.

Indian historical accounts often give an impression of barbaric invaders pouring into civilized India through the Khyber Pass and easily defeating weak local forces to set up rule in Delhi, until soon enough, a new set of invaders would come and displace them. The hapless native population would placidly carry on with their lives, acquiescing unresistingly in their own brutal exploitation.

However, this is not always an accurate representation of events. Rather than calmly accepting foreign rule, in many instances in history, local rulers would actually hold off invaders for centuries or, when the centre became weak, would push back, trying to reoccupy territories. This push-and-pull went on for centuries. Pushbacks happened after the death of Muhammad bin Tughlaq, when Vijayanagara reconquered most of the southern territories; after Timur's invasion, when many Rajput states expanded after Delhi was destroyed; and after the death of Aurangzeb, when the Marathas wrested control of most of India.

So it was for Iltutmish, who came to power in troubled times. He had to rebuild the empire which had splintered immediately after Aibak's death. He also faced a host of other troubles.

Nobles in Multan, Bengal and Sind all declared themselves independent rulers. The Ghazni ruler occupied Lahore. Some of the Rajput rulers used this opportunity to reoccupy their lands. Kings displaced by the Mongols attacked India. And the Mongols attacked India.

Most of Iltutmish's rule was spent slowly defeating first the breakaway provincial governors, then the reclaimed Hindu kingdoms and then making new conquests such as Gwalior. Not all his campaigns met with success – he was unable to conquer Gujarat, where he was defeated by the Chalukyas.

From 1219 onwards, the Mongols under Genghis Khan overran the Islamic heartlands of Asia, even killing the Caliph in Baghdad. A large number of Muslim refugees – scholars, soldiers, noblemen and adventurers of all sorts – fled to India, and Iltutmish presided over a cultural flowering of sorts. New buildings were constructed, including the Hauz Shamsi, Sultan Garhi and the Jahaz Mahal; the Qutb Minar was completed; and universities were founded.

Amir Khusro, the poet of Delhi, wrote later in the century:

> My abode was the Arch of Islam, the 'qibla' of the kings of the seven realms – Delhi, that twin sister of the blessed Heaven, a tract of paradise on the surface of the earth... Its lofty palaces raise their heads to the skies and overshadow the sun itself... Its green fields are bedecked with roses and its springs are brighter than bright eyes – running waters pleasant as life, like milk flowing through sugar. The tank of the Sultan, with its colours and illuminations looks like molten silver cast into stone. Its gardens are full of pleasure-seekers, rose-cheeked beauties with pierced ears, bright as the pearls of their earrings.

Iltutmish brought about many changes in governance. To reduce the powers of the traditional Turkish nobility, which had troubled him immensely on his path to kingship, he created a new ruling class of selected faithful slaves called the Shamsis (derived from his first name, Shamsuddin) and named them the Chahalgani, or the Chalisa (the Forty). They were mostly of Turkic origin, though a few were Mawalis (converted Indians). Although they were loyal to him while he lived, after his death in 1236 the power-hungry nobles formed groups that supported different successors, resulting in four of Iltutmish's descendants, including Raziya, having very short reigns.

Iltutmish's heir apparent was Nasiruddin Mahmud, the son of his chief queen Qutub Begum, the daughter of Qutubuddin. Raziya was also her daughter, and a favourite of Iltutmish – he did not hold his other sons, Ruknuddin Firuz and Muizuddin Bahram, both born from slaves, in high regard.

Unfortunately, Nasiruddin died suddenly in 1229, leaving Iltutmish bereft. The emperor now turned to Raziya and assigned her administrative responsibilities. Raziya had been given an excellent education and schooled in administration as well as in the skills of war. She was well versed in the Quran and had a fair knowledge of several other sciences, and even wrote Persian verses under the pseudonym 'Shirin'.

In 1231, to the disbelief of all, Iltutmish formally declared Raziya as his heir. Minhaj-i-Siraj, a contemporary scholar and the head of a university in Delhi during Raziya's rule, wrote of Raziya's appointment in his book, *Tabaqat-i-Nasiri*:

> The Sultán discerned in her countenance the signs of power and bravery, and, although she was a girl and lived in retirement, yet when the Sultán returned from the conquest of Gwalior, he directed his secretary, Táju-l Malik Mahmúd, who was director of the government, to put her name in writing as heir of the kingdom, and successor to the throne.

Unsurprisingly, his nobles were horrified at his actions as women were very much in purdah and women rulers unheard of among the warlike Turks. They asked Iltutmish for a justification, writes Siraj, and goes on to say:

> The king replied, 'My sons are devoted to the pleasures of youth, and no one of them is qualified to be king. They are unfit to rule the country, and after my death you will find that there is no one more competent to guide the State than my daughter.' It was afterwards agreed by common consent that the king had judged wisely.

However, when Iltutmish died in 1236, the nobles, still unhappy with a woman being placed on the throne, defied the departed sultan's decision and crowned his son Ruknuddin Firuz as sultan. Ruknuddin, as it turned out, was a terrible ruler. He squandered the kingdom's resources on his amusements and paid no attention to the business of the state. Of him, Siraj says:

> He was so entirely devoted to riot and debauchery, that he often bestowed his honours and rewards on bands of singers, buffoons, and catamites. He scattered his riches to such a heedless extent, that he would ride out drunk upon an elephant through the streets and bázárs, throwing tankas of red gold around him for the people to pick up and rejoice over

His mother, Shah Turkan, who had been a slave of Iltutmish, was now in a position to take revenge for all the real and imagined slights she had suffered from the other women of the harem. 'She now seized the opportunity of punishing them, and in blind fury and vindictiveness she put several of them to death... In addition to her other cruel acts she caused the young prince Kutbu-d dín, son of the late king, and a very excellent youth, to be blinded and afterwards to be put to death.'

Soon, several nobles began revolting against the mother and son, and the kingdom fell into confusion. Determined to subdue his detractors, Ruknuddin led his forces out of the capital, little realizing how much his misrule had affected the common people of Delhi, who looked upon Raziya with affection and admiration and also as the true heir to the throne. Upon his return, though, he found a different Delhi waiting for him. As Siraj describes it, 'When Ruknu-dín arrived at Kílú-gharí [then a luxurious suburb of Delhi, in the area that is modern-day New Friends Colony], he found that rebellion had broken out, and that his mother had been made prisoner.' What followed has been narrated by the Moroccan scholar Ibn Battuta who wrote a colourful account of Raziya's ascension a century after the event. Iltutmish had given an order that a wronged person who sought justice should wear white clothes and come out in the public, so as to be easily identified. When Raziya's brother was killed by Shah Turkan, Ibn Battuta says:

> Raziya... ascended to the terrace of the Old Palace, called Daulat-khána, close by the chief mosque. She was clothed in the garments of the wronged, and, presenting herself to the people, she addressed them from the terrace, saying, 'My brother has killed his brother, and also wishes to kill me.'
>
> ... Thereupon the auditors rushed tumultuously towards Ruknu-d dín, who was in the mosque, seized him, and brought him to Raziya. She said, 'The slayer must be slain.' So they massacred him in retaliation for his murder of his brother.

Raziya now took control as sultan; she refused to be addressed as sultana because the word meant 'wife of a sultan'. She took the regnal name Jalalat-ud-din Raziya. The populace of Delhi greatly supported Raziya but most of the Chahalgani could not tolerate the idea of having a woman as a ruler. The Nizam-ul-Mulk, or chief minister of the sultanate, violently opposed to a woman ruler, gathered many of the Chahalgani in a camp outside the fort of Delhi and besieged it. They also defeated nobles, like the governor of Oudh, who came to aid Raziya from the provinces.

After a long siege, Raziya decided to go on the offensive and led her forces to camp outside Delhi. They fought many battles with the besiegers. She cleverly managed to meet some of the rebel Chahalgani secretly at night and convinced them to come over to her side. In a weak position, the remaining fled, but they were tracked down and killed over time.

Thereafter, she subdued a recalcitrant Gwalior, and personally led out troops to quell the mutinous governor of Lahore. In fact, most of Raziya's brief rule was spent subduing rebellious nobles. However, she also established schools, academies, centres for research and public libraries that included the works of ancient philosophers along with the Quran and writings on Islam

As Siraj put it: 'Throughout its territories from Lakhnautí to Dewal all the princes and nobles made their submission. The country now enjoyed peace, and the power of the State became manifest.'

But this peace was not to last, for Raziya was about to break some cardinal societal rules that would once again make the hackles of the nobility rise. Siraj writes:

> About this time, Amír Jamálu-d dín Yákút, the superintendent of the stables [who was Ethiopian] was made a personal attendant of her majesty. This created

> jealousy among the Turkish generals and nobles. The Sultán Raziya now threw off the dress and veil of women. She put on a coat (kabá) and cap, and showed herself among the people. When she rode on an elephant all men clearly saw her.

She was soon suspected of having an affair with Yakut; perhaps because a little indiscreetly, she used to lean on him while mounting her horse. A conspiracy to dethrone her was hatched by the horrified Chahalgani once again. In April 1240 Malik Altuniya, the governor of Bhatinda, staged a revolt. Many later works written about Raziya say that Altuniya and Raziya were childhood sweethearts and he became jealous of Yakut, but the truth of these accounts cannot be verified. On being challenged, Raziya marched with an army to subdue Altuniya and his Chahalgani allies. She was defeated and captured. Yakut was killed and she was imprisoned by Altuniya in Bhatinda. The nobles then went back to Delhi and placed her half-brother Muinuddin Bahram on the throne.

In an unexpected twist, Raziya married Altuniya, and they gathered together an army, including many from the warlike Khokhar tribe which dominated Punjab at the time. They set out to reclaim Delhi and fought against her brother's forces in Kaithal in October 1240, where they were defeated and were forced to flee. 'The opposing forces met,' writes the eloquent Ibn Battuta of her tragic end,

> and Raziya was defeated and obliged to flee. Pressed by hunger and overcome with fatigue, she addressed herself to a man engaged in cultivating the ground and begged for food.

> He gave her a bit of bread, which she devoured, and then she was overpowered by sleep. She was dressed in the garments of a man; but when the peasant looked at her as she slept, he perceived under her upper garment a tunic trimmed with gold and pearls. Seeing she was a woman, he killed her, stripped her of her valuables, drove away her horse, and buried her corpse in his field. He then carried some of her garments to the market for sale. The dealers suspected him, and took him before the magistrate, who caused him to be beaten. The wretch then confessed that he had killed Raziya, and told his guards where he had buried her.

He goes on to say that her body was exhumed, and reburied near the river Jamuna, close to Delhi, and a small shrine built. Today a neglected, unpretentious grave in Bulbuli Khana in Old Delhi is thought to be her tomb.

Unfortunately, her successors appear to have considered a woman sultan an embarrassment; Firuz Shah Tughlaq in the 14th century went to the extent of omitting her name from the list of sultans that was prepared during his reign.

Her brother Muinuddin Bahram ruled only for two years before he was overthrown in favour of Ruknuddin's son Alauddin Masud in 1242.

Finally, in 1246, Balban, one of the Chahalgani, gained control of the sultanate. He placed his son-in-law, Nasiruddin Mahmud, son of Iltutmish's elder son and Raziya's brother, Nasiruddin, on the throne. This Nasiruddin was extremely religious and led an ascetic life: he spent most of his time copying the Quran while insisting that his wife, the sultana, cook his food with her own hands. The reins of the government were firmly in the hands of Balban; he ruled as the *nayab* (deputy) until Nasiruddin died without an heir in 1266. Thereafter, Balban ruled as the sultan until 1286. This was a period of relative stability for the sultanate till the Khilji dynasty took over in 1296, finally bringing the century-old slave dynasty to an end.

From Slave to Sultan

Military slavery among the Turks was a unique practice. Young men were bought as military slaves or *mamluk*s and given extensive war training. They were often given important posts, although they remained slaves. They lived well, with great prospects of promotion. Many became generals and viziers, and some even became rulers who founded dynasties. The ethnic origins of the *mamluks* were varied – Turkish, European, African. Egypt had a Mamluk dynasty, founded by slaves of white origin. The Ottoman Turks in Constantinople routinely took young white boys from Eastern Europe, who became the elite Janissary corps. In India the Slave dynasty, where most of the rulers were former slaves, ruled for a century.

The story Iltutmish gave of his origins goes thus – he belonged to the Ilbari tribe from Turkestan. He was, but obviously, high-born. His brothers became jealous as he was handsome and particularly intelligent. They eventually sold him off to slave merchants who took him to Ghazni. Bought by the sultan, because of his exceptional talents, he became the personal attendant of Muhammad Ghori and gradually became a much-valued administrator. This story closely echoes that of Joseph in the Bible – a sceptic would say it showed a certain lack of creativity on the part of Iltutmish, who was clearly keen to establish a noble ancestry.

Iltutmish shifted to the service of Qutubuddin Aibak when he came to power after Ghori's death. Aibak later manumitted him and married his daughter to Iltutmish. After a brief reign of four years Qutubuddin died in 1210 in Lahore, playing *chaugan*, a version of polo, when his horse fell on him. As he had no sons, a succession war arose among his various generals. Iltutmish, who was governor at Badaun, rushed to Delhi and occupied it after a battle with another would-be successor, Aram Shah, at Bagh-i-Jud (modern-day Jor Bagh in Delhi).

The Princess Who Became a Prince

Rudrama Devi

> This (Kingdom) was formerly under the rule of a King, and since his death, some forty years past, it has been under his Queen, a lady of much discretion, who for the great love she bore him never would marry another husband [sic]. And I can assure you that during all that space of forty years she had administered her realm as well as ever her husband did, or better; and as she was a lover of justice, of equity, and of peace, she was more beloved by those of her kingdom than ever was a Lady or Lord of theirs before.
>
> Marco Polo, Venetian traveller, *The Travels of Marco Polo*

Rudrama Devi (r. 1262–89 CE*) ruled Orugallu, present-day Warangal, in the 13th century for 40 years and presided over the golden age of the Kakatiyas. She is the only independent female ruler mentioned by Marco Polo in his journey across the world. But he was mistaken in thinking her a widow of the previous king; she had inherited the kingdom from her father, Ganapati Deva, who chose her as his heir over other male members of his extended family.*

In the 13th century, after the great empires of the Cholas and Chalukyas had battled each other to exhaustion over the course of three centuries, the Deccan came to be divided into four major kingdoms, which also fought each other incessantly. The boundaries of these southern kingdoms were close to the modern-day state limits – the Seuna Yadavas ruled over the Marathi-speaking regions which now form Maharashtra, with their capital at Devagiri (Daulatabad); the Hoysalas over today's Karnataka, with their capital at Dwarasamudra (Halebidu); the Pandyas over what is now Tamil Nadu and some of Kerala with their capital at Madurai; and the Kakatiyas over Andhra, with their capital at Orugallu (Warangal).

The Kakatiyas, who were feudatories of the Eastern Chalukyas from around the eighth century, established the first kingdom encompassing all the Telugu-speaking lands. Rudradeva I declared independence from the Chalukyas in 1163 CE and changed the official language of Orugallu from Kannada to Telugu. He built the wondrous thousand-pillared temple in Hanumakonda to commemorate his clan's independence.

A later king, Ganapati Deva, who ruled for about sixty years from 1199 to 1262 CE and is considered the greatest Kakatiya king, built the capital – then called Eksilanagaram (in Sanskrit) or Orugallu, which both mean single stone, referring to a large granite boulder in the fort – and greatly extended Kakatiya boundaries. He actively promoted foreign trade.

Orugallu was a rich kingdom, the only major source of diamonds in the world, as well as a producer of unimaginably fine fabrics. In the words of Marco Polo:

> No other country but this kingdom of Mutfili produces them [diamonds], but there they are found both abundantly

> and of large size. Those that are brought to our part of the world are only the refuse, as it were, of the finer and larger stones. For the flower of the diamonds and other large gems, as well as the largest pearls, are all carried to the Great Khan and other Kings and Princes of those regions; in truth they possess all the great treasures of the world...
>
> In this kingdom also are made the best and most delicate buckrams, and those of highest price; in sooth they look like tissue of spider's web! There is no King nor Queen in the world but might be glad to wear them. The people have also the largest sheep in the world, and great abundance of all the necessaries of life.

Ganapati Deva had no sons. His elder daughter, Ganapamadevi, was married to Betadeva, his feudatory from the Kota dynasty. Ganapamadevi ruled with her husband from 1241 to 1251, and upon his death, ruled independently from 1251 to 1264, as a loyal feudatory to her father. She had no children.

Ganapati Deva's younger daughter, Rudrama Devi, was brought up to rule as his heir and trained in all the requisite kingly skills. To improve her chances of being accepted as a sovereign ruler, Ganapati officially declared Rudrama Devi as his son via a Putrikayagna. This religious rite appoints a sonless man's daughter or his daughter's son as his own son. Her official depictions always showed her in male clothing and referred to her in the masculine, as Rudradeva. She attended all public meetings dressed as a man.

She was made a co-ruler with her father and given the male name Rudradeva Maharaja in 1259. Soon after, Ganapati Deva resigned from his position and she became the sole ruler of the kingdom in 1262. However, she only ascended Orugallu's 'lion throne' in 1269 CE after the death of her father.

Rudrama Devi was married to the Chalukya prince Virabhadra, a member of a minor Chalukya branch based in the Vengi area. They were an offshoot of the Eastern Chalukya dynasty, which had ruled the region before the Kakatiyas. The marriage occurred shortly after Ganapati Deva's conquest of Vengi in 1240. We do not hear of Virabhadra occupying any administrative position or playing any public role. Rudrama Devi and Virabhadra had three daughters – Mummadamma, Ruyamma and Rudrama – who were all married to local noblemen. At the end of her reign, Rudrama Devi, overlooking her daughters, designated Mummadamma's son, Prataparudra, as her heir.

Rudrama Devi came to power in troubled times. Her warring neighbours saw her accession as an opportunity to annex her kingdom. The Yadavas from Devagiri, the Gangas from Kalinga and the Pandyas from the Tamil region to the south all attacked the Kakatiyas. She also faced a great deal of opposition from her feudatory noblemen who could not stomach the thought of being ruled by a woman. She was, however, luckier than her near-contemporary, Raziya Sultan, who had been designated the ruler of the Delhi Sultanate by her father Iltutmish just 25 years before Rudrama Devi, and though possessed of all the attributes necessary for a king, had died battling against her own nobles after a brief rule of four years. Though much of Rudrama Devi's reign was spent pushing these kings back to their original boundaries, and controlling her nobles, she survived the onslaught and ruled for a long time.

In the early years of her reign, the Seuna Yadava king, Mahadeva, invaded Tailanga (Telangana today) and reached Orugallu. As per the 18th-century record, *Pratapachantra*, written by Ekamranatha, after 15 days of fighting she chased the Yadava army back to Devagiri and forced them to pay a large indemnity in money and horses. The Seuna and Kakatiya accounts vary, as can be expected. Seuna records show a Yadava victory in which Rudrama is spared by Mahadeva because she is a woman. In contrast, *Pratapachantra* mentions an indemnity of 1 crore being received by Rudrama. The coins received in the indemnity payment were apparently distributed by her among her officers, and a buried hoard of Seuna coins found deep in Andhra territory could possibly have been part of that loot. Rudrama Devi's victory is also borne out by inscriptions where local rulers pledge allegiance to her, which have been found in Bidar, deep in Yadava territory.

A title she adopted after the victory was Rayagajakesari, which literally means 'the lion who rules over the elephant kings'. She built a *rangamandapa* (pavilion) in the Swayambhu temple in Warangal to commemorate her victory. In it she is shown as a warrior mounted on a lion with a sword and shield in her hands and an elephant trunk holds up a lotus to her in submission.

In 1262, the Ganga king of Kalinga, Narasimha I, whose dynasty had proudly adopted the title of Gajapati after the famed elephants of Odisha, marched into the Godavari delta and occupied the Vengi region. Rudrama Devi was only able to recover it after 15 years. In 1278, her commanders, Poti Nayak and Proli Nayak, fought against Vira Bhanudeva I, son and successor of Narasimha I, and inflicted a crushing defeat on him. The commanders then assumed the titles Tangasimha, or the lion to the rutting elephant (referring to the Gajapati), and Oddiyarayamanamardana, or the destroyer of the pride of Oddiyaraya.

Over her 40-year rule, the toughest challenge Rudrama Devi faced was in the south. Within the first two or three years of her joint rule with her father, the kingdom had been thrown into disarray due to Jatavarma Sundara Pandya I's invasion of the south in which the Kakatiyas were disastrously defeated in the Battle of Muthukur, near Nellore. Rudrama Devi's loyal feudatories, the Kayastha chief Jannigadeva and his brother Tripurarideva later reoccupied some of this territory from the Pandyas and kept the Pandya king at bay. However, things changed with the succession of Jannigadeva's younger brother, Ambadeva, in 1273, who remained a thorn in Rudrama's side as he had ambitions to become an independent king. He allied with Kakatiya enemies like the Yadavas and the Pandyas, and started conquering the territories of neighbouring Kakatiya feudatories. He is said to have fought with 75 kings and amassed a substantial kingdom.

As mentioned earlier, according to the *Pratapachantra*, Rudrama Devi had to face rebellion from many of her nobles as well, including her family members, Hariharadeva and Murarideva. She defeated them with the help of loyal feudatories like Gona Ganna Reddy and Recherla Prasaditya. According to legend, Annamambika Devi, the wife of Gona Ganna Reddy was considered to be one of her best friends.

Even through the incessant warfare Rudrama Devi worked on many projects. She completed the construction of the nearly impregnable Warangal Fort, work on which had been begun by her father. The citadel was protected by an inner wall, one kilometre in diameter, and made of huge blocks of granite, irregular in size but perfectly fitted without the use of mortar. Rudrama Devi increased the height of this wall to over 20 feet. Forty-five massive bastions, from 40 to 60 feet on a side, projected outwards from the wall and into the waters of the moat. Amir Khusro in his typical style of *qasidaqari* (embroidery) thus described the granite wall: 'Its turrets rose up in air and soared up to the moon while its bottom passing below water reached the fish'. An earthen wall surrounding this, 2.4 kilometres in diameter, further surrounded by a moat 150 feet wide, was built by Rudrama Devi. In the 16th century a third wall was added, an earthen rampart nearly 13 kilometres in diameter.

There are beautiful temples and buildings in Warangal, much damaged by invaders, made of intricately carved hard granite. Most of the pillars and *toranas* (gateways) were carved out of single pieces of stone.

During Rudrama Devi's rule the Kakatiyas also brought large tracts under cultivation, which greatly increased their revenue. Before the 11th century, much of the dry Deccan interior was inhabited by herders. The Kakatiyas and their feudatories built more than 5,000 reservoirs or tanks by damming small streams. These tanks were often managed by small temples, which were endowed by the nobles. This caused the spread of agriculture and the settlement of the land by immigrants and herders. Most of these tanks are still in use today.

Rudrama Devi also introduced the recruitment of non-aristocratic warriors from diverse castes as officers and landowners, a practice that was continued by her heir, Prataparudra. The older feudal families were gradually supplanted and land grants were now given to new meritocratic officers. This policy was also used in the later empire of Vijayanagara, whose official language was also Telugu. A study by historian Cynthia Talbot shows that only 17 per cent of Rudrama Devi's subordinates were of noble background, perhaps because most of the hereditary nobles rejected her as a ruler for being female. She also created a class known as *angarakshakas* – designated warriors who were part of the queen's retinue, who then became a new class of warrior lords.

Rudrama Devi is credited with the introduction of the Nayankara system, in which prominent commanders received land grants, and became the feudatory Nayaks who were powerful semi-independent rulers. This system continued in the Vijayanagara Empire, which was founded later by erstwhile Kakatiya feudatories Hakka and Bukka. Even after the fall of Vijayanagara in the Battle of Talikota in 1565, this robust system allowed many Nayaks to hold out against the might of Deccan sultanates like Bijapur and even the Mughals.

Though Rudrama Devi was not very interested in the arts, she encouraged the practice of *Perini shivatandavam* by the soldiers, which is an extremely vigorous and powerful dance performed to the beat of drums by the soldiers as a prelude to war. It was part of the training of the royal forces. This dance form nearly died out after the end of the Kakatiya dynasty and has recently been revived by the celebrated dancer Nataraja Ramakrishna by studying the poses depicted in the Ramappa Temple at Warangal and other sources.

The famed fabrics produced by the Kakatiyas were an important export item to other Indian kingdoms and elsewhere in the world. Amir Khusro's description of the fine and glittering fabric he encountered in the Deccan is, unsurprisingly, far more poetic than Marco Polo's:

> The fineness of its cloths is difficult to describe: the skin of the moon removed by the 'executioner star' [Mars; *Akhtari Jallad*] would not be so fine. One could compare it to a drop of water if that drop fell, against nature, from the font of the sun. A hundred yards of it can pass through the eye of a needle, so fine is its texture, and yet the point of a steel needle can pierce through it only with difficulty. It is so transparent and light that it looks as if one is wearing no dress at all but has only smeared the body with pure water.

In spite of continuous warfare, the Kakatiya kingdom under Rudrama Devi was tremendously rich, not least because it was the only known source of diamonds in the world. (The first diamonds outside India were only discovered in the 18th century in South America.) Interestingly, while invading Telangana, Malik Kafur, the eunuch general of Sultan Alauddin Khilji's army, did not bother to dig for diamonds as they passed the famed mines – he said that strong warriors dig out diamonds with their swords and not with pickaxes! The Kohinoor, incidentally, was from the Kollur mines and is rumoured to have been the eye of an idol in Warangal during Kakatiya times. It is supposed to have been carried to Delhi by Malik Kafur and later passed on to the Mughals as part of the Delhi treasury.

In 1994, an inscription dated in the Saka calendar equivalent of 25 November 1289 was found in Chandupatla, Telangana, which gives an indication of Rudrama Devi's death. The inscription was laid down by Puvvula Mamidi, a member of Rudrama Devi's army, who donated a piece of land to the Somnath Temple, commemorating the recent death of Rudrama Devi and her army chief Mallikarjuna Nayakudu. Though there is no mention of the cause or location of her death, it is considered that the two probably died facing the armies of Ambadeva. The queen was then about 80 years old, but clearly still fighting wars in the forefront.

The Fall of the Kakatiyas

In 1289 Rudrama Devi was succeeded by her grandson Prataparudra, who later defeated Ambadeva. He was a great king who reconquered lost territories and was at the zenith of his glory 20 years into his reign in 1309 when he came across a threat unlike any the Kakatiyas had dealt with: the Turks.

Turkic invaders had already conquered north India, and established the Delhi Sultanate a century ago. Now the Sultan of Delhi, Alauddin Khilji, who fancied himself a great conqueror – an epithet he adopted was Sikandar Sani (the second Alexander) – looked to the south. In 1309, the army under Khilji's favourite slave, Malik Kafur (formerly known as Kafur Hazar Dinari, or Kafur who is worth 1,000 Dinars), besieged the strong fortress and, with their vastly superior siege machinery, broke through the outer mud wall. Prataparudra sued for peace. As Amir Khusro, who was himself part of a later Tughlaq campaign, puts it:

> He sent to the Malik an image of himself in gold with a rope round its neck in token of surrender and a humble request that his life be spared. 'If the king,' he said, 'desires treasures and presents, I have of gold enough to gild all the mountains of Hind, and it is at his service. If the object of the king be diamonds and pearls, I have collected so many of them that neither the eyes of the rocks have beheld nor the ears of the fish heard of a similar treasure.'

He agreed to an annual tribute. Kafur returned to Delhi along with 20,000 horses and 100 elephants. Another account says that there were 500 *mans* (20 tons!) of gems and gold. Never before had such treasure been brought to Delhi.

When the Khiljis were displaced by the Tughlaqs, Prataparudra stopped paying tribute. An army was dispatched under Muhammad bin Tughlaq, still a prince, in 1320, which returned unsuccessful in its endeavours. However, they were back in 1323 and, after many months of siege, finally conquered the fortress. The city was destroyed and the loot was taken back to Delhi. As an aside, the Delhi Sultan, Ghiyasuddin Tughlaq, died viewing the elephants captured from Warangal. The viewing platform he was sitting on – supposedly engineered by his son Muhammad bin Tughlaq – collapsed, resulting in his death.

Prataparudra was captured and sent in a cage to Delhi. He is said to have committed suicide en route by drowning himself in the Narmada. *Sic transit gloria mundi.*

Twice-Told Tales: Truth and Myth

The Heroines of Chittor

> There is a sanctity in the very name of Chitor, which from the earliest times secured her defenders.
>
> Lieutenant Colonel James Tod, *Annals and Antiquities of Rajasthan*

More often than not, tales about Rajput women who are immortalized in history show them either dying heroically defending their honour, or making amazing sacrifices or inspiring their menfolk to greater heroism. Seldom does one come across tales of these women as doers and warriors. However, there are instances of unusual women who were warriors, administrators, rulers and poets, and showed decisiveness and independence of thought.

Women such as Tarabai, Karmavati, Jawahirbai and Mirabai, daughters-in-law and granddaughters-in-law of Rana Raimal of Chittor, lived as members of the same family in the early 1500s. In fact, Karmavati, Jawahirbai and Mirabai were all women who flouted the norm in choosing not to commit sati and came into prominence only after being widowed.

At the beginning of the 16th century, north India was divided into warring states, many of which were formed after the

Tughlaq Empire fell apart following the destruction of its capital, Delhi, by Timur Lang in 1398. The Delhi Sultanate, now ruled by the Lodis, was only one of these states, and by no means the largest or the richest. Two of the most powerful kingdoms at the time were those of Mewar, with its capital at Chittor, and Gujarat, with its capital at Ahmedabad. Other prominent kingdoms included Bengal, Malwa, Jaunpur, Gondwana, Sindh and several Rajput kingdoms besides that of Chittor, all of which continuously battled against each other. Meanwhile, the Deccan sultanates and the Vijayanagara Empire faced off in the south.

In 728 CE, Bappa Rawal had established the Guhilot kingdom of Chittor. Though Alauddin Khilji had destroyed Chittor in 1303, as recounted in the much-romanticized bardic tale about Rani Padmini, it was re-established in 1326 by Veer Hammir from the Sisodia branch of the Guhilots. Sisodia kings like Rana Kumbha and Rana Sanga greatly extended the kingdom's territory. At the time of Babur's entry into India in 1526, Rana Sanga of Chittor was his strongest foe and ruled over a substantial part of Rajasthan, Madhya Pradesh and Gujarat.

At the outset, it is imperative to point out that the most popular tales about two prominent Rajput queens are, unfortunately, not borne out by hard facts. First, that of Rana Sangha's wife, Rani Karmavati, who, as the story goes, sent a rakhi to the Mughal emperor Humayun. He chivalrously rushed to her succour but arrived too late to save her from committing *jauhar* (mass self-immolation). Second, the story about the emperor Akbar and Tansen, travelling in disguise to listen to Mirabai sing. These stories are based on legends recounted by bards, some of which were popularized by Colonel James Tod, who recorded the legends of Rajasthan during his stint as the British resident in the early 19th century in his extensive account, *Annals and Antiquities of Rajasthan*.

Rana Raimal of the Sisodia dynasty ruled Chittor from 1473 to 1509. The story of Tarabai, the warrior wife of Prithviraj, his second son, is also told by Tod, who was quite prone to romanticism. Tarabai was the daughter of Rao Surthan Solanki, the erstwhile ruler of Toda, near Ajmer, who had been dispossessed by the Afghans.

Tod recounts a very unusual tale of Tarabai's valiant efforts to wrest Toda from the Afghans:

> Stimulated by the reverses of her family, and by the incentives of its ancient glory, Tara Bai, scorning the habiliments and occupations of her sex, learned to guide the war-horse, and throw with unerring aim the arrow from his back, even while at speed. Armed with the bow and quiver, and mounted on a fiery Kathiawar, she joined the cavalcade in their unsuccessful attempts to wrest Toda from the Afghan. Jaimall, the third son of Rana Raemall, in person made proposals for her hand.

Jaimall was looked upon as the heir to the throne of Chittor as both his older brothers, Sanga and Prithviraj, were in exile. Tarabai agreed to marry him if he redeemed Toda for her father, Rao Surthan. Jaimall, however, is said to have attempted to rape Tarabai instead, and was slain by her outraged father.

When Rana Raimal heard about the killing of Jaimall by Rao Surthan to save Tarabai's honour, in the words of Tod, 'The Rana, incited to revenge, replied with a magnanimity which deserves to be recorded, that "he who had thus dared to insult the honour of a father, and that father in distress, richly merited his fate"; and in proof of his disavowal of such a son he conferred on the Solanki the district of Radnor.'

Prithviraj, Rana Raimal's second son, now came forward to the aid of Tarabai and to redeem the honour of his family. He joined Tarabai's cavalcade in Toda during Moharram with 500 horsemen, and together they managed to kill the Afghan leader viewing the procession from the balcony. As described by Tod, 'the lance of Prithviraj and an arrow from the bow of his Amazonian bride stretched him [the Afghan ruler] on the floor.'

In the ensuing confusion they captured the fort, Tarabai successfully chasing off a war elephant with her sword. They restored the city to Rao Surthan and were granted the fort of Kumbhalgarh by the Rana, where they lived until, unfortunately, Prithviraj was poisoned by his sister's husband, whom he had punished for mistreating his sister. Thereafter, Tarabai committed sati on Prithviraj's pyre.

Rana Raimal was succeeded by Rana Sanga, his eldest son, who was an extremely powerful ruler. He was, however, defeated by Babur in 1527 in the Battle of Khanua and died later of his wounds in 1528. Rana Sanga's heir apparent, Bhojraj, who had been married to the saint-poet Mirabai, had already died on the battlefield the previous year. Rana Sanga was thus succeeded by his second son, Ratan Singh, who died soon after in 1531, in a quarrel with Surajmal Hada, who was the brother of his stepmother, Rani Karmavati. The throne now came to Rana Sanga's teenage son, Vikramaditya, under the aegis of his mother, Rani Karmavati of Bundi.

Vikramaditya was extremely unpopular. He insulted the Rajput chiefs, often playing practical jokes on them, some truly childish, like getting their clothes stitched together stealthily while they sat in court so that they would trip when they stood up. Not surprisingly, the nobles soon stopped attending court and went back to their provinces. Vikramaditya maintained an army of paid *pahalwans* or *paiks* (foot soldiers), who were not part of the feudal nobility.

Bahadur Shah, the king of Gujarat at the time, saw the young king's misrule as an opportunity. The two kingdoms had been feuding for centuries and he was still smarting over his father's defeat by Rana Sanga and the loss of the royal crown of Gujarat, which had been carried away by Rana. The relationship was, however, complicated – Bahadur Shah had briefly taken shelter in Chittor earlier in 1526 when he was fleeing from his father after a quarrel, and had collaborated with Rana Ratan Singh during the conquest of Malwa in 1531.

After Bahadur Shah ascended the throne of Gujarat in 1526 he set out on an extremely successful career of conquest. The Portuguese were now in Gujarat and he inducted foreign guns and gunners, especially Portuguese-made ones, into his army. Cannon made an explosive entry into India after

Babur used them to win the battle of Panipat in 1526. From a global perspective, after the invention of the cannon, forts stopped being able to resist prolonged sieges. Any wall would eventually crumble with prolonged bombardment – the walls of Constantinople, which had held out for a thousand years against hundreds of invasions and sieges, fell before the cannon of Mehmet II in 1453. In Europe, this is the time during which spacious palaces and mansions of the nobility began being built in the plains as there was not much advantage in living in cramped forts any more.

In 1533 Bahadur Shah moved on Chittor with a vast army, reinforced with Portuguese arms, for his first siege of the fort there. Rana Vikramaditya faced him en route with his *pahalwan* troops, but lost the battle and fled, and Bahadur Shah set up camp on the outskirts of Chittor.

Rani Karmavati, who was left defending her kingdom, began to ask for help from many quarters, including the Mughal emperor, Humayun. Humayun had ascended the throne of Delhi in 1530 after the death of his father Babur, and was having a hard time containing the wars across the country. The Afghans, who had dominated India under the Lodis, had fled to neighbouring kingdoms and were attempting to regain power in Delhi. Humayun's own family members were also becoming rebellious. To contain Bahadur Shah, in January 1533, Humayun moved to Gwalior with his troops and camped there for the next two months. Although the Mughals were breathing down his neck, Bahadur Shah did not raise the siege.

In March 1533, with no aid in sight, the queen concluded a humiliating treaty with Bahadur Shah which entailed the surrender of the conquered districts of Malwa, the famed jewelled crown and belt taken from Mahmud Khilji of Malwa by Rana Sanga, ten elephants, 100 horses and five crores of Tankas. He also conquered and kept the territories of Ranthambore, Ajmer and Nagore.

Rana Vikramaditya now came back to rule in 1533. In legend he is the king who tormented his elder brother's widow, saint Mirabai, who was living in Chittor at that time. As recorded in her poems, he sent her snakes and bowls of poison which could not harm her due to divine intervention. Her cousin, Rao Jaimal Rathore, the prince of Merta, came and took her away to Merta in 1534 to keep her safe. This was actually a blessing in disguise for her because of what was to transpire; had she remained in Chittor much longer she would not have survived.

In 1534, Humayun founded the city of Dinpanah in Delhi. He received a letter from Bahadur Shah congratulating him on the completion of Dinpanah in June 1534 and he responded by generously permitting Bahadur Shah to retain all his latest conquests: Malwa, Raisen, Ranthambore, Ajmer and Nagore (many of which used to be under the pre-Mughal Delhi Sultanate), and professed amity and good will.

In September 1534 Humayun set out eastwards from Agra to deal with the continuous Afghan rebellions in Bengal and Bihar, now spearheaded by the fearsomely competent Sher Shah Suri. With Humayun out of the way, Bahadur Shah now thought he had a good opportunity to become the most powerful king in India. He simultaneously attacked Chittor and the Mughals. He besieged Chittor again in November 1534 and sent troops under Tatar Khan, a scion of the dispossessed Lodi family, to attack Delhi. Many believe that Sher Shah Suri in Bihar and Bahadur Shah were coordinating activities to mount concerted attacks on Humayun.

As per Tod's retelling of events which is part of modern Indian legend, here's what happened: When Bahadur Shah, the sultan of Gujarat, attacked Chittor, Rani Karmavati asked the Rajput nobles for help. They agreed on the condition that Rana Vikramaditya, who had offended many of them, would be sent away. She duly sent off both her sons, Vikramaditya and Uday Singh, away from Chittor to Bundi. Realizing the danger they were in, Rani Karmavati sent a rakhi to Humayun in Bengal, claiming him as her brother who should now come to the rescue of his sister. Humayun, according to Tod, rushed back. However, he did not reach in time. The fort was breached by cannons with the help of *firangi* (possibly Portuguese) gunners and the defenders of Chittor, including Karmavati, committed *jauhar* in March 1535 – 13,000 women hurriedly burnt themselves while the men fought to death. (This was the second *shakha*, or *jauhar* of Chittor; the first was when Alauddin Khilji besieged it in 1303 and the third when Akbar finally destroyed it in 1568.) Humayun, grief-stricken at his failure to reach in time, marched to Chittor in April and defeated Bahadur Shah. He then conquered Gujarat and Malwa and restored Rana Vikramaditya to the throne of Chittor.

However, other histories written of that period tell a very different story; also, the dates of Humayun's movements are well-recorded and attested. One such important source is the *Vir Vinod* by Kaviraj Shyamaldas, the official history of Mewar commissioned by the Sisodia rulers of Udaipur in the 19th century, which he based on the Mewar documents available to him and the *Baburnama*. We reconstruct the sequence of events from these.

Rani Karmavati had moved from Chittor to the fort of Ranthambore along with her minor sons Vikramaditya and Uday Singh when her stepson, Ratan Singh, became the Rana in 1528. Worried for her children's safety, she asked Babur for protection for her children against their stepbrother, promising him Ranthambore in return for a safer territory like Bayana. One must remember that her husband, Rana Sanga, had died fighting Babur! Babur mentions receiving this proposition in the *Baburnama*, dating it 1528 (though calling the queen Padmavati instead of Karmavati). Nothing much came of it because Babur was busy fighting battles in the east and he died in 1530. Rani Karmavati's brother, Surajmal Hada, fortuitously killed Rana Ratan Singh, when the Rana attacked him during a hunt, and her son, Vikramaditya, came to the throne in 1531.

When Bahadur Shah besieged Chittor for the second time in 1534, Humayun was not in Bengal as recounted by Tod. He had only reached Kalpi, not far from Agra, when he heard of the siege of Chittor and the attack on Delhi. Humayun also learnt that Bahadur Shah had given shelter to the rebel Mughal general Muhammad Zaman.

Humayun immediately took action, sending his brother Hindal to Delhi, where he thoroughly defeated Bahadur Shah's forces under Tatar Khan. Humayun himself moved toward Chittor in January 1535. However, instead of rushing to the rani's rescue as per the legend recounted by Tod, he dawdled in Sarangpur and Ujjain (only 250 kilometres away from Chittor) for months, waiting for Chittor to fall. Bahadur Shah did not abandon his siege of Chittor because his ministers assured him that Humayun would not attack a fellow Muslim when he was engaged in war with an infidel. In any case, Bahadur Shah was confident of victory and saw no need to negotiate with Chittor this time.

A more likely reason for Humayun waiting patiently was that both these kingdoms of Gujarat and Chittor were his enemies. As a strategy it made sense for him to let them fight and destroy each other and then sweep in and easily defeat the weakened and exhausted victor.

The Rajputs heroically defended the fort. However, the walls of Chittor were breached in March 1535 after constant bombardment by Portuguese cannons. We hear of the tale of the queen mother Jawahirbai (from the Rathore family of Jodhpur), another of Rana Sanga's widows and mother of Rana Ratan Singh. She decided that to fight the enemy and kill as many of them as possible was more glorious (and useful) than dying by *jauhar*. She apparently led a cavalry charge of other like-minded Rajput women, in male dress and armour, and they died defending the breach. Meanwhile, 13,000 women, including Rani Karmavati, committed *jauhar*. As Tod puts it

'There was little time for the pyre... Combustibles were quickly heaped up in reservoirs and magazines excavated in the rock, under which gunpowder was strewed. Karmavati... led the procession of willing victims to their doom, and thirteen thousand females were thus swept at once from the record of life.' The gates were then thrown open and the men fought to death.

On 8 March 1535, Chittor fell. After a few days, when the triumphant Bahadur Shah started to return, he found that his way home was blocked by Humayun, who had moved to Mandsaur, about a hundred kilometres away from Chittor. Surrounded, Bahadur Shah's troops fortified their encampment with rings of carts. The two armies faced off against each other for days.

When supplies ran out, Bahadur Shah fled after destroying some of his prized possessions. The sultan shed bitter tears when his favourite elephants, Sharzah and Patsingar, and his main cannons (lovingly named Laila and Majnun), were destroyed. As he entered the abandoned encampment, Humayun was stunned to see the royal enclosure which had been left behind – one mile in circumference, made of velvet, silk and brocade, with ropes of silk and tent pegs of gold and silver. At the sight, Humayun is said to have echoed Sikandar Lodi, 'Why should it not be so, Delhi relies on its wheat and millets for revenue while Gujarat counts upon its corals and pearls.' He then followed Bahadur Shah's army and conquered Gujarat and Malwa, while Bahadur Shah took shelter with the Portuguese. But when Humayun returned to Agra, leaving his incompetent brother Askari in charge of Gujarat, Bahadur Shah recouped the territories within a year. Humayun, au contraire, lost all his lands to Sher Shah Suri, and had to flee India.

However, Bahadur Shah soon came to an ignominious end. He had gone aboard a Portuguese ship in 1537 to negotiate terms. There was a quarrel and the Portuguese simply threw this great conqueror overboard, and let him drown.

Meanwhile, the 18-year-old Vikramaditya and a small contingent of Rajputs had quickly reoccupied Chittor almost immediately after the flight of Bahadur Shah from Mandsaur. The demoralized Gujarati contingent gave it up without much of a fight. However, Vikramaditya was as disliked as ever by the nobles and was eventually murdered by his cousin, Banvir (an illegitimate son of his uncle Prithviraj, husband of Tarabai). Banvir also attempted kill Uday Singh, Rani Karmavati's infant son, who was kept safe by Panna Dhai, his wet nurse. In the ultimate sacrifice, she is said to have substituted her own son for the sleeping child. She then smuggled Uday Singh out in a basket and trekked with him secretly through the forests of the Aravallis, to chieftain after chieftain, unsuccessfully asking for protection, as they were all too scared to take on Banvir. Finally, the governor of Kumbhalmer agreed to rear the little prince, disguising him as his nephew. Uday Singh was later acknowledged by a conclave of nobles. Banvir was exiled and exited to the south. The Bhonsles of Verul, Shivaji's ancestors, claim descent from Banvir.

The saint-poet Mirabai, who had left for Merta just before the siege started, would probably have perished in the *jauhar* of Chittor in 1535 had she stayed. As it is, she lived till around 1547, and wrote many more poems in these 12 years. The story that Akbar sneaked into Chittor in disguise to hear her sing is, of course, a fabrication, since Akbar would have barely been five years old when she died.

History offers glimpses into the lives of these extraordinary, unusual women: Tarabai, who fought battles in male dress, not under duress but as a noble pastime; Jawahirbai, who preferred to die leading a cavalry charge rather than by committing *jauhar*; Karmavati, who held together her kingdom under attack and ensured the safety of her children and of her kingdom; Panna Dhai, who managed to save the heir of Chittor; and Mirabai, whose voice is still heard all over our land. Even more remarkably, these women were not ostracized for their valour, their independence and their strength but instead are revered even today.

Of Poetic Letters and Chivalrous Deaths

It is interesting to look at the diplomatic correspondence in those days. Humayun and Bahadur Shah wrote letters (which were quite poetic!) to each other in which Humayun asked him to return Muhammad Zaman; Bahadur Shah refused.

Humayun's letter is in the form of an allegory in which two philosophers are questioned: 'Who is the most helpless person in the world?

One of them answers, 'He who has no friend.'

The other, however, corrects him. 'No! The most helpless man is he who had a friend but has managed to lose him.'

Humayun himself then pointed at the moral of the story by saying that a thousand friends were too few and one enemy was too many, meaning that Bahadur Shah should not be so foolish as to lose his friendship.

Humayun ended his letter with an oft-quoted verse:

> Plant the tree of amity, that it may bear fruit, namely [the fulfilment of] the heart's desire,
> Uproot the sapling of hostility that yields countless ills.

A rude reply by Bahadur Shah contained the following verse:

> If thy sword hast no tongue (to speak of your valour),
> Do not trouble the sword of thy tongue by mere boast.
> If thy sword hast no lustre, my son!
> Do not brag of thy father's noble descent.

Another verse attributed to Humayun in this correspondence is:

From grief every fold of my heart has turned into blood,
(To think) that in spite of our oneness, duality is attributed
to us.
I never recollect you without weeping bitterly,
(Nay,) I seldom recollect you (for fear) that I may have to
weep much.

Diplomacy was certainly conducted differently in this age of poetry!

It was the third *jauhar* of Chittor which finally led to it being abandoned permanently. Rao Jaimal of Merta was the leader of the defence of Chittor against Akbar's siege in 1567. Uday Singh, whom Panna Dhai had saved by sacrificing her son, was the ruler, but not present in the fort. As per Abul Fazl, Akbar's favourite polymath, Jaimal was killed by a shot fired by Akbar himself one morning while inspecting the defences. When in a few hours, smoke started billowing from the fortress, veterans among the attackers understood a *jauhar* was in progress. Chittor fell with horrific massacre. To count the number of dead, as a shortcut, the *janeu* (sacred thread) from the Rajputs was weighed, which was 74½ *maund*s (about two and a half tons!). Chittor was destroyed permanently. For centuries, the number 74½ came to be seen as cursed, with Rajasthani merchants stamping it on the seals of their letters as a safeguard till quite recently. It was common superstition that whoever broke the seal would suffer the sin of the massacre of Chittor.

Impressed by Jaimal's defence of the fort, Akbar had a statue made of him and his co-commander Patta riding elephants, and had them placed outside his fort in Agra. These statues later stood outside the Delhi gate of the Red Fort right until the demise of the Mughal Empire.

The Defender of Her Realm

Rani Durgavati

> Durgavati... was distinguished for courage, counsel and munificence, and by virtue of these select qualities she had brought the whole of that country under her sway. She neglected no point of courage or capacity, and did great things by dint of her farseeing abilities. She had great contests with Baaz Bahadur and the Miyanis, and was always victorious. [...] There are stories current in Hindustan of her feasts and her frays. But she had one great fault, to wit, she, owing to a crowd of flatterers, became proud of her outward success, and did not submit herself at the threshold of the Shahenshah.
>
> Abul Fazl, *Akbarnama*

Rani Durgavati (r. 1550–64 CE), born in the Rajput Chandela dynasty, was the ruler of her husband's kingdom of Gondwana in central India in the 16th century, which became one of the earliest conquests of Emperor Akbar. She is still part of the legends of the region around Jabalpur, Madhya Pradesh, and her story was chronicled widely by the Mughals, and later the British.

Gondwana is a hilly and forested region of central India, named after the tribe of Gonds, an adivasi community, who speak Gondi, a Dravidian language. Geographically, it is located around present-day Jabalpur and the Kanha National Park in Madhya Pradesh.

In the Puranas, the Haiheya king Kartvirya Arjun ruled this region from his capital, Mahishmati. According to Hindu mythology, he was killed by Parshurama, one of the avatars of Vishnu. This region was also known as Chedi, ruled by Shishupal in the Mahabharata, who was killed by Krishna, another avatar of Vishnu.

A young man named Jadurai, who worked for the powerful Kalchuri king Gangeyadeva, had founded the Garha-Mandla dynasty in the fifth century CE. According to legend, Jadurai married the daughter of the Gond chief of Mandla and succeeded him. His descendants, the Garha-Mandla kings, were petty chiefs for a thousand years until Raja Sangram Shah Madawi, the 47th king, conquered a substantial area at the beginning of the 1500s. Under Sangram Shah, the kingdom contained 70,000 villages and 52 forts, and he moved his capital from Garha to the new town of Chauragarh, 90 kilometres from modern-day Jabalpur.

Abul Fazl, Akbar's closest companion and designated historian, has a not very complimentary tale to tell of Sangram Shah. Sangram Shah was born Aman Das, the elder son of the Garha-Mandla king. He was later awarded the title of Sangram Shah by Sultan Bahadur Shah of Gujarat for the aid he rendered him in conquering Raisen. Sangram Shah had been a dissolute youth, whom his father had had locked up to save him from himself. He managed to escape and joined the service of Birsingh Deo, the Baghela raja of Rewa, who effectively adopted him.

While his benefactor was away in Delhi serving Sikandar Lodi, Sangram Shah heard that his father was planning to give the throne to Sangram's younger brother. He went to his mother's palace by stealth, killed his father and declared himself king. Birsingh Deo, horrified, went to Garha to punish him. Refusing to fight – and certainly in no condition to withstand the Baghela forces – Sangram Shah pleaded that he had already lost one father and did not want to lose another, somehow convincing Birsingh Deo of the sincerity of his repentance. As Abul Fazl put it: 'Aman Das wept continually and expressed his abhorrence of himself for his evil action.' Birsingh left and Sangram started on his career of conquest. He soon had as his neighbour the Chandela Rajputs and their princess Durgavati, who later married his son Dalpat Shah.

Durgavati, born in 1524, was the daughter of Shalivahan, the Chandela Rajput king who ruled a small neighbouring kingdom called Mahoba in the mid-16th century. The founder of the Chandela kingdom was Nannuka, who had ruled a small territory around Khajuraho in the ninth century. Later bardic traditions traced Chandela ancestry to Chandravarman, a son of the Moon God and the Brahmin girl, Hemavati. The Chandelas are known today for the amazing temples they built in Khajuraho over a few generations.

The marriage of Durgavati, a Rajput princess, to Sangram Shah's son, Dalpat Shah, was quite unusual since the Gonds fell outside the Hindu caste system. Various tales abound as to why Durgavati's father agreed to her marriage into a 'low' caste. A popular story is that Durgavati had heard of how brave and handsome Dalpat Shah was and sent a private message asking him to come and win her with his sword. When her guru pointed out that Dalpat Shah was a Gond, Durgavati, it is said, replied, 'He might be a Gond by tribe, but his deeds make him a Kshatriya.' Dalpat Shah obliged and came, according to the story, with 50,000 troops (although that number is extremely unlikely to be accurate). Others say that Sangram Shah wanted the high-born and beautiful Durgavati as a bride for his son as part of his drive for upward mobility, and her father agreed, either because he gained a strong ally or simply because he was paid a large sum of money.

Many tales also position Dalpat Shah as actually belonging to a high caste, to make this marriage more digestible. According to Abul Fazl, Sangram Shah, who had no sons, convinced one of his employees, Govind Das, a Kachwaha Rajput, to let his wife give birth in the palace and then claimed the child as his own son, making Dalpat Shah actually of Rajput birth. Another retelling is more ambitious and goes back to the founder of the dynasty, Jadurai, making him a high-caste Hindu who had a dream in which Rama, Sita, Lakshmana and Hanuman promised him sovereignty. Jadurai was then selected by a *neelkanth* (Indian roller bird), which had been sent out to find the Gond raja a suitable son-in-law. Jadurai's guru, the Brahmin Surbhi Pathak, allowed him to marry the Gond princess on the condition he would not eat food from her hand. Other more intimate contact was presumably acceptable as they had a number of progeny!

Dalpat Shah became king shortly after his marriage, upon the death of Sangram Shah. In 1545, he fathered a son with

Durgavati, Veer Narayan. When Dalpat Shah died suddenly of illness in 1550, the infant Veer Narayan was declared king and Durgavati ruled as his regent with the help of her ministers.

All accounts of her reign describe her as an able and just ruler. Though she was not set on a career of conquest like her father-in-law, she quelled rebellions and fended off attacks from her neighbours by leading armies personally. Her bravery gained her the name Durga Shah.

This is what Abul Fazl had to say about her victories: 'She had 20,000 good soldiers with her in her battles, and 1,000 famous elephants. The treasures of the Rajahs of that country fell into her hands... It was her custom that when she heard that a tiger had made his appearance, she did not drink water till she had shot him.'

At the beginning of her reign she defeated the Miyana Afghans of Hoshangabad. They accepted her suzerainty, and many joined her service; from their clan, Shams Khan Miyana became an important general in her court.

In 1555, when Baaz Bahadur, who had taken over as the ruler of the neighbouring kingdom of Malwa, attacked Gondwana, he was soundly beaten back by Durgavati. The historian A.L. Shrivastava says, 'The defeat at the hands of a woman caused Baaz Bahadur so much humiliation that he lost every incentive for aggressive conquest and fell into sloth, and sought solace in music and sensual pleasures.'

Durgavati was devoted to her people and they loved her. She was a good administrator and undertook many public works like building tanks; one of the large reservoirs near

Jabalpur is still called the Rani Talao in memory of her. She increased the prosperity of her kingdom manifold; Abul Fazl says that the people were so prosperous during her reign that they paid their taxes in gold coins and elephants. There was enough surplus grain to export to Gujarat and the Deccan. The scholar Badauni, one of Akbar's *navratan*, puts it in his inimitable (and quite bigoted) style in *Tariq-i-Alfi*: 'All the dogs of that country were very faithful and devoted to her.'

She was also recorded as being very generous. A rock in Ramnagar has an inscription by later kings about the Garha-Mandla dynasty, which says in hyperbolic style: 'Durgavati, donated daily, millions of horses, elephants, and pieces of gold, and thus reduced the honour of the Kamadhenu [the divine cow which fulfils all wishes].'

Durgavati also patronized the arts, and important texts were written during her time. She invited several learned Maithil Brahmins to her court. One of them, Mahesh Thakur, was a brilliant scholar. Later, in 1577, he was appointed tax collector of Darbhanga by Akbar and went on to establish the dynasty of the rajas of Darbhanga, which survived till 1947.

Though major political changes took place during Durgavati's reign, all seemed well for her kingdom for nearly 14 years after a few initial attacks. In 1550 the Sur Afghan Empire in the north was embroiled in internal and external warfare after Sher Shah's death in 1545 at Kalinjar. The Surs were under attack from the exiled Mughal emperor Humayun, ruling from Kabul, and had no time to look south. The pleasure-loving Baaz Bahadur, who was no longer a threat to Durgavati, ruled Malwa. To Durgavati's north lay the kingdom of Panna, ruled by Bundela relatives, with whom she had good relations. To her south lay the Deccan sultanates, which were perpetually engaged in war with the great Hindu kingdom of Vijayanagara to their south.

In 1556 the Mughals decisively defeated Hemu, leader of the Afghan forces, in the second battle of Panipat. The young Akbar commenced his rule at just 13 years of age, under the able guardianship of Bairam Khan. At 18, an impatient and energetic Akbar began his career of conquest, which he kept up for the next 45 years, right till the end of his life. He had tripled his territories by the time he died in 1605.

Akbar unabashedly believed that expanding his territories was the duty of any worthwhile king. He said, 'A monarch should be ever intent on conquest, otherwise his neighbours rise in arms against him. The army should be exercised in warfare, lest from want of training they become self-indulgent.' An important objective of his conquests was acquiring gold; he amassed a great fortune in gold and silver coin, which filled a number of tanks in his palace. Akbar first conquered Durgavati's neighbour Malwa in 1561. Baaz Bahadur lost ignominiously and fled. Mandu was sacked. The fate of a city that resisted Akbar, especially in his younger days, was usually total annihilation in true Mongol style. After all, Akbar was a descendant of both Genghis Khan and Timur. All the defenders would be put to the sword, the women abused, all the wealth, horses, elephants appropriated and, more often than not, the city destroyed. The heads of the dead would be cut off and stacked in tall towers to strike fear far and wide.

In 1562 Akbar appointed the experienced Abdul Majid Khan, also known as Asaf Khan, as the governor of Kara Manikpur, which bordered Panna. Asaf Khan was from Herat and had been a trusted general of Humayun.

Attracted by Panna's famed diamond mines, the Mughals soon took over the territory, which submitted. Raja Ramchandra Baghela of neighbouring Rewa had to part with many treasures, including the gem of his court, the musician Tansen. The Mughals now bordered Durgavati's dominions; the wolf was at the door.

In the words of Abul Fazl:

> When Asaf Khan conquered the country of Panna, Durgavati, infatuated with the strength of her army, her courage and her war abilities, was not apprehensive of such a neighbour. When Asaf Khan was near at hand he kept open the gates of friendship and intimacy and sent spies and experienced traders into her country and made investigations about her revenue and her expenditure. When he knew the truth about her abundant collections of treasure, and her hidden stores, the desire of lordship over the country entered his mind.

Getting the nod from Akbar, Asaf Khan gathered together 10,000 cavalry and infantry and made a surprise attack on Durgavati's kingdom. The Mughal armies, particularly their artillery, were far superior to her forces. By the time the horrified queen realized that her relations with the Mughals were not as cordial as she had thought, the Mughals had already conquered Damoh, an important city in her domain.

She gathered what she could of her scattered army, many of whom deserted her to defend their families, and retreated from Singorgarh to buy time and to find a more defensible position.

She made a stand in a valley near Narrai with about five thousand men and the teenaged Veer Narayan. The valley was guarded by hills on one side and the Narmada and Gaur rivers on the other. The Mughals were chasing her and arrived at one end of the defile, albeit without their artillery. Her leading general Arjun Das had died and Durgavati herself led the troops mounted on her favourite elephant, Sarman.

After a prolonged fight Durgavati's troops managed to defeat the Mughals and chased them out of the defile. The fiery queen wanted to attack them again during the night but her advisors rejected the idea. The next day, however, the Mughal artillery arrived, and blasted through the valley. The battle went on the entire day, moving from arrows and muskets to daggers and swords as the armies came closer. Veer Narayan was badly injured, and the queen sent him to a safe place. There were now only 800 soldiers left with the queen and she ordered a retreat. An arrow struck her on her left temple. She drew it out herself; it broke, leaving the point behind. Her retreat was blocked because of the sudden rise of the water level in the river, which had been dry in the morning. An arrow then struck her neck. She said to one of her warriors, Adhir, riding in front of her on the elephant: 'Today is a day in which I am overcame in battle. God forbid that I be also overcome in name and honour, and that I fall into the hands of the enemy; act like a faithful servant, and dispose of me by this sharp dagger.'

Adhir could not bear to do it. She then unhesitatingly stabbed herself with the dagger and died on the spot.

Two months later, Asaf Khan, after thoroughly looting the country, finally besieged Chauragarh, the capital. Veer Narayan defended it valorously, but with certain defeat in sight, decided on *jauhar* – the men would fight to death, while the women burnt themselves alive.

Abul Fazl, in a rare detailed description we have of a *jauhar*, says:

> He had appointed Bhoj Kaith and Miyan Bhikari Rumi to look after the jauhar, for it is the custom of Indian rajahs under such circumstances to collect wood, cotton, grass, ghee, and such like into one place, and to bring the women and burn them, willing or unwilling. This they call the jauhar.
>
> Whoever out of feebleness of soul was backward (to sacrifice herself) was, in accordance with their custom, put to death by the Bhoj aforesaid. But four days after they had set fire to that circular pile, and all that harvest of roses had been reduced to ashes, those who opened the door found two women alive. A large piece of timber had screened them and protected them from the fire. One of them was Kamlavati, the Rani's sister, and the other the daughter of Rajah Puragadha, whom they had brought for the Rajah, but who had not yet been united to him. These two women, who had emerged from that storm of fire, obtained honour

> by being sent to kiss the threshold of the Shahenshah [i.e., were sent to Akbar's harem!].

The loot from Durgavati's kingdom was enormous: 'There were coined and uncoined gold, decorated utensils, jewels, pearls, figures, pictures, jewelled and decorated idols, figures of animals made wholly of gold, and other rarities.' Surprisingly, the loot was said to include a hundred large pots full of gold ashrafis of Alauddin Khilji.

A greedy Asaf Khan kept much of the wealth, and of the 1,000 elephants acquired, he only sent 200 to Akbar. A little later, Asaf Khan panicked when he realized he would have to give the accounts for Gondwana and went and joined Akbar's rebellious relatives. In the course of time, Akbar forgave him and reinstated him as the governor of Kara. Asaf Khan was later with Akbar at the siege of Chittor (another *jauhar*) and was made the governor of Chittor when it fell in 1568.

Dalpat Shah's brother, Chandra Shah, was reinstated as the ruler of Garha-Mandla a few years later, on accepting Akbar's suzerainty and ceding the region of Bhopal to the Mughals. The dynasty continued, gradually weakened by the Bundelas, until they were deposed by the Marathas in 1781. The last we hear of them was during the great uprising of 1857. The British blew up a descendant with a cannon, to punish him as he went about killing Englishmen in Jabalpur by pushing their heads into sacks of red chilli powder accompanied by an invocation to Kali!

The 1560s saw the destruction of the most important Hindu kingdoms of India. Gondwana was plundered in 1564.

Vijayanagara fell to the Deccan sultanates in the Battle of Talikota in 1565. Chittor was permanently destroyed by Akbar in 1568. Many Hindu rulers, however, continued to rule under Akbar's suzerainty. His liberal religious policies and inclusion of the kings in his court made them his loyal allies.

Although Garha and Chauragarh were thoroughly destroyed, ruins of Durgavati's buildings remain in Chauragarh, Singorgarh, Garha and Jabalpur. A memorial was made to Durgavati where she fell. A 19th-century British traveller, Alexander Cunningham, had this to say:

> She was interred at the place where she fell; and on her tomb to this day the passing stranger thinks it necessary to place, as a votive offering, one of the fairest he can find of those beautiful specimens of white crystal, in which the hills in this quarter abound. Two rocks lie by her side, which are supposed by the people to be her drums, converted into stone; and strange stories are told of their being still occasionally heard to sound in the stillness of the night by the people of the nearest village.

Durgavati lives on in folk memory to this day. Folk songs still talk about the three great things of the Garha-Mandla kingdom and the Gondwana region: the fertile land, the Narmada River and Rani Durgavati.

Friendly Fire, a Guru's Legacy and a King's Travails

Soon after Durgavati's marriage to Dalpat Shah, Sher Shah Suri, the founder of the Sur Empire in the north, besieged the fort of Kalinjar ruled by Kirat Singh Chandela. The strong fortress withstood six months of siege. Finally, Sher Shah decided to lay mines to blow up the fort. On 22 May 1545, as he stood on a tall tower supervising the attack, a rocket which had been fired against the fort ricocheted off the wall and hit a heap of ammunition, causing an enormous explosion which fatally injured Sher Shah. The assault on the fort, however, continued and Kalinjar was finally taken at sunset. The garrison was massacred. The news of the victory was taken to Sher Shah in his tent, who is supposed to have smiled with joy, and then died. Without this accident, there may have been no Mughal rule in India, as it was only Sher Shah's death that allowed Humayun to recapture Delhi from Sher Shah's incompetent successors.

An important guru who stayed in Durgavati's kingdom for a few years was the Gosain guru Vitthalnath, the son of the saint Vallabhacharya. Many in Gujarat and Maharashtra, particularly the wealthy merchants, still follow the Krishna-centred Pushti Marg of Vallabhacharya. There is a legend that Birbal, who hailed from the town Kalpi in the region, was still poor and obscure when he visited the guru. He was given a vest by the guru as a blessing and, wearing it, ascended to his later heights of royal favour. Vitthalnath is supposed to have left Gondwana just before the Mughal invasion. Birbal later helped

Vitthalnath get grants of land rights in Gokul. The Gosain's descendants were patronized by the next few generations of the Mughal kings until they fled with their idol of Krishna holding up the Govardhan, called Srinathji, during the reign of the iconoclastic Aurangzeb and established the important temple at Nathdwara, which is run till today by the same family. This story also illustrates the continuity of life in India, in spite of so many political changes and conquests over the centuries.

The conquest of Mandu, and the romance of Baaz Bahadur and Roopmati, has passed into legend, with a proliferation of films and books recounting the tale. Akbar sent his foster brother Adham Khan to conquer Mandu. Baaz Bahadur fled and his queen, Roopmati, chose to poison herself rather than submit her virtue to Adham Khan. Adham Khan kept most of the enormous loot for himself, and sent a pittance to Akbar. An enraged teenaged Akbar rushed to Mandu, Malwa's capital, and made Adham Khan give up the plunder, but forgave him at the request of Adham Khan's mother, Maham Anaga, his childhood nurse. Next year, however, he had Adham Khan killed by having him thrown head first over the walls of Agra Fort (twice, to make sure he was quite dead) when Adham Khan tried to attack him at night after being asked for accounts. The defeated Baaz Bahadur roamed about for the next 15 years, unsuccessfully trying to get support from neighbouring kingdoms to win back his kingdom, and finally surrendered to Akbar. Akbar generously gave him a position in his court, where he became known as one of the best musicians along with Tansen, and evolved a special style of music called the Baazkhani!

The Admiral Queen

The Rani Abbakkas of Ullal

> Her complexion was as black as that of a natural Ethiopian... She was girded at the waist, with a plain piece of thick white Cotton, and barefoot... From the waist upwards the Queen was naked... In brief, her aspect and habit represented rather a dirty Kitchen wench, or Laundress, than a delicate and noble Queen; whereupon I said within myself. Behold by whom are routed in India the Armies of the King of Spain which in Europe is so great a matter!
>
> Pietro della Valle, Italian traveller

Rani Abbakka Chowta was the legendary queen of Ullal near Mangalore, who fought off the Portuguese during the sixteenth and seventeenth centuries. Historically, it is believed that there were at least two queens of the same name who ruled Ullal from the 1540s to at least the 1620s, and there are many tales of valour associated with each of them. There was a queen Abbakka who fought the Portuguese in 1557 and 1568. There is another queen Abbakka who gained a great naval victory in 1618 and who was 40 years old when Italian traveller Pietro della Valle met her in 1623. In legend, Rani Abbakka is commemorated as one great queen, Abbakka Mahadevi, a little like the Phantom in the comics by Lee Falk. She was known as the Abhaya Rani, for her fearlessness, and is considered the first Indian woman freedom fighter against European colonialism.

In the early 1500s, the glory days of the Vijayanagara Empire, many kings on the Arabian Sea coast of Karnataka were their feudatories but functioned almost independently. The Portuguese had reached India in 1498 and within a couple of decades had a string of forts along the west coast of India. They dominated trade on the Indian Ocean and were able to set terms with Vijayanagara, the Deccan sultanates, the Gujarat Sultanate and later, even the Mughal kings. After the fall of Vijayanagara at the hands of the Deccan sultanates in the Battle of Talikota in 1565, the coastal kingdoms lost their protector and in order to survive they had to independently manage the Deccan sultanates, the Portuguese, the Dutch and other small kingdoms.

Many of these kingdoms grew rich on European trade – the silver and gold that had been looted from the Aztecs and Incas poured into India as payment for spices and textiles. Ocean trade routes with the Arabs had been established as early as the seventh century CE and there were many local Muslim trading communities, like the Moplahs of Kerala and Byaris of Tulu Nadu, who were involved in the maritime trade of pepper and ginger.

Rani Abbakka belonged to the Chowta dynasty which ruled over a small but fertile part of coastal Canara called Ullal, situated 10 kilometres from Mangalore, an ancient port mentioned by both the Roman Pliny and the Alexandrian Ptolemy 2000 years ago. Like the other coastal kings, the Chowtas too were feudatories of the great Vijayanagara kingdom and remained under the supervision of the Nayaks of Keladi (also former feudatories of Vijayanagara) even after the destruction of Vijayanagara in 1565. Mangalore was a crucial port for the kingdom of Vijayanagara, through which they imported their all-important source of power: war horses brought in by the Arabs. The port was also important for the export of spices and textiles since antiquity.

On to this fertile spice coast descended the Portuguese; they were the first Europeans to finally find a sea route to India in 1498 under Vasco da Gama. With their superior naval technology, they quickly established total dominance of the Indian Ocean, creating a ring of forts around it from Mozambique to Sri Lanka, and eventually farther to West Bengal, the Malaccas, the Indonesian islands, Macau in China, and even Japan. The Portuguese controlled the entire spice route within 20 years of Vasco da Gama's voyage.

For the whole of the 16th century, the Portuguese monopolized trade on the Indian Ocean. No other European power challenged them – the Dutch and English only managed to make their way there by the beginning of the 17th century. The Portuguese would not let any other ships trade on the Indian Ocean unless they had a Portuguese *cartaz* (permit), which they charged for (naturally!). The Indian Ocean, which had hitherto been a free-trade zone with Arab, Egyptian, Persian and Indian ships, now became a Portuguese pond. Even the great Mughal king Akbar had to take a *cartaz* from them for any ships travelling on the Indian Ocean. During this time, the Portuguese engaged in a number of battles with Indian navies several times their size, but Portuguese superiority in weapon technology meant that they invariably won.

The Portuguese advance on the smaller kingdoms along the coast met with fierce resistance. Kingdoms like Ullal and Calicut (now Kozhikode) which had traded directly with the Arabs, bitterly fought the Portuguese and refused to knuckle under. There were naval engagements and their cities were often attacked and cannonaded by the Portuguese but they did not give up. They managed to survive for hundreds of years. The British finally annexed most of these kingdoms, but only after the fall of Tipu Sultan of Mysore in 1799.

In 1526, the Portuguese, under their viceroy Lopo Vaz de Sampaio, took possession of the Mangalore port. Ullal was just across the water from Mangalore. It was then ruled by Thirumala Raya III of the Chowta dynasty.

The Chowtas were a Digambar Jain dynasty and they had migrated from Gujarat around the 12th century. Their main centre was Moodabidri, known as the Jain Dakshin Kashi, as it was a cultural centre with beautiful Jain temples and a seat of Jain scholarship. Descendants of Chowta kings still live in the Chowta Palace in Moodabidri with its beautifully ornate carvings.

The Chowtas followed a matrilineal system, which is still followed among some communities like the Nairs in Kerala, whereby the inheritance descends through the female line; it is the man who rules, however, and not the woman. The ruler's sister's son becomes the king. Unusually, since Thirumala Raya III had no nephews, he trained his niece Abbakka in princely crafts like military science, archery and sword fighting. Such training was normally reserved for men. According to local legends, she was a visionary child, unequalled in her capabilities in all the arts and sciences.

A strategic match was arranged for her with King Lakshmappa Bangaraja II of Mangalore. As per the system in matrilineal societies, Abbakka continued to live in her own home. The married couple met occasionally and her three children stayed with her. The marriage was fractured, as per legend, because of Abbakka's desire to fight the Portuguese, and her husband's wish to compromise. She is supposed to have sent back her wedding jewellery to her husband over this dispute, which was tantamount to a divorce.

This Abbakka Devi is said to have ruled Ullal from 1544 to 1582, while Lakshmappa Bangaraja II ruled Mangalore from 1545 to 1556. His nephew, Kamaraya III, who was believed to have conspired with the Portuguese against his uncle, and later supported them against Rani Abbakka, was in power in Mangalore from 1556 to 1612.

Rani Abbakka ruled over a multi-religious kingdom. Though she was Jain, her people and her administration largely consisted of Hindus and Muslims. Her army was also diverse; in particular, the Muslim fishermen community was a great strength for her while fighting naval battles with the Portuguese.

Since Rani Abbakka was not willing to accept the Portuguese embargo on her ships travelling to Arabia, she would trade in spices and fabrics with the help of the Zamorin ruler of Calicut. She also refused to pay the Portuguese the tribute they demanded despite her ships being continually attacked at sea.

In 1555, the Portuguese finally sent Admiral Don Alvaro da Silveira against Ullal. Rani Abbakka fought hard and managed to hold them back. The battle ended with an uneasy truce.

Once Vijayanagara fell in 1565, the Portuguese became emboldened in their attacks on its erstwhile feudatories.

In 1567 the Portuguese army attacked Ullal under General Joao Peixoto. He captured the city and occupied the palace. However, the queen escaped and hid in a mosque. At night, with 200 soldiers, she managed to kill General Peixoto and 70 Portuguese soldiers. The invaders fled to their ships. She followed them and killed the Admiral Mascarenhas.

In 1570, Rani Abbakka formed an alliance with the sultans of Bijapur and Ahmednagar, and the Zamorin of Calicut against the Portuguese, holding off their attacks for a while.

In 1581, the Goa viceroy Anthony D' Noronha led an attack against Ullal with a grand armada. Ullal fell and was destroyed. The queen also died, after leading her men from the front with a battle cry exhorting them to save the motherland and push the invaders back to sea, according to legend.

But this was not the end. There rose from the ashes, like a phoenix, another Abbakka in the dynasty. She gained great fame throughout the Indian Ocean by attacking and burning the Portuguese fleet in 1618.

In keeping with family tradition, she continued defying the Portuguese and trading directly with the Middle East. When the Portuguese captured a rich ship of hers returning from Mecca she planned a secret attack on their fleet. On a dark night, her fishermen soldiers, the Mogaveeras and the Moplahs, got into boats, sneaked in among the Portuguese ships, and used thousands of *agnivans* or fire arrows, and coconut torches to set the ships on fire (probably the last recorded use of fire arrows in battle). The Portuguese navy had to retreat after having incurred heavy losses. This was akin to the defeat of the Spanish Armada by the British just two decades ago – Abbakka, however, was unaided by any divine storm, unlike the British.

Her fame resounded around the Indian Ocean. Pietro della Valle, an Italian traveller, toured India's west coast between 1621 and 1624. He had earlier met the great Persian emperor Shah Abbas, who had praised Abbakka, and asked Pietro to meet her when he went to India. Shah Abbas, along with the other kings around the Indian Ocean, was greatly impressed by Abbakka's unprecedented defeat of the dreaded Portuguese.

Pietro della Valle managed to run her to earth in the village of Manel, where the 40-year-old queen had gone to supervise some irrigation work. She asked him about his journeys, and then said, 'After seeing the Great Turk, Persian Emperor, Mogul Emperor and Venkatappa Nayaka [her Keladi overlord] what is there to see in this wilderness?'

'I came only to see you, Your Majesty. You are so well known in my part of the world!' was Pietro's answer.

He notes that she had a very small and humble entourage. 'We beheld the Queen coming alone in the same way without any other woman, on foot, accompany'd only with four, or six, foot Soldiers before her, each of them had a Sword in his hand, or at most a Sword and Buckler; there were also as many behind her of the same sort, one of whom carry'd over her a very ordinary umbrella made of Palm-leaves.'

He was not at all impressed by her appearance, but quite appreciated her bearing.

> She was corpulent and gross, particularly in regard to her person below the waist where her corpulence, owing to the cotton cloth which she wears, which, according to Indian fashion, is worn very tight, is very evident, but not heavy, for she seemed to walk nimbly enough; her Age may be about forty years, although the Portugals had described her to me as much older. She was cloth'd, or rather girded at the waist, with a plain piece of thick white Cotton, and bare-foot, which is the custom of the Indian Gentile Women, both high and low... From the waist upwards the Queen was naked, saving that she had a cloth ty'd round about her Head, and hanging a little down upon her Breast and Shoulders... her voice was very graceful in comparison with her Person, and she spoke like a prudent and judicious Woman. I imagine she was handsome in her Youth; and, indeed, the Report is that she hath been much of a Lady, of majestic beauty, though stern rather than gentle.

Pietro della Valle, however, was very impressed by her dedication to her work.

> She was little at home, but, rising at break of day, went forthwith to her Works and there stayed till dinner; and as soon as dinner was done returned thither again and remained there till night... active and vigorous in actions

> of war and weighty affairs. Moreover they said that at night she was employ'd a good while in giving Audience and doing Justice to her Subjects; so that it was better to go and speak to her in the field, while she was viewing her Workmen, than in the house.

Rani Abbakka's story, where the tales of the two queens are fused into one legendary character, lives on in folk memory in southern Karnataka, through folk songs and performances of *Yakshagana*, the local theatre form. In *Bhuta Kola*, a local ritual dance, a person in trance recounts the great deeds of Abbakka Mahadevi. In all these, Abbakka is portrayed as dark and good-looking, always dressed simply as a commoner.

In 2012, the Indian Coast Guard acknowledged India's rare woman naval hero and named a patrol vessel *Rani Abbakka* after her.

Sea Wolves

Other famous naval heroes in the war against the Portuguese were the Marakkars. Kunjali Marakkars were the Muslim naval admirals for the Zamorin or Samudrin of Calicut. They were of Arab origin, and held the Portuguese at bay, generation after generation, for 100 years. Kunjali Marakkar IV finally surrendered to the Portuguese in 1600, under assurance of safety. However, he was taken to Goa, and cut into four quarters, his head pickled in brine.

It is interesting that Kunjali's main lieutenant was a Chinese boy called Chinale, who was probably from Malacca and had been enslaved by the Portuguese. He was rescued by Kunjali. Chinale was a Muslim, and Kunjali's feared right-hand man. After Kunjali's death, Chinale yielded to the persuasion of the Fathers and became a Christian with the baptismal name of Bartholomew. This, however, did not save him – it just ensured his burial in consecrated ground after he was hanged.

Indian naval training centres are named after Kunjali Marakkar, and the government has issued a stamp to commemorate him.

The Challenger of Mughal Might

Chand Bibi

Chand Beeby, put on armour, and with a veil on her face, and a naked sword in her hand, flew to defend the breach. The feats of the valiant heroine... became the subject of universal admiration and conversation in the enemy's lines. During the whole night she superintended in person the repairs of the breach, and by dawn of day it was built up to the height of seven or eight feet.

Mohammad Kasim Ferishta,
History of the Rise of Mahomedan Power in India

Chand Bibi (r. 1579–84 CE and 1595–99 CE) ruled as the regent in Bijapur, her husband's kingdom, as well as later in Ahmednagar, her father's kingdom. Most know of her as the brave heroine who successfully saved her tiny kingdom from the mighty Mughal forces. However, that was merely an episode from the end of her life. She lived a rich and unusual life before that and has many achievements to her credit.

In the 1500s, the Deccan was divided into five independent sultanates: Ahmednagar, Berar, Bidar, Bijapur and Golconda towards the north, and the mighty empire of Vijayanagara to the south. The sultanates had a ruling class which was one of the most ethnically diverse ever seen. There were the Wilayatis or Afaqis, who came from *'Wilayat'*, the land beyond the Hindu Kush, and were of Turkish, Afghan, Persian or Central Asian origin; the Deccanis or converted native Hindus; and the Habshis or Abyssinians (Ethiopians). The many factions in these courts constantly battled each other for control, the Habshis typically siding with the Deccanis.

Incidentally, lakhs of Ethiopians migrated to India and were seamlessly absorbed into the local population. Arab traders would procure slaves from Ethiopia, some from raids, and some sold to them by local kings, in exchange for Indian textiles and other luxury goods. The Habshis would then be sold in Baghdad or brought to India, where they were much in demand as military slaves in the Deccan. They would be converted to Islam and trained in warfare and would often join special Habshi contingents. Malik Ambar, the Ethiopian vizier of Ahmednagar, had an elite troop of 10,000 Abyssinians. They were often freed and many went on to occupy important posts as generals and ministers. They intermarried with local communities and even married into royal families.

These kingdoms were perpetual battlegrounds. Factions of nobles fought each other for control within the sultanates. The sultanates also warred against each other continuously, forming and breaking alliances and intermarrying; soon they were all related to each other. Vijayanagara kings like Krishnadevaraya played them off against each other, aligning with some against others, to maintain the balance of power.

In 1562, the four sultans of Ahmednagar, Bijapur, Golconda and Bidar got together and formulated a plan to launch a concerted attack against Vijayanagara. As part of the deal, Chand Bibi, the 12-year-old daughter of Hussain Shah of Ahmednagar was married to King Ali Adil Shah of Bijapur. It is worth mentioning here that Ali Adil Shah had previously conducted many joint campaigns with King Rama Raya of Vijayanagara against Ahmednagar and had visited Vijayanagara as an honoured guest. Ibrahim Shah, the ruler of Golconda, had lived in Vijayanagara for many years when he was fleeing from his brother; Rama Raya had given him refuge. But in politics there are no permanent friends or permanent enemies, only permanent interests.

In January 1565, when Chand Bibi was 15, the Battle of Talikota took place, with Vijayanagara on one side and the combined forces of the four sultans on the other side. During the battle, King Rama Raya was captured and beheaded, causing his troops to lose heart and flee. Within a few days, the sultanate armies reached Vijayanagara, then the largest city in India, and the second-largest in the world, and tore it apart, permanently destroying it. Their conquest complete, the sultans went back to their own territories.

The destruction of Vijayanagara was horrific. As Robert Sewell, a historian, puts it:

> Never perhaps in the history of the world has such havoc been wrought, and wrought so suddenly, on so splendid a city; teeming with a wealthy and industrious population in the full plenitude of prosperity one day, and on the next

seized, pillaged, and reduced to ruins, amid scenes of savage massacre and horrors beggaring description.

Chand Bibi, meanwhile, continued to live in Bijapur, a prosperous city with lakhs of inhabitants. Her education continued for many years after her marriage; she was skilled in Persian, Arabic, Turkish, and Urdu and fluently spoke the dialects in current use in the army. She drew and painted well, played the veena with skill, and had other accomplishments suited to royal women. She was also considered very beautiful and elegantly dressed. She used to ride astride a richly caparisoned horse when travelling in the city or while hunting, with her face slightly concealed by a wisp of a veil of very fine material.

After their brief collaboration, the sultanates resumed their internecine conflicts. After a few initial battles Chand Bibi's husband, Ali Adil Shah, came to an agreement with her brother, Murtaza Shah, who had been named the sultan of Ahmednagar after her father's death in 1565. The agreement stated that they would not interfere with each other as they extended their respective territories in other directions. Murtaza Shah ruled for more than 20 years, conquering Berar in 1574 and killing its sultan. Ali Adil Shah focused on conquering the Nayak kingdoms one by one, which had been Vijayanagara's feudatories.

An interesting incident took place during his campaigns, highlighting the number of assertive women chieftains in the region. He held an assembly where he bestowed robes of honour on the Nayaks who had accepted his suzerainty. He had men's clothes made for the male rulers and women's for the female rulers. The women, however, protested and said that they wanted the same clothes as the men, whereupon he immediately changed their robes of honour to the same as that of the men.

Ali Adil Shah had no children, neither from Chand Bibi nor from anyone else, a possible reason being that his preferences quite openly lay elsewhere. Ferishta, the official historian of Bijapur in later times, relates this surprisingly uncomplimentary tale, which puts a bizarre twist on the classic story of the virtuous queen versus the rapacious attacker.

> About this time, Moortuza Nizam Shah [the king of Ahmednagar] determined to reduce the fort of Bidur, Ally Bereed Shah [the king of Bidur]... solicited Ally Adil Shah [the king of Bijapur] to march to his aid. The latter consented, but required, as a preliminary, that Ally Bereed should give up a certain young eunuch, celebrated for his beauty throughout the Deccan, and to whom he was much attached... Ally Bereed reluctantly agreed to the demand of Ally Adil Shah. When the latter heard of the approach of this youth, he went out to meet him, and appointed an elegant palace for his reception. But on his first interview, the young man was so incensed at the behaviour of Ally Adil Shah, that, drawing forth a dagger, he stabbed the king to the heart. This event happened on April 20, AD 1579. The eunuch, as might be expected, fell a victim to his conduct.

With Ali Adil Shah's unexpected and scandalous death, nine-year-old Ibrahim Adil Shah II, son of his brother Tahmasp, was crowned the sultan; earlier that year, Ali Adil Shah had declared the boy as his heir. The 29-year-old Chand Bibi was declared his guardian and put in charge of Ibrahim's education. Nobleman Kamil Khan Dakkhani was appointed regent. For a while Kamil behaved well but, as Ferishta puts it:

> At length, intoxicated with power, he became guilty of some disrespect towards Chand Beeby, who turned her thoughts to effect his destruction. She therefore secretly sent a message to Hajy Kishwur Khan, an officer of high rank, observing, that as the Regent was unfit for his office, she wished to remove him, and to bestow it upon himself. Hajy Kishwur Khan, allured by these hopes of advancement, formed a plot, with several chiefs, to seize Kamil Khan.

Kamil Khan tried to flee, but was caught and beheaded. However, Kishwur Khan soon got into a quarrel with the other nobles. Worried that Chand Bibi would replace him with the senior noble Mustafa Khan, Kishwur Khan had him assassinated. When Chand Bibi protested, he had her imprisoned in the fort of Satara. He was, however, defeated by an army led by the Habshi noble Ikhlas Khan, who then became the regent and invited Chand Bibi back as Ibrahim's guardian.

Taking advantage of this conflict, the armies of Ahmednagar and Golconda joined forces and besieged Bijapur with 40,000 cavalry in 1580. There were very few defenders, as many of the nobles belonging to other factions refused to support the Habshis. Chand Bibi, however, sustained a spirited defence. In the words of a later chronicler, Captain Cecil Cowley:

> The queen, accompanied by her nephew the king, used to go from post to post at night, cheering, encouraging and directing all... After days of... bombardment by the enemy, a portion of the city wall gave way. Notwithstanding the torrential downpour the queen guarded the breach in person, collected the masons of the city, and personally superintended the work of repair, leaving the spot neither by day nor night till it was safe against attack by storm. Her devotion and spirited personal valour inspired confidence in all, which now amounted to positive enthusiasm.

Regent Ikhlas Khan Habshi, now at his wit's end, went to her and asked her to solve the internal conflict among the nobles. She asked him to resign and appointed a new Afaqi regent, a nobleman named Abul Hasan. With his help, Chand Bibi was able to bring together the Bijapuri nobles who had refused to work with Ikhlas Khan, and gathered a force of 20,000 cavalry. She also managed to persuade her Maratha vassals to disrupt the supply lines of the besiegers. The siege was finally lifted after nearly a year and the troops from Ahmednagar and Golconda returned home, pursued and plundered all the way by the army of Bijapur, led by Dilawar Khan, another high-ranking general in the Bijapuri army.

On his return to Bijapur, Dilawar Khan felt empowered to execute a coup. He had both Ikhlas Khan and Abul Hasan killed, and declared himself regent. He was very successful in wresting total control and ruled Bijapur for the next eight years until Ibrahim Adil Shah attained maturity.

Chand Bibi now felt superfluous in Bijapur and when Ibrahim's sister was sent to Ahmednagar in 1584 to marry

Murtaza's son Meeran, she went along and stayed on in Ahmednagar. Her brother Murtaza had started displaying signs of madness. Ferishta, the historian, recounted a very peculiar incident. Murtaza had asked his chief minister to give the priceless jewels captured in the battle against Vijayanagara to his favourite dancer, Fattey Khan. When the jewels were laid out for his inspection, Murtaza grew suspicious that some were missing and, in a rage, threw them all into the fire. The chief minister managed to save most of them except the pearls, which were burnt. The incident led to him being called 'Murtaza dewana' by the commoners in the kingdom. He once tried to kill his teenage son Meeran by setting fire to his room while he slept. Meeran escaped to Daulatabad. Soon, all the ministers defected to support him, and he returned to Ahmednagar and arrested his father. A short while later, Murtaza was murdered by his son, who locked him into a steam room with the fires turned up.

The teenaged Meeran Shah became king in 1588 and established a reign of terror along with a group of other drunken teenaged companions. To eliminate potential rivals, he killed off all his male relatives he could lay his hands on. It is said that 15 princes were killed in a single day. In less than a year, the nobles who could no longer bear the oppression executed a coup and his head was cut off and put up on a pike.

From 1589 to 1595, the kingdom witnessed wars of succession, and the short reigns of three kings. In 1595, after the death of the last king, Ibrahim Shah, four opposing groups set up candidates for kingship and Ahmednagar readied itself for another period of warfare.

But things were about to change.

After the death of Muhammad bin Tughlaq in 1351, for a period of 150 years, the northern kings had not looked south; they were too busy facing invasions from beyond the northern borders and fighting each other. In 1526, the Turko-Mongol Babur finally established the Mughal Empire by conquering Delhi, but it was his grandson Akbar who started to aggressively expand his kingdom from 1560 onwards. After conquering all the kingdoms north of the Vindhyas he finally looked south in 1591. Emperor Akbar wanted to conquer the rich Deccan sultanates, as well as throw the Portuguese out of India by capturing their seaports, like Goa, which could only be accessed through these sultanates.

He sent a message to the four Deccan sultanates to submit and pay tribute to the Mughal emperor. They were, of course, not inclined to do so. Ahmednagar was the northernmost among the Deccan forts and thus became Akbar's first target (he was also positively insulted by the measly gift of 15 elephants, and the few jewels and textiles they had sent back for him along with their refusal to submit to his reign). Viewing the ongoing succession wars as a perfect opportunity, Akbar instructed his son Murad to proceed to Ahmednagar along with the great general Abdur Rahim Khan-e-Khana.

Murad was elated when he received a request from Mian Manju, the chief minister of Ahmednagar, for his help in installing as king his candidate Ahmad, who was of doubtful lineage. On 14 December 1595, the mighty Mughal war machine appeared at the gates of the Ahmednagar Fort to lay siege. Akbar had not failed in a single conquest he had attempted in the last 40 years of his rule. He was considered invincible and was even thought to possess supernatural powers. The people of Ahmednagar now turned to Chand Bibi. Mian Manju fled the fort, with the boy pretender, to Bijapur to get help. Chand Bibi had the infant grandson of her brother crowned as Bahadur Nizam Shah and ruled in his stead. Instead of submitting, Chand Bibi decided to defend the fort. She sent messengers to Bijapur and Golconda, asking for help, since only a combined effort from the Deccan sultanates could possibly keep the Mughals at bay – it had to be one for all and all for one. Golconda and particularly Bijapur, ruled at that time by her erstwhile ward Ibrahim Adil Shah II, responded and sent out large armies to aid her. She also convinced Nehung Khan, the Habshi general who had set up his own candidate for the throne of Ahmednagar, to help her withstand the siege. He managed to break through the Mughal encirclement and join her in the fort.

As news spread of more than 30,000 cavalry forces from Bijapur and Golconda gathering near the town of Shahdurg, the Mughals decided to capture the fort as soon as possible. Their expert sappers secretly dug five tunnels full of explosives under the walls of the fort. When Chand Bibi came to know about this, she ordered two of them to be countermined, to remove the explosives. However, Murad ordered the third to be blasted, and a section of the city wall came down. In the words of Ferishta:

> Immediately as the breach was made, many of the principal officers of the besieged prepared for flight. Chand Beeby, on the contrary, put on armour, and with a veil on her face, and a naked sword in her hand, flew to defend the breach. This instance of intrepidity brought back the fugitives, who now one and all joined her...
>
> An obstinate defence took place at the foot of the breach, where the assailants suffered severely from the heavy fire of the besieged. The ditch was nearly filled with dead carcasses; and although several storming parties succeeded each other from four o'clock in the evening till nightfall, they were successfully repulsed.

The Mughals marvelled at Chand Bibi.

> The feats of the valiant heroine, Chand Beeby, who had been seen by all defending the breach, became the subject of universal admiration and conversation in the enemy's lines... During the whole night she superintended in person the repairs of the breach, and by dawn of day it was built up to the height of seven or eight feet.

Meanwhile, the sultanates' troops started marching to Ahmednagar from Shahdurg. The Mughals had thoroughly looted the nearby towns by then and were now short on supplies. There was also dissension in the camp between Murad and Abdur Rahim. As historian Vincent Smith puts it: 'The jealous hostility which marked the relations of Prince Murad with the Khan i Khanan continued to exist undiminished.'

According to Ferishta, the Mughals made overtures, and according to Abul Fazl, author of the *Akbarnama*, Chand

Bibi reached out to the enemy. A deal was struck – Bahadur Nizam Shah would be recognized as king of Ahmednagar by the Mughals under the suzerainty of the emperor; jewels, elephants, and other valuables would be handed over, as also the province of Berar. For Chand Bibi this was a very good deal, because had her allies lost, she would have no chance of survival. Murad's willingness to sign the treaty was surprising to a lot of his contemporaries. In fact, Abul Fazl in the Akbarnama heavily criticized it later:

> A party of men, owing to ignorance, and some, from interested motives, accepted these improper proposals. Though able men represented the want of food, the dismay and the trickery of the garrison, it was of no avail. Owing to the influence of bribes, and the listening to idle tales, the peace-proposals were accepted on 28 February, 1596, and fighting was laid aside.

The Mughals retreated to Berar and started to establish their administration. The allied armies reached Ahmednagar three days later. Chand Bibi was fully supported in her nomination of Bahadur Nizam Shah by Ibrahim of Bijapur, who told Mian Manju to desist from championing his candidate, Ahmad. Ibrahim wisely gave Ahmad an estate and invited Mian Manju to join his court in Bijapur, relieving Chand Bibi of his presence.

Chand Bibi then appointed her long-time associate Mahomed Khan as the new peshwa (Persian for chief minister; the Marathas borrowed this term). However, when he promptly started purging his rival nobles in a now-familiar scenario, Chand Bibi asked Ibrahim for help again. Ibrahim sent troops led by the eunuch Sohail Khan, who besieged the fort for four months. Mahomed Khan treacherously sent a message to Abdur Rahim in Berar that he was willing to hand over the kingdom to the Mughals. When the garrison inside the fort found out, they immediately handed over Mahomed Khan to Chand Bibi, who then made Nehung Khan the new peshwa.

Meanwhile, the Mughals were already intruding into Ahmednagar. Under Sohail Khan 60,000 troops from Bijapur, Golconda and Ahmednagar now moved to fight the Mughals, who had a much smaller contingent. They met in the Battle of Sonpeth in January 1597. After two days of intensive battle the Deccani army was destroyed and Sohail Khan barely escaped with his life. The Mughal army could have moved on to besiege Ahmednagar, but Prince Murad and Abdur Rahim started bickering again. Sick of receiving Murad's complaining letters, Akbar recalled Abdur Rahim and deputed Abul Fazl to the Deccan instead.

With this going on, the Mughal army was in stasis. Murad was by now quite sick due to his drunken excesses and he finally died in 1599, at the age of 32. Akbar now deputed his youngest son Daniyal to the Deccan to besiege Ahmednagar, and he himself, at the age of 57, moved south with 80,000 horses to accomplish his long-time dream of conquering the Deccan.

The Deccan kingdoms watched apprehensively as the Mughal juggernaut rolled in. Akbar stopped to conquer Khandesh and besiege Asirgarh. He sent Daniyal and Abdur

Rahim on to Ahmednagar. The new peshwa, Nehung Khan, who was having a tussle of wills with Chand Bibi, had left with his troops and this time Chand Bibi had a much-reduced garrison with which to hold the fort. She realized that there was absolutely no hope of successfully defending the fort and decided to negotiate terms with the Mughals whereby she would surrender Ahmednagar and continue to rule under Mughal suzerainty from Junnar. She made the mistake of discussing this with a senior officer, the eunuch Humeed Khan. As per Ferishta's account: 'Humeed Khan ran out into the streets, declaring that Chand Sooltana was in treaty with the Moguls for the delivery of the fort; and the shortsighted and ungrateful Deccanies, headed by Humeed Khan, rushed into her private apartments, and put her to death.'

Thus ended the life of Chand Bibi, who had always suffered more because of the infighting among her power-hungry nobles than from external threats. She was buried in an unnamed grave. Again and again, when things got out of hand, the people and nobles of both Bijapur and Ahmednagar had turned to her for a solution, relying on her good sense and commitment to the welfare of the kingdom. She would invariably solve their problems and settle things, until another short-sighted and ambitious nobleman would start the cycle again.

The fort did not surrender instantly, but the Mughals could not be resisted. Mines were tunnelled under the walls, filled with gunpowder and exploded. The walls were breached, the Mughal forces poured in, and the town sacked. The royal family was taken prisoner, and sent to the Mughal fort at Burhanpur. This was Akbar's last campaign. He died in 1605 and his son Salim was crowned as Jahangir.

This, however, was not the end of the Ahmednagar kingdom. The Habshi general Malik Ambar crowned a prince, Murtaza, as the new Nizamshahi king and held many forts and much of the countryside against the Mughals for nearly 30 years, to the frustrated rage of Jahangir. The Mughals had to struggle for almost another hundred years to conquer the Deccan, finally succeeding under Aurangzeb in 1687, but the victory was pyrrhic and brief. Within 25 years, the Marathas effectively threw them out again.

The Deccan Sultanates

After the death of Muhammad bin Tughlaq in 1351, the south quickly broke up into many independent kingdoms. Vijayanagara, founded in 1336 in south Karnataka by the Hindu warriors Hakka and Bukka, and the Bahmani Sultanate, founded in 1347 in Daulatabad in north Maharashtra, by an erstwhile Tughlaq governor Alauddin Hasan Bahman Shah, went on to become the two most powerful states of the Deccan region.

In 1481, the Bahmani Sultanate splintered into five kingdoms, often called the successor states or the Deccan sultanates. The five founders of the Deccan sultanates came from a variety of backgrounds: the prosperous Bahmani court was a magnet for adventurers from all over the world.

The sultanate of Ahmednagar (1490–1633) was founded by Malik Ahmad, the son of a converted Telugu Brahmin from Vijayanagara, who had risen to become the Nizam-ul-Mulk (chief minister) of the Bahmani kingdom. The dynasty was thus called the Nizamshahi.

The sultanate of Bijapur (1490–1686) was founded by Yusuf Adil Shah, about whose origins there were many legends. Ferishta reported that Yusuf was the son of the Ottoman emperor Murad II and that his mother had saved him from strangulation by his brother by replacing him with a slave. He then escaped to Persia, finally making his way to India. Other accounts state that he was of Georgian or Persian origin. (One should note, however, that almost all the slaves who became kings around this time always claimed to be of noble, if not royal, origin.)

The sultanate of Berar (1490–1574) was founded by Imad-ul-Mulk who was by birth a Kannada Hindu Brahmin.

The sultanate of Golconda (1512–1687) was founded by Quli Qutb-ul-Mulk, a Central Asian Turkoman. He belonged to the colourfully named tribe of 'Black Sheep Turkomans', of Turkic Shia origin.

The sultanate of Bidar (1489–1619) was founded by Ali Barid, descended from Qasim Barid, from the modern-day Georgia, and of either Turkic, Armenian or Hungarian descent. A smaller sixth state of Khandesh in central India was founded by an Arab.

The Chess Player

Nur Jahan

> Day by day her influence and dignity increased... No grant of lands was conferred upon any woman except under her seal... Sometimes she would sit in the balcony of her palace, while the nobles would present themselves, and listen to her dictates. Coin was struck in her name... [and] on all farmans [Persian for grants or permits] also receiving the Imperial signature, the name of 'Nur Jahan, the Queen Begam,' was jointly attached. [Until] at last her authority reached such a pass that the King was such only in name.
>
> Mirza Muhammad, *Ikbal-nama-i Jahangiri*

Nur Jahan (r. 1611–27 CE*), wife of the Mughal emperor Jahangir, was the de facto ruler of the largest, richest and most powerful empire ever controlled by a woman. Queen Victoria certainly ruled a larger empire but she was a constitutional monarch, functioning only as a figurehead; the decisions were taken by the parliament and ministers. Though Nur Jahan was not the crowned ruler, it was well established that she took all the decisions and her nominees occupied all the major posts in the empire for 15 years. She was a master strategist in the game of political chess. Beyond her administrative and political skills she was tremendously creative and stylish, setting lasting precedents in the fields of fashion, jewellery, cuisine, entertainment, literature, architecture, gardening and interior design, and indeed, almost anything she touched.*

The Mughal court was by far the richest court in the world at the beginning of the 16th century. As Nicholas Withington, a European traveller, recorded in his journal, 'The greatnesse of this Kinge, the Greate Mogul... is soe greate in comparison of most Christian Kinges that the report would be almost incredible.'

The Turko-Mongol ruler Babur from Central Asia founded the Mughal Empire in India in 1526. In 1556 his grandson, 13-year-old Akbar, reclaimed it after 15 years of Afghan rule by Sher Shah Suri and his descendants. Akbar was the true founder of the Mughal Empire. He was a ferocious warrior and never lost a campaign. He tripled his territory to include all the area north of the Vindhyas.

Salim (who later took the regnal name Jahangir), Akbar's beloved son, was born in 1569 after many prayers and pilgrimages. His mother was the Hindu princess of Amer. Salim was intelligent and able and had a broad education from the best of tutors. He studied languages including Persian, Turkish, Arabic and Hindi, as well as subjects including arithmetic, history, geography, music and painting. Like any well-brought-up prince, he was taught archery, riding, swordsmanship and rifle shooting as well. He was a good shot and an enthusiastic hunter and once estimated that he had killed 28,532 animals!

However, from the age of 18, Salim became addicted to alcohol. He was childishly self-indulgent, short-tempered and capable of great cruelty. In 1599 he rebelled against his father, setting up an alternate court in Allahabad, styling himself as

Salim Shah, and living a life of great self-indulgence. By his own confession in his autobiography *Tuzuk-e-Jahangiri*, he drank six litres of hard spirits a day, along with a few glasses of opium. He weighed about 120 kilos. His life and health were devastated by his addiction.

In 1602, Salim had Akbar's favourite Abul Fazl, the grand vizier of Akbar's empire and author of *Akbarnama*, assassinated, and to add insult to injury, threw his head in the toilet. Akbar watched his beloved son's doings in great despair. As per Rahul Sankrityayan, in 1604, when Akbar heard that Jahangir had a writer skinned alive in his presence, he lamented, 'Sheikhu baba, I cannot even see a goat being skinned! Where did you learn this hardheartedness from?'

Daniyal, Akbar's youngest son, died in April 1604; Murad had died earlier. Salim was now his only son left alive. Akbar persuaded Salim, via intermediaries, to come to Agra and submit to him. Salim, apprehensive that his eldest son, 17-year-old Khusrau might be declared the heir instead of him, agreed to go to Agra. Akbar received him publicly with affection, and holding his hand, withdrew with him to a private room. He then, as historian Vincent Smith put it, 'inflamed by intense passion, administered several violent slaps on his son's face, showering upon him bitter reproaches for his unfilial conduct, and mocking him because when he had 70,000 horsemen at call, he had been fool and coward enough to cast himself at his father's feet as suppliant.'

Akbar had Salim confined to a room under the charge of a physician and two servants, in an attempt to cure his alcohol and opium dependency. After this period of drug detox, Salim was allotted appropriate apartments and lived in apparent amity with his father until the death of Akbar due to a lingering dysentery infection a year later, in October 1605. There was some suspicion that Salim might have poisoned him.

At the age of 36, Salim became the Mughal emperor and took the regnal name of Jahangir. He put down a revolt by Khusrau, blinding and imprisoning him, and settled down to rule, continuing Akbar's policies of toleration and inclusion. His reign was the most peaceful and prosperous period for the Mughal Empire.

Jahangir was an aesthete to his core and was fond of life's luxuries. He utilized the time afforded him by a peaceful kingdom by patronizing the arts, specially painting. He had a superb atelier of artists, and would even get European paintings replicated so well that they were impossible to distinguish from the original. Designing clothes was one of his many interests, and he invented new styles, including the first version of the modern kurta. He called this the *kurdi* because it was based on a Kurdish style. He was always lavishly dressed. The English visitors were stunned at this rotund vision dripping in jewels, mentioning that he apparently wore a different set of jewels every single day of the year, each of them extremely elaborate.

While he continued Akbar's policy of general religious tolerance, celebrating Hindu and Parsi festivals and banning cow slaughter, he would not hesitate to get a holy statue broken if it offended his aesthetic sensibility.

Niccolao Manucci, an Italian traveller in Mughal India, commented on his sentimental nature: 'Weeping came easily to Jahangir, for without any reason at all he would burst into tears. Anything and everything made him cry.'

And so was Jahangir at the time of his marriage to Nur Jahan, childlike and charming, but whimsical and capable of acts of great cruelty. To put it simply, he would do exactly what he wanted.

Nur Jahan was the daughter of Ghiyas Beg, a nobleman from Persia. Ghiyas Beg's father had been the Vizier of Isfahan and was very cultured and a well-regarded poet. Upon his death in 1576, Ghiyas Beg had to flee Persia and decided to migrate to India. Persians were much admired in India and he had relatives in Akbar's court. Persian culture in India had similar status as French culture did in latter-day Europe – their poetry, manners, cooks, embroidery and other arts were admired, imitated and treasured. The official language of the Mughal court was Persian, even though the rulers were Turko-Mongol and the nobility of diverse origin: Turk, Persian, Arabic, Afghan and Indian.

On his way to India in 1577 with his pregnant wife and children, Ghiyas Beg was robbed of all his possessions. In Kandahar, his pregnant wife, Asmat Beg, gave birth to a girl, whom they named Mehrunissa. Destitute, they abandoned her but were later reunited. A popular version of this story is dramatically recounted by Alexander Dow, a British official who wrote *The History of Hindostan* in the 18th century:

> When they had advanced about a mile from the place, and the eyes of the mother could no longer distinguish the solitary tree under which she had left her daughter, she gave way to grief; and throwing herself from the horse on the ground, exclaimed, 'My child! my child!'... Ghiyas Beg promised to bring her the infant. He arrived at the place. No sooner had his eyes reached the child, than he was almost struck dead with horror. A black snake was coiled around it; and Ghiyas believed he beheld him extending his fatal jaws to devour the infant. The father rushed forward. The serpent, alarmed at his vociferation, retired into the hollow tree. He took up his daughter unhurt, and returned to the mother.

A snake sheltering a sleeping person is the classic Indian portent predicting future rule and must have been added later to the story.

Ghiyas Beg made his way to Fatehpur Sikri and managed to get an audience with Akbar. Because he was polished and well-spoken, as well as from a good family, Akbar started him off with a 300 *mansab*, which was a rank that gave him a salary enough to maintain 300 horsemen, and he was soon promoted to the post of diwan of Kabul. He rose quickly up the ladder and moved back to Akbar's court in 1596. He clearly had great people skills. Contemporary chroniclers say that he 'was considered exceedingly clever and skillful, both in writing and in transacting business'. As per Jahangir, 'no one ever went to Itmad-ud-daula [Ghiyas Beg's title later] with a petition or on business who turned from him in an injured frame of mind. He showed loyalty to the sovereign, and yet left pleased and hopeful him who was in need. In fact, this was a speciality of his.'

Famous as he was for his sense of fairness and accessibility, Ghiyas Beg was also known for the weakness that made this generosity possible: greed. According to the *Tatimma-i Wakiat-i Jahangiri* by Muhammad Hadi, 'in the taking of bribes he certainly was most uncompromising and fearless.'

Nur Jahan was educated in all the domestic arts and cultural accomplishments that a well-brought-up daughter of a Persian nobleman was expected to know. She was considered a rare beauty. They lived well; Ghiyas Beg's compound had a reputation as 'a delightful place and enchanting residence'.

Nur Jahan and her mother would visit the royal women like other noblemen's wives. Jahangir recounts a story of how Nur Jahan's mother invented the technique of making a fabulous *attar* of roses, which became very popular with the royals.

At the age of 17, in 1594, Nur Jahan was married to the eminently suitable Persian nobleman Ali Quli Beg Istajlu. Ali Quli had been a table attendant of Shah Tahmasp of Persia. He had migrated to India and taken service with Akbar. After his marriage, he accompanied Jahangir on his campaign to Mewar. There he saved Jahangir's life by grappling with a tiger and was given the title of Sher Afgan (or tiger tosser) by Jahangir in 1599. However, when Jahangir rebelled against Akbar, Sher Afgan quietly slipped away and went back to Akbar's service.

When Jahangir acceded to the throne in 1605, Ghiyas Beg was given the title of Itmad-ud-daulah, meaning 'pillar of the state', and his *mansab* was increased to 1,500. Sher Afgan was forgiven for what Jahangir saw as his 'desertion' six years ago, and given a *jagir* (territory) in far-off Burdwan in Bengal. He moved there with Nur Jahan and their newly born daughter, Ladli Begum.

Jahangir was suspicious of many of his nobles. In May 1607 he asked his favourite foster brother, Qutubuddin Koka, the governor of Bengal, to investigate Sher Afgan. A notoriously hot-tempered Sher Afgan was enraged when he saw Qutubuddin coming with many soldiers, got into an altercation, and then ran his sword through Qutubuddin, killing him. Sher Afgan was immediately killed by Qutubuddin's soldiers, his body cut into pieces.

As she was from an influential family, Nur Jahan was safely escorted back to Agra along with her infant daughter.

Her family, however, was in trouble. Her brother Mohammad Sharif had been executed for being part of Khusrau's plot to assassinate Jahangir. Her father had been charged by one of his underlings of embezzling 50,000 rupees. When told of this, Jahangir placed Itmad-ud-daulah in the custody of the informant. Later, after his son's treachery, Jahangir was inclined to execute Itmad-ud-daulah but forgave him after the payment of 2 lakh rupees as compensation.

Meanwhile, Nur Jahan was very lucky to get a post as the powerful Ruqayya Begum's companion in the royal harem. Ruqayya Begum was Akbar's cousin and had been his first and principal wife, the Padshah Begum, or head of the women's harem, during Akbar's rule. Nur Jahan soon became a favourite of Ruqayya Begum. The Dutch merchant Pieter van den Broecke says, 'This Begam conceived a great affection for Mehr-un-Nissa; she loved her more than others and always kept her in her company.'

Four years later, in 1611, on the occasion of the Persian new year Nowruz, always elaborately celebrated by the Mughal court, a 'Meena Bazaar' was held. This was a peculiar custom initiated by Akbar where noblemen's wives and daughters, unveiled, would have stalls in which they sold precious wares. The royal ladies and men, and the emperor, would be the buyers and jokingly negotiate with them. It also brought attractive women to the emperor's attention.

This is exactly what happened with Nur Jahan. Jahangir, who was then 42, saw Nur Jahan, 34 – by Mughal norms, positively middle-aged and old enough to possibly have grandchildren – and suffered a coup de foudre. Impulsive as ever, he married her in short order on 25 May 1611 and gave her the title of Nur Mahal. She was given the title Nur Jahan in 1616. He had, at that time, 19 previous wives and about 300 concubines.

A more controversial tale about Jahangir and Nur Jahan's love was popularized by many later writers like Khafi Khan. According to this story Jahangir and Nur Jahan were in love before she was married. Akbar disapproved of it and made her marry Sher Afgan. A heartbroken Jahangir was permanently estranged from his father. When Jahangir became emperor, he had Sher Afgan killed and finally the childhood sweethearts were reunited. However, this story is quite unlikely for many reasons. There was no reason for Akbar to disapprove of this eminently suitable marriage. Had Jahangir's sweetheart been forcibly married to Sher Afgan, Akbar would hardly have asked him to accompany Jahangir to Mewar. Jahangir would have been most unlikely to laud his rival and give him the title of Sher Afgan. On becoming emperor, Jahangir could have immediately asked Sher Afgan to divorce Nur Jahan; he would not have needed to kill him. And lastly, though Nur Jahan was back in court in 1607, Jahangir only married her four years later, in 1611.

Nur Jahan became Jahangir's 20th and last wife. It was a stroke of great good fortune for her family. Her father was forgiven all his indiscretions and his *mansab* was increased from 1,500 to 2,500. He soon became Jahangir's chief vizier. Her brother Abul Hasan received the title Itiqad Khan and one of Jahangir's special swords, called Sarandaz.

Nur Jahan's big coup was the marriage she then engineered between the 20-year-old Khurram, the heir apparent, and her 18-year-old niece Arjumand Bano, Abul Hasan's daughter, which took place the next year, in 1612. Arjumand Bano was renamed Mumtaz Mahal and Khurram loved her obsessively all her life, forsaking all other women and eventually building the exquisite Taj Mahal as her tomb.

Khurram was Jahangir's favourite son and clearly expected to be emperor. Jahangir called him 'the first of my sons,' and said 'gradually, as his years increased, so did his excellencies', 'inasmuch as the signs of rectitude and knowledge of affairs were evident in him.' As for his other sons, Khusrau was blind and in confinement, Parviz was considered dull and incapable, and the youngest, Shahryar, was only seven years old.

Nur Jahan slowly gained tremendous ascendancy over Jahangir. A junta of sorts was created which wielded all power in the empire; it consisted of Nur Jahan, her father Itmad-ud-daulah, her brother Abul Hasan (soon titled Asaf Khan), and Khurram. This is how it worked, as Dow points out:

> If anyone with a request to make at Court obtains an audience or is allowed to speak, the King hears him indeed, but will give no definite answer of Yes or No, referring him promptly to Asaf Khan, who in the same way will dispose of no important matter without communicating with his sister, the Queen, and who regulates his attitude in such a way that the authority of neither of them may be diminished. Anyone then who obtains a favour must thank them for it, and not the King.

By 1622, her family had a stranglehold on the government. Her father was the vizier, Asaf Khan was the vakil, and her relative Iradat Khan was the *mirbakshi*, or head of military. In addition, seven of the 12 provinces were under the governorship of her extended family – Lahore, Kashmir, Multan, Thatta, Agra, Gujarat and Odisha.

A gold coin of a hundred *tolas*, the highest denomination ever issued, was named the Nur Jahani. The inscription on it read: 'By order of the King Jahangir, gold has a hundred splendours added to it by receiving the impression of the name of Nur Jahan, the Queen Begam.'

Most unusually, Nur Jahan's powers were formal, legalized and visible to all. She approved all *farmans* (orders) and grants of appointment that went out under the king's name, and her name – 'Nur Jahan, the Queen Begam' – was jointly attached to the imperial signature. She also controlled all promotions and demotions that were issued by the royal government.

Mughal chroniclers like the contemporary Mutamid Khan have praised Nur Jahan's capabilities: 'It is impossible to describe the beauty and the wisdom of the queen. If a difficulty arose, she immediately solved it. Whoever threw herself upon her protection was preserved from tyranny and oppression.'

Jahangir was quite happy to shuffle off his dreary responsibilities to the junta headed by his wife, of whom he said 'than whom I did not think anyone was fonder of me'. He also thought she did an excellent job: 'From the date on which Nur Jahan Begam entered into the bond of marriage with this suppliant... she had made such arrangements as were becoming to the State, and knew what were the requirements of good fortune and prosperity.'

He also ignored horrified old comrades like Mahabat Khan, a prominent Mughal general and statesman, who remarked that 'the whole world is surprised, that such a wise and sensible emperor as Jahangir should permit a woman to have so great an influence over him'. On the contrary, Jahangir used to brag that having bestowed sovereignty on Nur Jahan, he required nothing else but a *ser* (about a kilogram) of wine and half-a-*ser* of meat.

They had a very caring relationship and Nur Jahan, who was personally very disciplined, managed to restrict Jahangir's drinking substantially in an effort to improve his health. As he records, 'She, by degrees, lessened my wine, and kept me from things that did not suit me, and food that disagreed with me... Her skill and experience are greater than those of the physicians.'

Controlling his drinking was not always easy, as shown in a later tale by that inveterate purveyor of bazaar gossip Manucci in his *Storia do Mogor*. The story also throws an interesting light on the relatively equal nature of their relationship. Jahangir, the story goes, was listening to the singing of his musicians when he came to the end of his allotted nine cups of wine. He turned to Nur Jahan to ask her for more, and when she said no, 'he fell into a passion, laid hold of the queen and scratched her, she doing the same on her side, grappling with the king, biting and scratching him, and no one dared to separate them.' The musicians created a diversion by pretending to weep and cry in the room outside. The couple heard and, coming out to see 'that it was a feigned plot... they fell a-laughing, and the fight ended.' The musicians were rewarded but Nur Jahan would only forgive Jahangir if he fell at her feet, which he did symbolically by having his shadow cross her path one day in the garden.

Nur Jahan also shared her husband's passion for the finer things of life such as painting, clothes and architecture, and together they set new standards in the art of living. Nur Jahan devised excellent new dishes; many of the finest Mughlai dishes today are named after her – Nur Jahani Biryani, Nur Jahani Kofta, Murg Nur Jahani, among others. She also designed new patterns for carpets, brocades and laces. She wrote poetry under the pen name Makfi and patronized many poets, including a woman poet called Mahri.

Even in their middle age, Jahangir and Nur Jahan often behaved like a young couple in love. The Englishman Thomas Roe, who represented England in the Mughal Empire, reports seeing them driving about alone on a bullock cart, with Jahangir holding the reins. They travelled all over the country together, especially to their beloved Kashmir, building beautiful buildings and gardens and devising the most spectacular entertainments. They also went hunting often. Nur Jahan was generally considered the better shot. In 1617, she shot four tigers with a total of only six shots. Jahangir says of this feat, 'Until now such shooting was never seen, that from the top of an elephant and inside of a howdah six shots should be made and not one miss... As a reward for this good shooting I gave her a pair of bracelets of diamonds worth 100,000 rupees and scattered 1,000 ashrafis [over her].'

But this seemingly idyllic environment was about to change.

The junta had functioned smoothly for many years. Khurram was given many military commands and was very successful. In 1617, Jahangir gave him the title of Shah Jahan for his Deccan victories, which were celebrated elaborately by Nur Jahan in Mandu. By 1620 Nur Jahan's daughter, Ladli Begum, was 15 and ready for marriage. Nur Jahan wanted her to be empress. Unfortunately for her, Shah Jahan was too deeply in love with her niece, Mumtaz Mahal, to marry anyone else. Khusrau, Jahangir's other son who had been blinded for his rebellion, had had his eyesight partially restored by medical treatment but he had apparently refused to marry Ladli, since he was devoted to his wife, Mirza Aziz Koka's daughter. In 1621, Nur Jahan finally married her daughter to the youngest prince, the 15-year-old Shahryar. He was not highly regarded, comments on him varied from 'docile nature, feeble mind, and imbecile character', 'without sense or understanding, and not fit to govern a kingdom' and 'want of capacity and intelligence'. He also had the unfortunate nickname of '*Nashudani*', good-for-nothing. Nur Jahan, however, was confident of her ability to rule on his behalf in the future.

Thus, in 1621 the junta finally broke up as Nur Jahan's interests and those of Shah Jahan and Asaf Khan diverged. Her mother and father, who could have possibly kept the family together, died in quick succession. In addition, Jahangir gave the whole of Itmad-ud-daulah's estate, after his death, to Nur Jahan, cutting out Asaf Khan totally, which would hardly have endeared her to her brother.

In 1621 Shah Jahan was posted in Burhanpur in the Deccan, battling Jahangir's old enemy, Malik Ambar of Ahmednagar. Khusrau, who had been entrusted to Shah Jahan's care, was strangled on his orders to eliminate potential rivals. It was put about that he had died of an illness. This considerably upset Jahangir. At Nur Jahan's instigation, in 1622, he commanded Shah Jahan to proceed to Kandahar to take up the battle against the Persians who had attacked it. Not wanting to leave his power base in the Deccan behind, Shah Jahan refused to move from Mandu until after the rains. Jahangir was upset and gave the Kandahar command to Shahryar, as well as depriving Shah Jahan of some territories. Things got worse and finally in 1623, Shah Jahan marched to take control of Agra and the treasury.

From earlier endearments of 'baba Khurram', 'beloved Khurram', Shah Jahan was now permanently renamed Bidaulat (the wretch) by Jahangir, who never saw him again. Shah Jahan was roundly defeated in Baluchpur by Jahangir's troops, led by Mahabat Khan and Shahryar, and fled down south with his family, taking refuge in Golconda. He then orchestrated an invasion of Mughal Odisha and captured territory right till Bengal. Defeated by imperial forces again, he had to retrace his steps to the Deccan, and teamed up with Malik Ambar, Jahangir's bête noire, and a Mughal enemy for 50 years, to attack Burhanpur. Shah Jahan lost again and finally wrote to Jahangir asking for pardon.

In 1626, Jahangir, or rather, Nur Jahan, agreed to let him be, provided he gave up his forts, sent his sons to Jahangir, and retired to the small province of Balaghat, which they now allotted him.

Meanwhile, Mahabat Khan, Jahangir's old and loyal commander, was deputed to Prince Parviz, Jahangir's second son. Mahabat had successfully quelled Shah Jahan's rebellion and was becoming increasingly powerful. Nur Jahan and Asaf

Khan were both apprehensive of his power and persuaded Jahangir to transfer him to Bengal. Mahabat Khan came rushing up to Lahore to plead his case with Jahangir; Jahangir was already on his way to Kabul, near the Jhelum River. Finding Jahangir in the process of crossing the river, with his troops already on the other side, Mahabat Khan captured him. Mahabat Khan now started ruling, issuing orders on behalf of Jahangir. The imperial troops under Asaf Khan were too scared to attack in case Mahabat Khan injured Jahangir. Nur Jahan then crossed over to join Jahangir and persuaded Mahabat Khan to move to Kabul. There, over a period of time, she managed to subvert all of Mahabat's associates, until after a reign of 'a hundred days', Mahabat had to flee. Jahangir was thus freed by Nur Jahan. Mahabat made his way to join Shah Jahan in the Deccan, who welcomed him.

In 1626 Prince Parviz died. In 1627, on the way from Kashmir to Lahore, the ailing Jahangir finally passed away. Asaf Khan, who secretly sympathized with his son-in-law Shah Jahan, immediately swung into action. He had his sister Nur Jahan placed under arrest in her tent, allowing her no communication with anyone. He sent a messenger to Shah Jahan but knew it would take him months to reach Delhi from the Deccan. He then had Dawar Bakhsh, Khusrau's son, crowned emperor to keep the power out of Shahryar's hands.

Shahryar was in Lahore and quite well placed for the succession battle, with troops and treasure in hand. He had also crowned himself king. However, he was incompetent, and without Nur Jahan there to advise him, he lost the battle against Asaf Khan's troops when they reached Lahore. He was captured and blinded.

Shah Jahan now marched to Agra, declaring himself king. Setting a dangerous precedent, which would finally destroy the Mughal Empire through fratricidal warfare carried out generation after generation, he sent a message to Asaf Khan to kill all putative heirs. Shahryar, Dawar Bakhsh and the three sons of Jahangir's brother Daniyal were then duly strangled.

Nur Jahan was now retired to a private house in Lahore, with her widowed daughter Ladli Begum, and her granddaughter, the child of Shahryar. While royal widows normally lived at court in the harem, both Shah Jahan and Asaf Khan were wary of Nur Jahan and wanted to cut off her access to power and keep her as far away from court as possible. She was given an allowance of 2 lakh rupees a year, which wasn't very generous; it is unlikely that her great wealth stored in the Agra treasury was handed over to her. She lived a retired life for the next 18 years until she died in 1645, spending her time visiting the grand tomb Shah Jahan was constructing for Jahangir in Lahore, and building her own tomb with her meagre resources. She was not involved in matters of the state at all after the death of Jahangir.

Her lasting legacy is the many beautiful buildings she had constructed: Shalimar Bagh in Srinagar, Serai Nurmahal in Punjab, and her own tomb in Lahore. The most significant is the tomb she had made for her father, Itmad-ud-daulah, in Agra. It set new standards in opulence and beauty, and many concepts used in its building were later imitated in the Taj, particularly the lavish use of white marble all over the building, rather than as an accent, and the use of pietra dura, the inlay of precious stones, in the marble walls. This great empress who had set new aesthetic standards and ruled so generously and well, thus died in obscurity, though her brother, who had risen to power riding on her coattails, was the chief vizier of the empire.

The melancholy epitaph on Nur Jahan's tomb reads:

> On the grave of this poor stranger, let there be neither lamp nor rose.
> Let neither butterfly's wing burn nor nightingale sing.

The Intemperate Emperor

Jahangir's reign began with a bloodbath. Almost immediately after Jahangir's accession to the throne in 1605, there was an attempt by Khusrau, Jahangir's son by his first wife, Man Bai, to overthrow him. Khusrau was supported by Akbar's stalwarts like Raja Man Singh, Mirza Aziz Koka and Abdur Rahim Khan-e-Khana. Jahangir defeated him comprehensively and brutally punished his son along with his supporters. Khusrau was blinded and kept in confinement. Guru Arjan Dev, the Sikh guru who had blessed Khusrau, was tortured and killed. Many were crucified; Abdur Rahim Khan-e-Khana, the son of Bairam Khan, the grand vizier of the Mughal Empire, a great scholar and Jahangir's erstwhile tutor, was sewn up in the freshly flayed skin of an ass and paraded around town as the skin shrank and nearly killed him. He was let off, though, before he died, and somewhat reinstated. He always had an uneasy life after that – Jahangir later even had his son's head presented to him, saying it was a melon.

Manucci says about the emperor's religious proclivities:

> This king did many things against the Mohamedan religion, in drinking wine, in eating pig's flesh... The learned in the Mahomedan law gave him to understand repeatedly that wine and pork were prohibited... Enraged at so many warnings, he sent out orders one day to assemble all the learned men. He inquired from them the religions in which it was allowable to drink wine and at the same time eat of pork. They replied that only the Christians had that liberty.

He [Jahangir] then said publicly that he meant to become a Christian... The learned men were in amazement, and taking counsel together, said that the king might eat and drink whatever he liked. I have met persons who were present at the time.

The Queen Who Chopped Off Noses

Rani Karnavati of Garhwal

Shah Jahan dispatched a general at the head of thirty thousand horsemen besides infantry. The prince allowed his enemy to penetrate into the mountains, retreating as they advanced. When the soldiers of Shah Jahan had got a certain distance he closed the roads, so that they could neither advance any further nor retreat... the prince... sent to say that he would grant them their lives, but his soldiers required their noses... Shah Jahan's soldiers... issued one by one, leaving their noses behind them on the spot... Shah Jahan... gave an order that ever afterwards this prince should be spoken of as the Nactirany.

Niccolao Manucci, *Storia do Mogor*

A little-known story of Indian history is that of Rani Karnavati of Garhwal (r. 1631–40 CE*), called 'nak-kati rani', or the queen who cut off noses, by Mughal emperor Shah Jahan and numerous Mughal chroniclers like Niccolao Manucci, Francois Bernier, Jean-Baptiste Tavernier and Shahnawaz Khan. A Mughal force sent to invade her kingdom was decisively defeated by her and sent back after their noses were chopped off!*

In the aftermath of the Muslim conquest of India that began in the 12th century, indigenous kingdoms survived only in difficult terrains such as hills and deserts where they were able to defend themselves effectively despite having smaller forces. The inhospitable terrain in which their kingdoms were located gave them tremendous advantage over attacking forces. Sensing this advantage, many erstwhile rulers from the plains fled to the hills and deserts to found kingdoms, like the Rathores of Kannauj who settled in the desert kingdom of Jodhpur.

Mountainous terrain in particular has conferred a massive defensive advantage for territories across the world. In 480 BCE, 300 Spartans (along with some Thespians and Thebans who are ignored by praise singers) held off a Persian army of hundreds of thousands at Thermopylae for many days. Mountainous countries like Switzerland, Afghanistan and Vietnam have been the graveyard of reputations of invading empires, their geography making them extremely difficult to conquer and still harder to hold on to. Thus it was for the hill states of Uttarakhand, particularly Garhwal. In fact, Garhwal managed to defy two great Mughal emperors – Shah Jahan and Aurangzeb – and survive!

Garhwal was ruled by the Paramar kings. Their dynasty had been founded in the ninth century by Kanakpala, a Paramar Rajput prince, who had migrated from his ancestral kingdom of Dhara in central India and married a local princess. A later Paramar king of Dhara, the multifaceted scholar Raja Bhoj (r. 1010–55 CE), is an important figure in Indian history, legend and literature. The city of Bhopal was founded by him as Bhojpal.

Garhwal had its capital at Srinagar, on the Alaknanda River, a tributary of the Ganga, about a hundred kilometres upstream from Rishikesh. Its 52 *garhs*, or forts, had been unified by the Paramar king Ajaypal in 1358 CE and a later descendant, Balbhadra, took the Persian title 'Shah'. Persian historian Ferishta described it as a prosperous kingdom made rich by the gold wash collected from the rivers Alaknanda, Bhagirathi and Sona. Besides this, Garhwal had mines of gold, copper and lead. So prosperous was the region that William Finch, a British traveller who visited India between 1608 and 1611, said that the king dined off solid gold plates.

Though invasions from the plains were held off, the local rulers of the region fought incessantly among each other, with Garhwal regularly fighting the kingdoms of Kumaon, Sirmaur and Tibet.

Mahipat Shah, Karnavati's husband, ascended the throne in 1622. Little is known about the origin of Karnavati, though she is supposed to have been a princess from Kangra, which had been conquered by Jahangir a couple of decades earlier. Mahipat succeeded Shyam Shah, his uncle, who had been a pleasure-loving king and had drowned while indulging in one of his favourite pastimes – hosting risky moonlit boat parties on a tiny, relatively quiet, stretch on the Alaknanda, just before it descended into rapids.

Mahipat Shah was a quintessential warrior obsessed with conquest. He was considered a very arrogant and headstrong man. A local saying about him was '*Trin barabar sabko janahi, Kahi kahu ki kabhi nahi manahi*' (He considers everyone equivalent to a piece of straw and never listens to what anybody else has to say). He was forever at war with his neighbours, who were equally belligerent. In 1624, to punish Tibetan raids, he attacked Tibet with 12,000 men but had to retreat when faced with heavy snowfall. The Portuguese Jesuit missionary António de Andrade, who passed through Srinagar that year on his way to Tibet, mentions that Mahipat Shah invaded Tibet three times. Andrade incidentally also mentions that Jahangir's decree enjoining all officials to provide assistance to him in his travels was ignored by the people in the Garhwal region, which indicates that the people residing in the area considered themselves to be independent from the Mughals.

On Shah Jahan's accession to the throne, in 1628, it is said that an invitation was sent out to all kings and feudatories to attend the ceremony. When the Mughal messenger reached Garhwal with the invitation and opulent gifts, Mahipat Shah chose to interpret the invitation as an attack on his sovereignty and a signal that Shah Jahan considered Garhwal a feudatory. He gravely insulted the messenger. This was in spite of the fact that earlier Garhwal rulers had called on the Mughal emperor and even attended his court. This gratuitous rudeness certainly created bad blood with Shah Jahan.

In 1631, after nine years of incessant warfare with his neighbours, Mahipat Shah died on the battlefield while invading Kumaon. His seven-year-old son Prithvipat Shah was crowned king in 1631, with Karnavati appointed as regent.

As regent to the throne of Garhwal, Karnavati inherited a kingdom ravaged by war. She ruled over a tolerant, multicultural society and was lucky to have capable and loyal ministers and commanders from all communities to guide her – Madho Singh Bhandari, Rikhola Lodi, Banwaridas and Daulat Beg. Garhwal also allowed many churches to be set up. An old Tantric Hindu record, *Sanwari Granth*, mentions her patronage of the Tantric Kalikula and Shrikula systems. A *vidvat sabha* (congregation of wise men) held in Srinagar during her reign attracted Tantrikas from Gujarat, Magadha, Kashmir, Kerala and Andhra.

Though she did not share her husband's passion for warfare, Karnavati had to contend with neighbours who, with the usual perception of a woman ruler being weak, continuously launched attacks on her kingdom.

There are many *pawadas*, or folk songs, about the heroism of Karnavati's general Madho Singh Bhandari. In the battle of Chhota Chini with Tibet in 1635 he fell fatally sick and decided that his army should retreat. However, rumours of his death emboldened the Tibetans to attack. He asked his commanders to embalm him in hot oil, tie his body to the horse and show it to the enemy. He died in the process, of course, but the enemy held back and the army retreated safely. This seems to be a favourite stratagem adopted in similar circumstances by legendary generals in history like El Cid in medieval Spain and Hari Singh Nalwa in 19th-century Punjab.

Karnavati also concentrated on public works, especially irrigation, and she constructed many tanks and canals. The

Rajpur canal of Dehradun, the first canal to irrigate the region, is said to have been built by her. This created a boost in agriculture. She also established Karanpur village in Dehradun.

In 1638 the unusually named Baz Bahadur Chand ascended the throne of neighbouring Kumaon. In spite of his Persian name, he was a devout Hindu who had built many temples. However, he was an aficionado of Mughal culture and introduced many elements of it in his court – attire, court customs and names, as is evident from his own. He also attacked Garhwal repeatedly. It is said that he convinced the Mughal governor of Kangra, Najabat Khan, to attack Garhwal, promising rich pickings and full cooperation from him and the raja of Sirmaur. Najabat Khan, in turn, convinced Shah Jahan that this would be a lucrative conquest and had additional troops sanctioned, perhaps because the emperor still remembered being insulted by the Garhwal king at the time of his accession.

To put things in context, this was a small border issue for Shah Jahan; Mughal sources typically referred to the 'zemindar' of Srinagar, rather than 'king'. Shah Jahan ruled over the richest kingdom in the world; he is in fact estimated to have been one of the richest men who ever lived. His heart lay in creating objects of unparalleled beauty like the Taj Mahal, the Red Fort and the single-most expensive object in history, the Peacock Throne (which cost 1 crore rupees, twice as much as the Taj Mahal).

In 1640, Najabat Khan set off with 30,000 troops, with the raja of Sirmaur acting as a guide, and crossed the Ganga at

Haridwar. Though Karnavati could have asked for a truce and paid off the Mughals, she chose to fight and defy their might. What transpired became the subject of legends which floated around Mughal India, and is variously recorded by historians and travellers.

This is what the Italian traveller Manucci had to say about the conflict in his *Storia do Mogor*, although he mistakenly refers to the queen as the male 'prince of Srinaguer':

> The prince allowed his enemy to penetrate into the mountains, retiring as they advanced. When the soldiers of Shah Jahan had got a certain distance, he closed the roads so that they could neither advance any farther nor retreat, and there was no way of deliverance for them. Finding himself in this danger, the general sent proposals for peace negotiations, but the Hindu prince returned the answer that his resolve to retreat was too late. Already the commander had a deficiency of supplies, and all his camp was in great confusion. He therefore requested from the prince permission to withdraw, and although the rajah could have destroyed them every one, he did not wish to do so.

The queen took an unprecedented step, and truly showed her contempt for Mughal might, and her lack of fear of retribution. She asked that the noses of all the soldiers be cut off!

> He sent to say that he would grant them their lives, but his soldiers required all their noses as a memorial of having given them a gift of their lives. Shah Jahan's soldiers finding

> themselves in such dreadful straits, rather than lose their lives were content to lose their noses.

The soldiers threw down their weapons and left one by one, leaving their noses behind. Shah Jahan gave an order that ever afterwards she should be spoken of as the '*nak-kati*' rani – that is to say, 'Cut-nose'. The general, Najabat Khan, who could not endure coming back with his nose cut off, took poison and put an end to his life, writes Manucci.

The story is repeated in essence by Tavernier, and by Shahnawaz Khan in *Ma'asir al-Umara*, though there are differences over whether the general escaped before losing his nose, or committed suicide, or went back to court and was stripped of his rank and possessions.

When the *nak-kata* troops trudged back to the Mughal court, it was a huge blow to Shah Jahan's prestige. He sent a couple of punitive expeditions, especially one under Khalilullah Khan, but none of them were able to reach Srinagar as the fighting season was very short – just a few months before the terrain became impassable due to rain and snow. Karnavati's guerrilla troops succeeded in delaying them until the monsoon rains came, which would soon be followed by the snows of winter. An unexpected fallout of Karnavati's defeat of the Mughals was that Srinagar became a symbol of defiance against the Mughals and a safe haven for fugitives. Mughal princes including Dara Shikoh's son took refuge there, and Aurangzeb mounted military expeditions, which never managed to reach Srinagar.

Karnavati, however, became a beacon of resistance for small kingdoms in Mughal India, inspiring them to preserve their kingdoms from an invasion by one of the mightiest armies in the world. We hear no more of her after this.

Her son, Prithvipat Shah, was a wise and honourable ruler. After he acceded to the throne, he arrived at a truce with the Mughals. He sent his son Medini Rai to the Mughal court and managed to get Princess Jahanara and Dara Shikoh, Shah Jahan's favourite children, to intercede with Shah Jahan and normalize the relationship. He could then maintain his status as an independent ruler with no threat of invasion. The kingdom was preserved till 1947.

The Indian Nose

Cutting off noses as a means of punishment has existed in India since the days of yore. It is mentioned in the Ramayana, as the treatment meted out by Lakshmana to Ravana's sister Shurpanakha, and was considered to be one way of truly humiliating a defeated enemy. In fact, '*nak katana*' is still a colloquial phrase used in Hindi to indicate utter humiliation. Unsurprisingly, nasal reconstruction has always been good business in India because there were always plenty of clients. The tracts by Sushruta written as early as the fifth century BCE describe the process. The first modern plastic surgery technique – reconstruction of noses – travelled to Britain from India in an interesting way. East India Company surgeons Thomas Caruso and James Findlay saw a nose reconstruction process carried out on a Company bullock-cart driver called Cowasjee, whose nose had been cut off when he was captured by the Mysore troops during the Third Anglo-Mysore War (1789–92 CE). This procedure was carried out by a potter in Pune using hereditary knowledge. The surgeons minutely documented it and published it in the *Madras Gazette*. In 1794, seven months later, another surgeon published the text of it in the *Gentleman's Magazine*, London, as a letter to the editor. This inspired an English surgeon, Joseph Carpue, to try out the procedure on his patients – giving birth to the flourishing plastic surgery industry today. He named it the Indian Nose.

Other cultures also used this mode of punishment. The Byzantines used blinding or the cutting off of noses to make contenders ineligible for rule. There is a tale from the seventh century CE of a deposed king, Justinian II 'Slit Nose', who had his nose cut off but had it reconstructed (apparently by an Indian surgeon) and successfully came back to power.

The Builder of Highways

Rani Mangammal

> The Regency of Mangammal is remarkable for her careful stewardship of the affairs of the kingdom. Though she had to go to war on many occasions, she was fonder of the victories of peace.
>
> R. Sathyanatha Aiyar, *History of the Nayaks of Madura*

The year was 1689 CE*. India was entirely occupied by the Mughals under Aurangzeb, apart from some small kingdoms of the indomitable Nayaks at the southern tip of the country who still held out stubbornly against the invaders. There was immense tension and instability in these kingdoms of Mysore, Madurai and Tanjore; they constantly fought each other, besides fighting the Marathas and Mughals. Among them was the queen of Madurai, Rani Mangammal (r. 1689–1706* CE*), alternately battling and befriending her neighbours, walking a tightrope to preserve her kingdom for 18 years.*

Most histories of India do not mention the Nayaks, chieftains who ruled small kingdoms in the extreme south of India after the Vijayanagara Empire was taken over by the Deccan sultanates in the Battle of Talikota in 1565. The period from 1565 till the rise of Haidar Ali in Mysore in 1761 is often ignored.

It is important here to understand the background of Madurai. The Pandyas had ruled in Madurai from time immemorial; they have been mentioned in the Ramayana and Mahabharata, in Sangam literature and by the Greek historian Herodotus in the fifth century BCE. The longest reigning Indian dynasty, they held on to the throne of Madurai for nearly two thousand years. They were defeated in 1311 by Malik Kafur, Alauddin Khilji's general, in a lightning raid from the northern Delhi Sultanate. During the raid, Kafur ransacked the ancient Meenakshi temple. The Pandyas were finally displaced from Madurai by Muhammad bin Tughlaq in 1323, after which they retreated farther south and ruled from Tenkasi until 1650. The Tughlaq governor of Madurai later declared independence from Muhammad bin Tughlaq and created the sultanate of Madurai in 1335.

The great Vijayanagara kingdom, under General Kumara Kampanna Nayak, conquered Madurai in 1378. The conquest is described lyrically by his wife Gangadevi, a rare woman poet of her time, in the epic poem *Madura Vijayam*. Kampanna ruled the kingdom as a Nayak on behalf of Vijayanagara.

Akin to 'Duke' and 'Count' in medieval Europe, 'Nayak' was a title given to semi-independent feudal governors in the Vijayanagara Empire. The governors, belonging to diverse families, owed fealty to the king, paid a certain fixed revenue and made their troops available for battle. Though initially appointed at the king's pleasure, in the great Indian tradition, the posts eventually became hereditary.

Vishwanatha Nayak, the son of an important minister, had been appointed the governor of the southern lands by Krishna Deva Raya, the king of Vijayanagara. Soon after the Battle of Talikota and the subsequent prolonged sack and destruction of Vijayanagara at the hands of the Deccan sultanates, Vishwanatha Nayak declared his independence, with his capital at Madurai. He rebuilt the ancient Meenakshi temple, which was dedicated to Meenakshi, the mythical woman ruler of the Pandyas who had been deified as an incarnation of Parvati.

Other Nayaks also declared their independence, and indulging in the true sport of kings, these kingdoms of Mysore, Tanjore and others incessantly battled each other as well as the Sultanate of Bijapur.

Vishwanatha's descendent Chokkanath Nayak became the king of Madurai in 1662 at the age of 16. He inherited a shrunken kingdom, as his father, Muttu Virappa Nayak II, had lost territory to the Wodeyar king of Mysore, to the Nayaks of Tanjore and to the sultanate of Bijapur.

He was married to Mangammal, the daughter of Tupakula Lingama Nayak, a general in the Madurai army. Chokkanath Nayak started off his reign with some good luck – he won a few battles and recovered some territories. His signal success was the conquest of Tanjore. The legend of the destruction of Tanjore goes thus: Chokkanath sent a proposal of marriage to the daughter of the Tanjore king, Vijayaraghava, who not only refused but was also deeply offended at the temerity of Chokkanath, whom he thought a lower kind of Nayak. He treated Chokkanath's emissaries with disrespect. Enraged, Chokkanath attacked Tanjore and Vijayaraghava died on the battlefield after sending off a signal to blow up his entire family and harem!

Chokkanath, however, did not enjoy his conquest for long. In a dramatic twist, Vijayaraghava's son, who had escaped and been secretly sheltered by a merchant, requested the sultan of Bijapur to reinstate him. Troops were sent to Tanjore under Venkoji Bhonsle, the great Maratha king Shivaji Bhonsle's half-brother, who worked for the Bijapur Sultan. Venkoji predictably crowned himself king instead and founded the Maratha Bhonsle dynasty of Tanjore, which ruled till 1855 when the British annexed it under the doctrine of lapse, which postulated that without a direct blood heir, the state would lapse to the British Raj.

In the tragic absence of the suitably royal Tanjore princess, who was now dead, blown up with the other royal ladies, the non-royal Mangammal came to be Chokkanath's chief queen. Chokkanath now suffered reverses in the many wars he habitually initiated. To add to his problems, Shivaji arrived in the south in 1677 and began carrying out plundering raids. He captured many fortresses from Bijapur, including the important one of Gingee, and carried away much wealth from all the kingdoms. When Chokkanath died in 1682 his kingdom was financially distressed, bled by all the wars he had fought with his neighbours and lost.

His young son Virappa Nayak now came to power. He was guided by his mother Mangammal, who had staunchly refused to commit sati. He had a short but successful reign and was known for his energy in handling both external and internal issues. He died of smallpox in 1689, leaving behind a disconsolate pregnant wife, whom Mangammal forcibly restrained from committing sati. After giving birth to a son, Vijaya Ranga, Virappa's wife Mutuammal committed suicide.

In 1689, Mangammal assumed power as regent on behalf of her infant grandson.

Mangammal's rule was quite different from that of her husband Chokkanath. Where he had been constantly embroiled in futile, impractical and expensive wars, which had drained the country of its resources, Mangammal often concluded treaties with former foes, and was more interested in the fruits of peace and the welfare of her subjects. She is considered a great ruler of Madurai, one who preserved her kingdom in troubled times and truly cared for the people.

Mangammal invested heavily in infrastructure. She focused on providing roads and clean water for her people. She was particularly known as a road-maker as she supervised the building of numerous roads lined with inns, wells and trees. The highway she had had built from Kanyakumari to Madurai was named after her and is still called Mangammal Salai. In fact, almost every fine avenue in every town in her erstwhile kingdom is still ascribed to her. She built many canals and tanks as well as a number of *choultrys* – residences for pilgrims.

She was also very liberal in allowing the practice of all religions. When pressured to persecute Christians by other rulers she is supposed to have said that just as some were allowed to eat rice and others meat, so also was it lawful for each man to practice or adopt whatever religion seemed to him the best. She endowed the Meenakshi temple in Madurai, where she instituted the *unjal* (swing) festival and built pavilions like the Rani Mangammal Mandapam. A painting that adorns the temple's wall even today shows the temple priest handing over the royal sceptre to the queen. A copperplate inscription of 1692 records a grant to a mosque. In 1701 she gifted some villages for the upkeep of a dargah. Her own summer palace in Madurai, Tamukkam Palace, now houses a museum.

Mangammal was not only an able administrator, but she was also a shrewd negotiator when it came to military affairs. Bijapur and Golconda had fallen to Aurangzeb in 1686 and 1687 respectively, and now the Mughals were at her door. Chikka Devaraja Wodeyar of Mysore and Shahuji Bhonsle of Tanjore had accepted Mughal dominance and Mangammal could read the writing on the wall. In 1697, she agreed to pay tribute to the Mughals and cleverly exploited the relationship by sending beautifully written letters and expensive gifts to Mughal generals like Zulfikar Khan, who was in the region besieging Gingee, keeping them firmly on her side. She solicited troops from them to fight her other enemies like the Marathas of Tanjore and thus recovered lost territory. In an extremely fluid and dangerous environment, she fully used all the *kutniti* (stratagems) options prescribed in Indian polity – *saam*, *daam*, *dand* and *bhed*, that is, negotiation, bribery, force and espionage. She continuously evaluated her options with her foes, often fighting them, sometimes buying them off, and sometimes creating allies to counter her enemies. Her prudence substantially prolonged the life of her kingdom.

However, as was the case with other women rulers, who are typically perceived as weak, on her accession to the throne, neighbouring kingdoms began to attack her, and some tributaries promptly stopped paying the kingdom their tribute. Yet, Mangammal managed to hold her own against the many threats to her kingdom.

She held off Chikkadevaraya of Mysore, whose troops attacked her kingdom and invaded her capital. They had to withdraw due to the Maratha threat they faced in Mysore.

When the king of Travancore, Ravi Varma, stopped paying tribute, Mangammal would send an army each year to Travancore, which would then successfully collect the tribute. An organized resistance by the Varma king in 1697 was also firmly quashed, with much transfer of wealth to Madurai.

The dreaded Marathas of Tanjore continued raiding Madurai under Shahuji Bhonsle and Mangammal eventually declared war on him in 1700. As his army spilled into the kingdom, Mangammal realized that her army would be unable to hold off the excellent Maratha cavalry. In a stroke of genius, she decided that offence was the best form of defence and stealthily sent off her troops to harry Tanjore in the absence of the troops that would defend it. As Shahuji's troops turned back to defend their territory they were ambushed at a river crossing and forced to sue for peace. This happened at a time when even Aurangzeb was having trouble fighting off the Marathas! Madurai and Tanjore ended up signing a peace treaty.

Their new-found friendship was soon put to the test. In 1700, in an early edition of the modern-day Kaveri water dispute, the king of Mysore built a dam that stopped the flow of the river into Madurai and Tanjore. The erstwhile foes together planned a war against Mysore but were fortunately spared the effort as unprecedented rains washed off the dam and solved the problem.

Mangammal's major military failure was her inability to suppress the rebellion of Raghunath Sethupathi, the king of Ramnad in Tamil Nadu, who declared himself an independent ruler in 1702.

Her death in 1705 is shrouded in mystery. Oral legend says that her grandson, Vijaya Ranga, when he came of age, wanted total control of the kingdom. According to some accounts, he is supposed to have locked her in a room where she starved to death. There are, of course, no official records to support this version. Vijaya Ranga assumed the throne in 1706. The kingdom was finally annexed by the nawab of Arcot in 1739.

The Origin of Sambar

The Maratha Bhonsle dynasty of Tanjore gave rise to one of India's national culinary favourites. Few people know that the ubiquitous south Indian dal sambar is actually not south Indian at all, but a modified form of the Maharashtrian *amti*.

The story goes as follows. Sambhaji, Shivaji's son, visited Tanjore during the reign of his cousin Shahuji (1684–1712 CE). He was served a tweaked version of the favourite Marathi dal *amti*, which used local ingredients tur dal and tamarind, instead of the usual mung dal and kokum. He loved it, and the dish was named after him – sambar!

A later Tanjore king, Serfoji II, who was clearly passionate about food, actually had the recipes of the Tanjore Maratha royal kitchen compiled in the 1820s, to create the manuscript *Sarabhendra Pakasasthram*, which is one of the few records available of royal Indian cuisine.

The Queen Who Challenged Aurangzeb

Chennamma of Keladi

Do not go back on your words... Do not be partial to your kinsmen... Do good deeds... Have compassion for all living objects... Give protection to those who come to you seeking it... Conduct yourself in the world with your senses under control... Do not lose fortitude even in the face of danger... When you come by riches, do not be conceited... Do not lose opportunities... Consider this life as a dream... Laugh, but in such a way that you do not become a laughing stock... Let your speech be a string of pearls.

Rani Chennamma's advice to her son
Basavappa on her deathbed

Rani Chennamma ruled the small kingdom of Keladi on the west coast of Karnataka for 25 years from 1671 to 1696 CE. She is best remembered for her quixotic act of sheltering the fugitive Maratha king Rajaram, the great Maratha king Shivaji Bhonsle's son, and of facing the wrath of the Mughal emperor Aurangzeb.

Never has the Chinese saying 'May you live in interesting times!' been more apropos than to the lifetime of Rani Chennamma. The Portuguese had already dominated the

Indian coast for 150 years by then, and Chennamma herself witnessed the rise of Shivaji and the Marathas in the 1650s; the advent of the British and the Dutch and the establishment of the British in Bombay in 1668; and the conquest of her neighbours, the Bijapur Adil Shahis, by the Mughals in 1686. She dealt with, and often fought, almost all these powers and managed to maintain a prosperous kingdom made rich by foreign trade. The Portuguese called her the Reina de Pimenta, or the pepper queen, for her efforts in conducting trade in pepper with overseas lands. Indeed, the kingdom survived till 1763 when it was finally taken over by Haider Ali of Mysore.

After the defeat of Vijayanagara in the Battle of Talikota in 1565 by the Deccan sultanates, many of its erstwhile vassals now established smaller independent kingdoms and grew prosperous by conducting trade across the Indian Ocean in pepper and textiles. Keladi, one such kingdom, was founded by Chowda Nayak in 1499. They were vassals of Vijayanagara kings and declared independence after Talikota. Over the centuries the capital moved to Ikkeri and later to Bidnur (modern-day Nagara in Karnataka), from which Chennamma ruled.

The Chowda Nayaks, now known as the Keladi Nayaks, kept expanding their kingdom at the expense of their neighbours, subsuming smaller kingdoms until they ruled over a territory of about 26,000 square kilometres by the beginning of the 18th century, with a long coast stretching the length of Karnataka, from Goa to Kerala.

Times were hard for the Chowda rulers. Of the 11 successions that took place in Keladi between 1660 and 1760, in only two cases did the king die a natural death and was succeeded by an adult male relative. The rest of the successions saw a mise en scène of poisoned kings, widows and children as successors, and bloodbaths of relatives, generals and would-be kingmakers. Chennamma was one such widow.

Much of the wealth of these coastal kingdoms came from the pepper trade with the Portuguese. Keladi, however, had a difficult relationship with the Portuguese – Keladi sold them pepper and bought horses from them but also warred with them over terms, winning some and losing more. Other players on the west coast at the time were the Dutch and the British East India companies.

In 1664 Somasekara Nayak became the ruler of Keladi. While at the fair at the Rameshwar temple in Keladi, which housed their family deity, his eye fell upon the young Chennamma, who was the daughter of a Lingayat merchant, Siddappa Shetty. She has been described in later biographies as having the complexion of a pearl, with bright eyes, a broad forehead, a long nose and curly hair.

Stricken by a coup de foudre, Somasekhara overruled the objections of his ministers who were horrified by her non-royal background, and married her regardless.

Chennamma now received a royal education in politics and administration, warfare, weaponry, music, arts and literature. She also started participating in the administration, interceding for various supplicants. She did not have any children.

The Vijayanagara kings had celebrated Dussehra with great pomp and their former vassals continued the tradition. (The Mysore Wodeyar kings were also vassals of the Vijayanagara kingdom and the Mysore Dussehra is still famous.) The Dussehra celebrations in Keladi were accompanied by performances by artists who gathered from all over the region.

King Somasekhara was clearly subject to sudden passions; at one such *nada habba* (Dussehra celebrations), he became enamoured with a dancer, Kalavathi of Jambukhandi, and set her up as royal dancer and royal mistress. Her family, including her stepfather, Bharame Mahut, accompanied her to Keladi.

According to folklore the obsessed king moved in with Kalavathi, Bharame Mahut began to control the king with drugs and he gradually fell sick. His ministers had to visit the king at his paramour's residence for any discussions.

The administration was hence more or less run by Chennamma with the help of her ministers, the chief of whom was Thimanna Naik, a trusted retainer from her father-in-law Shivappa Naik's time. The ministers were quite worried about the succession and variously pressured her to adopt one of their sons. The queen resisted these pressures, perhaps hoping for a miracle and the return of the king. Thimanna Naik eventually left in a huff because she disregarded his advice regarding adoption.

The sultan of neighbouring Bijapur saw this as an opportune moment to finally acquire the kingdom he had tried to conquer for a century and sent an agent, Jannopant, to talk terms with Chennamma. This was a ruse, as the agent was actually followed by an army intent on conquest.

To stave off an invasion, Chennamma gave Jannopant 3 lakh rupees. But Jannopant apparently bribed Bharame Mahut to finally poison and finish off the king as the Bijapur army arrived at Chennamma's doorstep.

Bereaved and overwhelmed by the strength of the Bijapur forces, the queen secretly left with her troops and her treasure for Bhuvanagiri, a fort hidden deep in the jungles of Keladi.

There she was joined by Thimanna Naik, who came back in an agony of remorse – in his absence, his king had passed away and the kingdom had been occupied by the Bijapur forces. Thimanna Naik gathered an army and managed to ambush the Bijapur forces, which had ventured into the jungle to catch the queen. The Bijapur army was destroyed and Chennamma triumphantly returned to Bidnur. She had Jannopant and Bharame Mahuta executed and purged their followers and supporters. This victory must have helped with what followed – Chennamma was crowned ruler in her own right in 1671. Unusually, she was not a regent, as she had no heir of the blood she was representing. Chennamma eventually chose a successor – Basavappa, the three-year-old son of a relative, Markappa Shetty, instead of a Nayak boy.

Her ascent to the throne was in spite of the presence of many other family members who were eligible to be king, and they, unsurprisingly, brought forward their claims. Many plagued her to the end of her days, asking for help from neighbouring kings and other powers to displace such a monstrosity as a woman who ruled over men, made worse by the fact that she was the daughter of a merchant, with not a drop of royal blood in her.

For example, in Dutch East India Company records, there is a letter received in 1689 from a Sadashiv Nayak, purporting to be the true king of Ikkeri. He gave an elaborate genealogy of eminently royal ancestors and assured the Dutch that he had the support of the nobles of Ikkeri, who abhorred the thought of a woman ruling over them. He wanted military help from the Dutch, which they did not proffer. He had been roaming about for 17 years trying to find support for his claim to the throne!

He was, by no account, the only claimant to the throne. Chennamma's ascent became an opportunity for neighbours to declare war on Keladi, often under the pretext of supporting some other claimant. Among them was Chikkadevaraya Wodeyar, the king of Mysore, who attacked Keladi, supporting the claims of Andhaka Venkata Nayak as the king of Keladi. A number of battles were fought between Keladi and Mysore, which finally ended in a friendship treaty between Chikkadevaraya and Chennamma. In fact, Keladi survived by maintaining a policy of neutrality with its neighbours and grew rich on the back of Portuguese trade. The Portuguese exported spices and rice from the Keladi ports of Mirjan and Honavara, and Chennamma allowed them to settle there and build their churches. In 1675, Chennamma entered into a truce with Shivaji, and he offered her his protection against the Portuguese and the Adil Shahis.

Chennamma had a punishing schedule – every morning after her bath, prayers and breakfast, she would go to the court and listen to the complaints of her subjects. She would then confer with her ministers on matters of state, with Basavappa Nayak in attendance, as part of his training. After midday prayers, she would spend an hour giving alms to priests and the needy. She would also personally supervise Basavappa's training and education.

Great changes were now afoot in the Deccan. Shivaji, who had dominated the landscape of the Deccan for 35 years, died in 1680. Aurangzeb immediately made a push to conquer the Deccan and moved to the south of the Vindhyas – never to return to the north till his death a quarter of a century later. The Mughals had been unsuccessfully trying to conquer the Deccan kingdoms since the time of Akbar. Aurangzeb was finally successful – he completed the conquest of Bijapur in 1686 and Golconda in 1687. He then turned his attention to the Marathas, captured their king Sambhaji in 1689 and brutally tortured him to death. The Mughal behemoth now moved into Maratha strongholds, capturing fort after fort. The 19-year-old Rajaram, Shivaji's younger son, now crowned king of the Marathas, decided to flee to the fort of Gingee in the deep south, often considered the most impregnable fort in India.

But he had to traverse thousands of kilometres of Mughal territory to reach there. He and a few companions, disguised as Lingayat pilgrims, started moving south, clinging to the Western Ghats. On his way, he showed up at Keladi, at Chennamma's daily alms-giving ceremony and asked her for shelter.

As per her *rajdharma*, her royal code of conduct, Chennamma felt bound to give shelter to any supplicant, especially the son of her benefactor Shivaji. Against the advice of her aghast ministers, but with the enthusiastic consent of her young heir Basavappa, in whom she had inculcated her chivalric code, the rani aided Rajaram and facilitated his passage to Gingee, putting her kingdom at the risk of destruction by Aurangzeb who had a visceral hatred of the Marathas. Rajaram, not without some narrow escapes, managed to reach Gingee and directed the Maratha resistance against the Mughals, later continued by his wife Tarabai.

This then is what Chennamma is really remembered for – this great quixotic act of courage and principle – to take on the wrath of the all-conquering Aurangzeb on a matter of dharma, against her own best interests.

It is interesting to imagine an alternative-history scenario wherein Rajaram is unable to escape capture. In such a case, the Maratha resistance may not have survived; Aurangzeb would not have emptied out his treasury and decimated his armies trying to fight them; the Mughal Empire may not have declined; the British would not have been able to kick open a rotten door; and India may not have been beggared. China, after all, was never directly ruled by European powers.

As Rajaram fled, Keladi geared up to face the might of Aurangzeb, fully expecting to be destroyed by the Mughals as effortlessly as an elephant stepping on an ant.

Aurangzeb, of course, came to know that Rajaram was in Keladi. He sent a letter to the queen along with rich gifts, asking her to hand over Rajaram, else face the wrath of the Mughal army. The queen wisely replied that Rajaram was no longer in Keladi, though he had passed through.

Aurangzeb was not convinced – he sent an army commanded by Janissar Khan to attack Keladi and capture Rajaram. The army made its way through the dense forest on the way to Bidnur.

Just as Russia's greatest general is considered to be its winter, India could possibly lay claim to the monsoon as its saviour. A significant factor in Alexander's armies turning back was the relentless monsoon rain and the innumerable bugs, aches and fevers it generated. So it was with the Mughal army, which foundered about, sick and quagmired, continuously harried by guerrilla attacks by the rani's forces. Aurangzeb called her a 'female bear'.

To Chennamma's great relief, Aurangzeb redirected his army on hearing that Rajaram had reached Gingee. The army moved on, collecting a tribute and some border forts from the rani and concluding a peace treaty.

In her last days Chennamma handed over administration to Basavappa Nayak and devoted herself to religion. She went on pilgrimage and endowed temples at Kashi, Rameswaram, Shrishaila and Tirupati. She had an *agrahara* – an entire street with houses on either side – formed, and invited scholars to settle down there. It was named Somashekharapura, after her husband. She also rebuilt a fort in Hulikere which Basavappa Nayak later renamed Chennagiri in honour of the queen. The kingdom was well maintained. Dr Fryer, the British doctor who visited Kanara at this time, says: 'The people have good laws and obey them and travel without guides on broad roads, not along byepaths as in Malabar.'

Chennamma died in 1696 and her kingdom was then ruled by Basavappa Nayak, later known as Keladi Basavraj. He ruled well and long and wrote about the history of that period in a Sanskrit tome called *Sivatattva Ratnakar*. She had educated him well.

Keladi through Italian Eyes

The indefatigable Italian traveller Pietro della Valle accompanied a Portuguese ambassador to Ikkeri to meet the then king of Keladi, Venkatappa Nayak, in 1623, and recorded his observations about the kingdom of Keladi. From his accounts one gets a sense of a rich and verdant world which followed all the customs of the Vijayanagara kingdom – its festivals, its devadasi tradition, processions, music and dance, with the temple as the centre of public life.

He was, however, not impressed by the king, hardly deeming him one: 'I style him King because the Portugals themselves and the Indians do so; but, in truth, Venkatappa Naika... by reason of the smallness of his territory, deserves not the Appellation of King; and the less because he pays Tribute to Adil Shah.'

He also describes the people and festivals:

> We saw going along the streets several companies of young girls, well cloth'd, after their manner, with some of the above-mentioned wrought and figured Silk from the girdle downwards; and from thence upward either naked, or else with very pure linnen, either of one colour, or striped and wrought with several, besides a scarf of the same work cast over the shoulder. Their heads were deck'd with yellow and white flowers form'd into a high and large Diadem, with some sticking out like Sun-beams, and others twisted together and hanging down in several fashions, which made a pretty sight.

Afterwards they went to the Piazza of the great Temple which is moderately large, and there danc'd in circles, singing their songs till it was late. Walking about the City I saw a beam rais'd a good height, where, in certain of their Holydayes, some devout people are wont to hang themselves by the flesh upon hooks fastened to the top of it and remain a good while so hanging, the blood running down in the meantime, and they flourishing their Sword and Buckler in the Air and singing verses in Honor of their Gods.

The Matriarchs of Travancore

The Attingal Queens

I was introduced into her majesty's presence. She had a guard of above 700 Nair soldiers about her; the Queen's attire being no more than a piece of callicoe wrapt around her middle, the upper part of her body appearing for the most part naked, with a piece of callicoe hanging carelessly round her shoulders. Her ears, which were very long, her neck and arms were adorned with precious stones, gold rings and bracelets and her head covered with a piece of white callicoe.

She was past her middle age, of a brown complexion, with black hair tied in a knot behind, but of majestick mien, she being a princess who shew'd a great deal of good conduct in the management of her affairs.

On Umayamma Rani, in Dutch representative
Johann Nieuhoff's *Voyages and Travels*
to the East Indies (1653–70)

Umayamma Rani (r. 1678–84 CE) was one of a long line of Attingal queens, the mothers of the kings of Travancore, but who ruled their own territory of Attingal independently for 400 years. More is known about Umayamma Rani in particular because many Europeans encountered her and wrote about her, although other Attingal queens would have had equally interesting histories.

Kerala has a special identity in India as *pennu-malayalam*, or the kingdom of women. Its matrilineal systems still survive, whereas almost everywhere else in India and indeed the world, they have been overwhelmed and wiped out by patrilineal systems. *Marumakkathayam*, or inheritance traced through the female line (literally, the word translates into inheritance by nephews and nieces), is followed mostly by the Nair community. In this system, both male and female siblings continue to live in the *tharavad* (family home) where they were born, all their lives. The oldest male sibling looks after the management of the property. The men visit their wives, who live with their own siblings; the women are visited by their husbands who continue to live with *their* sisters and brothers. The children stay with the mother and carry her surname. Often the father of a Nair woman's children could be a Nambudiri Brahmin, who has formed a *sambandham*, or relationship, with her, but it is only the mother's blood which is important in terms of inheritance. This makes the society matrilineal, where property and surnames are inherited through the mother, presumably based on the adage 'Motherhood is a fact, fatherhood presumption.' It is also matrilocal: people genetically related through their mothers live together. Matrilocal societies have existed since Neolithic times all over the world; genetic analysis of many ancient family gravesites has shown people related to each other through the maternal side buried together. The Kerala society, however, is not matriarchal, since typically, the decision makers here are men, not women.

Marumakkathayam was also followed by many royal families. There would be an official queen, whose brother would exercise power on her behalf; his heir would be the queen's son; *his* heir would be the queen's daughter's (his sister's) son and so on. The kingdom would essentially pass from mother to daughter, with power being exercised by the nearest male relative. Sometimes the women themselves would exercise power, especially as regents.

In 1314, two princesses from the Kolathiri dynasty, related to the Cheras, Pandyas and Cholas by blood, were adopted by Vira Udaya Martanda Varma (r. 1313–33), the son of Ravi Varma, the king of Travancore who had founded the Kulasekhara dynasty, and enlarged and consolidated the kingdom. Being closely related, the Kolathiri dynasty was particularly suitable for the purpose of adoption. Both these dynasties were descended from the ancient Mushika dynasty.

The princesses were made rulers of Attingal, a principality of Travancore north of Trivandrum, installed in a new palace there and officially called the senior rani and junior rani. Their own homeland was recreated for them. Their family goddess, the Bhagwathi, was consecrated in a temple, and soldiers, retainers, artisans, craftsmen and slaves were brought in from their homeland. The princesses ruled Attingal directly, the rule passing from mother to daughter. Their son would rule Travancore. Their husbands came from four or five designated noble families, colloquially known as 'son-in-law houses'. Every generation, two among their daughters would become the new Attingal ranis, or Attingal queens. Only the son of a designated Attingal rani could become the king of Travancore. If no daughters were born, they would be adopted from designated families.

For the next few centuries, these queens ruled Attingal independently and exercised great influence over Travancore. They also periodically ruled Travancore directly or as regents.

The Attingal ranis were known for their bravery. There is a ballad about how one Attingal rani refused to let an armed escort accompanying the ruling king of Travancore on a pilgrimage (who must have been her brother or some close relative!) pass through her kingdom. This clash of egos caused a battle royal with much bloodshed in which both were killed.

Tales are also recounted by early Europeans about the Attingal ranis. In 1516, Lopo Soares de Albergaria, the third governor of Portuguese India, signed a treaty with the queen of Quilon who was related to the then Attingal rani. The two queens had allied together to invade Travancore, and the queen of Quilon told him, 'We are going to invade our neighbouring kingdom of Travancore, for which we start tomorrow. As we are now greatly pressed for money, please do not ask us about the church endowments now.' A few years later, in 1519, these two queens banded together to attack the Portuguese with a combined force of 20,000 soldiers.

John Wallis, an English trader, in 1727, specifically says in his book *A Short Treatise by Way of Essay of Attinga* that 'Attinga is Governed by a Queen', also noting that this was 'an instance peculiar only to this part' of Kerala. He also says that Attingal was outside the control of the prince who ruled Travancore.

By the late 17th century, the kingdom of Travancore was in great flux, with rival factions laying claim to the throne and some even ruling their principalities independently. A group of eight noble families, called the Ettuveetil Pillamar, now controlled Travancore. The kings were quite weak, and thoroughly dominated by the fractious nobles.

Aswathi Thirunal, popularly known as Umayamma Rani, was the junior Attingal rani. Her sister, Makayiram Thirunal, was the senior queen, and her son Ravi Varma was the heir to the king. The then ruler of Travancore, Adithya Varma, had been adopted from the Cochin royal family, breaking the tradition of adopting only women, and was thus not related to the Attingal ranis.

As per a semi-official Travancore history written in the 19th century by Shungoony Menon, Adithya Varma was of a 'very quiet and mild disposition, and led a retired and religious life'. He had little control over his nobles. Because of his religious convictions, he was trying to reform the administration of the Sri Padmanabhaswamy temple, which did not suit the nobles in control. His Trivandrum palace was burnt down one night, and he moved to a little fort nearby called Puthenkotta. According to Menon, the nobles started sending 'every day, Nivedyams, i.e., sweetmeat offered to the image of Padmanabhaswamy for pooja, and one day this being mixed with poison, the king, partook of it, became ill and died suddenly.'

The Ettuveetil now went to Umayamma Rani, who had six male children and lived in Puthenkotta palace, and swore allegiance and support. However, they were actually conspiring against her, and soon perpetrated a horrific crime. In the words of Shungoonny Menon:

> On a certain moonlight night, a few boys of the confederate party, who were of the same ages as the five Princes, were playing with them at the Puthenkotta palace. One of the boys proposed to the Princes (doubtless at the instigation of the confederates), to go to a tank or reservoir, situated a few furlongs distant from the western side of the palace, and to play on a white sandy plain and bathe in the crystal water. The young Princes proceeded with the boys, without the knowledge of their unfortunate mother, and while they were bathing, shocking to relate, some men from the confederate party appeared there under the pretext of bathing, and seized the Princes and suffocated them under water: they left the bodies to float in the tank and went away, telling the boys to inform the people at the palace that the Princes were unfortunately drowned in the tank while bathing.

Puthenkotta was cursed by the distraught rani, and became a cremation ground; the tank was abandoned as a bathing place by the locals, and became a burial place for animal carcasses. However, this theory has been disputed by many recent historians who say that Adithya Varma died a natural death and Umayamma Rani had no children!

Umayamma Rani became the regent in 1677 for her surviving son Ravi Varma. There are no accounts of what happened to her older sister, the senior queen. She moved to Nedumangad with her household and the palace officials, all her energies concentrated on preventing the murder of her son, the king. The unruly nobles now started fighting each other and anarchy prevailed.

Sensing an opportunity, a petty Mughal adventurer, Sardar 'Mugilan' (which simply means 'Mughal' in Malayalam) captured Travancore with some horsemen. The nobles fled. As per legend, some loyal Pathans attached to the house of Travancore managed to convince him not to loot the Sri Padmanabhaswamy temple. He could not have had any inkling of the one trillion dollars equivalent of gold in the basement. He would have become richer than Aurangzeb! He was also persuaded not to convert people to Islam. However, he did insist on the women covering up their shoulders in public.

Umayamma Rani, now left with no support from her nobles, needed an able commander to throw out the invader. She invited the exiled Kerala Varma from the Kottayam royal family to be the leader of her small army. He was a poet and scholar, and a brilliant military commander, who had been forced out from his homeland for attempting a rebellion. He raised armies of archers and slingers, and attacked the invader. The rocky forest terrain rendered the Mughal cavalry useless, and gave many points of vantage to the Travancore slingers and archers. As per legend, in an interesting twist on the David-and-Goliath tale, a slinger hit a nest of wasps hanging over the Mughal sardar's head, who was then beset by a swarm of those wasps. Stung badly, he fell off his horse, and was immediately shot through by arrows. The remaining forces fled; Kerala Varma captured 300 horses and several weapons, which gave him a decisive advantage in quelling the Ettuveetil nobles.

The rani now rebuilt the palace at Trivandrum and started living there. Kerala Varma soon cowed the Ettuveetil Pillamar and the powerful temple committees. Ravi Varma was crowned at the age of 16; the rani ceased to be regent but continued to rule in Attingal. Kerala Varma managed the kingdom of Travancore well until he was assassinated by the nobles in his palace in 1695.

Throughout this period, the Attingal ranis ruled and made treaties with the pepper- and calico-hungry Europeans, playing them off against each other for better terms. As per the Dutch historian Louise Ouwerkerk, 'great was the surprise of [these] merchants, when they found themselves negotiating trade treaties with bare-bosomed but dignified and capable Indian queens.'

In 1688, Umayamma, known as Queen Ashure in British records, granted Vettoor ('Rettorah') and Vizhinjam ('Brinjohn') in Travancore to the English to establish factories. However, soon afterwards, she cancelled the lease since 'They were troublesome to my people and therefore I ordered that they should goe from there and make no more Contracts in my Land,' as quoted in a letter to Sir John Gayer in 1695.

It was only after they reassured her that they had 'Intention to doe good to my Country and to bee in good ffriendship with mee' that the Rani gave them the fort of Anjengo (now Anchuthengu) in 1694. She also set the customs duty and annual tribute due to her, as well as fixed a 50 per cent share of any loot recovered from shipwrecked vessels nearby. All these grants were made in her own name, without reference to Ravi Varma. The English agreed to carry on their trade 'without any manner of Impudence' and 'to obey Her Highness'. They kept the queen in good humour with annual presents. Anjengo was extremely profitable and important for them; for many years, it was second only to Bombay on the west coast.

A picture of Umayamma Rani can be built through the interesting Europeans reminiscences about her. She comes across as very strong-minded and dominating. In 1677, Hendrik van Rheede, an administrator in the Dutch East India Company, wrote of her:

> of such noble and manly conduct that she is both feared and respected by everyone... she not only rules Attingal but Travancore itself, within whose bounds no princess may set her feet according to their laws, nor pass the river Canimani, on pain of forfeiting their rights, but this young Amazon has lately violated those customs and made even the king fly before her.

In 1694 he said that she could gather an army of 30,000.

The Europeans also had comments about the personal lives of the Attingal ranis. These may be taken with a pinch of salt, since one wonders if they were playing to their audience at home which thirsted for the exotic. John Henry Grose in his *A Voyage to the East Indies* records that 'whom and as many as she pleases to the honour of her bed' could be taken by the rani as lovers, adding, 'The handsomest young men about the country generally compose her seraglio.' James Welsh would note that the rani could 'change them whenever she is tired of one by sending him away and selecting another'.

The British, it seems, turned this to their advantage. In 1685, as per the British chronicler Pinkerton, the envoy who carried the East India Company's annual present was 'a young beautiful English gentleman' and 'her black Majesty' took a fancy to him. He 'satisfied her so well that when he left her court, she made him some presents'. The grant of Anjengo, according to some accounts, was one of those presents! Clearly the British performed above and beyond the call of duty.

This side of the queens is of course not mentioned in the 19th-century histories written by Travancore officials, who were now completely under the sway of Victorian morality. They preferred to cast Umayamma as a damsel in distress – downplaying her fiery independence to conform to the Victorian ideal of womanhood.

The rani, now middle-aged, needed children as future heirs, since any children Ravi Varma had could not succeed to the throne under the *Marumakkathayam* system. In 1688, she adopted two boys and two girls from the highly reluctant Kolathunadu king, who feared for his children's safety during a potential scramble for the throne.

Umayamma Rani died in July 1698; the junior rani, who is referred to in historical records only by the title Pooruruttathi Thirunal from Kolathunadu, became the queen of Attingal, since her elder sister had died within a year of the adoption.

After King Ravi Varma's death in 1704, there were the inevitable succession wars. Finally in 1729, Marthanda

Varma, the son of Poororuttathi Thirunal, became the king.

In 1721, a horrific massacre of the English took place in Attingal. Though it is often painted as the first uprising against the British, it cannot be called that since they were not the rulers then.

The queen who succeeded Umayamma in Attingal was weak, and her nobles essentially controlled the kingdom.

The British in Anjengo had by then started misbehaving with the locals, and not paying the tribute due to the queen. The chief factor, William Gyfford, was particularly noxious. In his three years there he had, along with his aide, Ignatio Malheiro, enraged the local population by cheating them, displaying contempt for their customs and committing petty atrocities like pelting traders with rotten eggs, and throwing dirty water on them as they passed by! Unsurprisingly, he soon found that the locals were unwilling to do business with him. Wishing to ingratiate himself with the rani, Gyfford offered to pay up the seven years of arrears in tribute, along with other presents. He was invited to the Attingal fort, six kilometres upriver, for the Vishu festival in 1721 by the nobles, who were by now thirsting for revenge against Gyfford and Malheiro. Gyfford left with the entire contingent of 120 Englishmen and 40 servants, leaving only four Englishmen behind with the womenfolk.

He successfully distributed presents in Attingal, and accepted the invitation to stay overnight in the fort, overruling the apprehensions of other Englishmen, who felt something strange in the air. That night, the entire English party was attacked and killed; the ammunition had been removed from their guns and they had been sleeping in small groups in different rooms. The hated Malheiro was 'gradually dismembered, while Gyfford had his tongue torn out, was nailed to a log of wood, and sent floating down the river', as recounted in *The Pirates of Malabar, and an Englishwoman in India Two Hundred Years Ago* by John Biddulph.

Anjengo was attacked by the locals, but was not captured, as British relief arrived quite soon.

The queen was accused of playing a part in this murderous scheme, and retired to Kollam. She was replaced by another sister of the then king, Rama Varma.

The British then renegotiated their treaty with the queen in 1722 and 1729. They were willing to overlook the past because of commercial interests: there was no retribution for the massacre, which was blamed on refractory nobles. The fact that they were willing to forgive and forget also throws light on the relative bargaining position of the British at that time. Thirty years later, there would have been no way that such a massacre would be so easily forgiven.

Marthanda Varma, who became king in 1729, is considered the father of the modern state of Travancore. He brutally suppressed all dissent and subdued the refractory nobles simply by beheading hundreds of them. In 1731, he forced his aunt, the Attingal rani at the time, to sign a silver-plate treaty with him, relinquishing all her sovereign rights to Attingal to the raja, after four centuries of independence. The treaty, however, guaranteed that only the sons of the Attingal ranis would succeed to the throne of Travancore and that the senior rani would remain the owner of the 15,000 acres of freehold land originally assigned to her ancestors in the 14th century. Attingal was now merged with Travancore.

Until 1749, the English continued to pay the rani an annual tribute. In 1751, when the then Attingal rani died, they fired a twenty-gun salute from the ramparts of Anjengo Fort, as they would for a sovereign, keeping flags at half-mast and shutting business for five days in official mourning.

Even as late as 1810, the British resident in Travancore would remark in a letter that, legally, the Attingal rani was 'the supreme authority in the State, her mandates are paramount to those of the Rajah, and her elevation to the situation of the Tumbratty [i.e., senior rani] is made in a manner as formal and solemn as that of the instalment of a Rajah'.

Later Attingal ranis ruled Travancore successfully as regents, and introduced many progressive reforms, especially in education, slowly making Travancore the leading state in literacy and other quality-of-life indicators. Gowri Lakshmi Bayi ruled in her own right from 1810 to 1814. Her sister, Gowri Parvathi Bayi succeeded, ruling for a remarkably visionary 14 years. In 1901, Sethu Lakshmi Bayi had a very successful rule. Kerala still has among the best quality-of-life indicators in India, due in no small part to the educational reforms introduced by the queens, and the relatively better position of women as a legacy from its matrilineal past.

The Contrasts of Kerala

Kerala was a study in contrasts, where some of the most tolerant and inclusive behaviour coexisted with some very narrow practices with respect to religion, caste and gender. Because it was the main entrepôt for the spice trade in India with the rest of the world, it was exposed to influences from all over the world. Jews traded here since the time of Solomon, c. 1000 BCE, and took refuge during the diaspora after the fall of Jerusalem in 70 CE. Christianity here is as old as in Europe; the first Christian converts date from the arrival of the apostle St. Thomas in 52 CE; the first European conversion was only in 50 CE by St. Paul at Phillippi. The first mosque in India was built by the Arabs in 629 CE; the third mosque ever to be built in the world, this was in the lifetime of the prophet, who passed away in 632 CE. Substantial populations of all these religions lived together in Kerala without persecution for millennia.

However, Kerala was extremely caste-ridden, with some of the worst institutionalized discrimination in the country. Lower-caste people had to call out as they walked so that upper-caste people could avoid being 'polluted' by seeing them. Lower-caste women were required to pay *mulakkaram* (breast tax) to be allowed to cover their breasts in public; the tax amount was calculated according to the size of the breast! Mannapeddy and Pulapeddy were unique customs where if a higher-caste woman was seen by a lower-caste man after dusk, she would be expelled from her caste and he could take her with him. Lower castes were taxed on marriages, childbirth, and even on death. Caste defined a person; even the people of the book (Jews, Christians, Muslims) were allocated a caste, Anjuvannam (or the fifth caste).

Perhaps these ancient customs survived because Kerala was still ruled by the descendants of the Cheras who had ruled here since the first millennium BCE. It was also relatively protected from the rest of India by the hills and sea enclosing it, especially Travancore in the south. To give an idea of this continuity, the Sri Padmanabhaswamy temple in Travancore has never been looted in the last 2000 years, unlike almost any other major temple in India. The treasure recently found in its basement is worth an estimated 1 trillion dollars (65 lakh crore rupees! Enough to wipe out India's internal and external debt). It is interesting to note that if a temple only patronized by the quite small but clearly rich kingdom of Travancore could accumulate so much, how much wealth there must have been in the major national pilgrimage centres like Somnath!

The Empire Builder

Rani Tarabai

[The Mughals felt] that it would not be difficult to overcome two young children and a helpless woman. They thought their enemy weak, contemptible and helpless; but Tara Bai, as the wife of Rajaram was called, showed great powers of command and government, and from day to day the war spread and the power of the Mahrattas increased.

Khafi Khan, *Muntakhab al-Lubab*

People say that I am a quarrelsome woman.

Tarabai

Tarabai, the Maratha queen (r. 1700–61 CE*), can perhaps be considered one of the most important factors that contributed to the breaking up of the Mughal Empire after Aurangzeb's death. She prevented the Maratha confederacy from disintegrating when it was at its lowest ebb, with almost all its forts in Mughal hands and the Mughal emperor Aurangzeb personally directing operations against it. Not only did she survive the Mughal onslaught, but also carried the battle over into Mughal territory, first raiding it and then creating permanent outposts, thus laying the foundations of Maratha hegemony in the 18th century. The Marathas effectively controlled the Mughal emperor for half a century before they were displaced by the British in the 19th century.*

In the second half of the 17th century, Emperor Aurangzeb's rule was experiencing a million mutinies across India. In particular, the Marathas had been honed as the ultimate fighting machine by the great Shivaji and had emerged as a significant force in the Deccan.

Born in 1675, Tarabai was the daughter of Hambir Rao Mohite, Shivaji's commander-in-chief. At the age of eight, she was married to Shivaji's younger son Rajaram, as his second wife. Shivaji had died in 1680, soon after crowning himself the ruler of the independent Maratha kingdom he had established.

In 1682, when Aurangzeb arrived in the Deccan, little did he know that over the next 25 years, the Deccan ulcer would bleed him and the Mughal Empire to death.

After the fall of the wealthy kingdoms of Bijapur and Golconda to Aurangzeb in 1686 and 1687, Aurangzeb now turned all his energies towards the Marathas who had retreated to forts built on the steep-sided Western Ghats. Shivaji's son, Sambhaji, was the Maratha king and had continued his father's depredations on Mughal territories as well as the kingdom of Bijapur.

As the Mughals entered western Maharashtra, the forts started falling like ninepins in front of Aurangzeb's might and wealth, and the Marathas took to hiding in their highest forts and in the most impenetrable forests. Sambhaji was captured from his forest hideout in Sangameshwar in 1689 and Aurangzeb vented his full fury on him. When he was asked to convert to Islam, Sambhaji flippantly replied that he would if

Aurangzeb married his daughter to him. As punishment, his tongue was cut off and his eyes gouged out. He was tortured over a long period and finally executed.

Aurangzeb continued capturing Maratha forts. Sambhaji's infant son, also named Shivaji, who was now officially the Maratha king, was captured when the capital Raigad fell. Aurangzeb decided to bring the child up in the royal harem and handed him over to his daughter Zeenat-un-Nissa. Aurangzeb, however, changed the boy's name to Shahu from Shivaji, a name quite unbearable to him. He thought Shahu would be a useful hostage in his wars against the Marathas.

Sambhaji's younger brother, 19-year-old Rajaram, who was still free, was hurriedly crowned the king of the Marathas. With Aurangzeb's armies swarming all over Maharashtra, he realized that he had to escape the region. In a ruse borrowed from his father, Rajaram and a few of his companions disguised themselves as Lingayat pilgrims and made their way to the deep south, to the most invincible Maratha fort they knew, the fortress of Gingee in modern-day Tamil Nadu.

Rajaram finally reached Gingee in November 1689 and began directing long-distance guerrilla operations in Maharashtra, led by his general Ramchandra Nilkanth. Tarabai spent her teenage years in Panhala under the tutelage of Ramchandra Nilkanth, gaining civil and military experience. After a few years, Rajaram's three queens, including Tarabai, joined him in Gingee by taking a ship from the Konkan coast, landing at Honavar port, and making their way to the fortress overland.

The impregnable fort of Gingee was besieged by the Mughals under the general Zulfikar Khan. However, the siege was as porous as a sieve since Rajaram was able to conduct his entire guerrilla operations rather like a modern-day don running his empire from prison.

The siege continued for eight years and Aurangzeb finally gave an ultimatum to Zulfikar Khan, warning him that he would be in dire trouble if the fort was not captured soon. Zulfikar Khan tightened the siege and food supplies grew scarce. Rajaram managed to escape to Vellore in 1697 and made his way back to Maharashtra with his family. He established his new capital at Satara near Pune. Gingee fell to Zulfikar Khan.

An enraged Aurangzeb, now increasingly senile at the age of 82, personally laid siege to Satara. He used all the stratagems he could come up with to capture the fort. In one instance, he dressed up in finery and participated in a parade in front of the fort in the hope that the besieged soldiers would give in to curiosity, come over to the parapet to see what was going on and he could then blow them up with a hidden mine.

In 1700, Aurangzeb received the news that Rajaram had died of a chest disease. The Marathas now had no adult king – they had been left with just the king's widows and two infant sons as heirs. The senior wife had committed sati.

Aurangzeb was overjoyed. The Maratha menace was finally quelled – or so he thought!

It was at this time that the 25-year-old Tarabai came into her own. She declared her four-year-old son king under the name

Shivaji II, throwing aside the claim to the throne of Sambhaji's son Shahu, still in Mughal captivity, with the argument that a king in hand was worth any number in the bush. She bribed, cajoled and convinced the Maratha generals to support her and threw Rajaram's other surviving wife, Rajasbai, and her son Sambhaji into prison, to eliminate potential rivals.

As the Mughal historian Khafi Khan put it: 'The chiefs then made Tara Bai, the chief wife [and] the mother of one son [of Rajaram], regent. She was a clever, intelligent woman, and had obtained a reputation during her husband's lifetime for her knowledge of civil and military matters.'

In the seven-year period from 1700 to 1707, Tarabai single-handedly directed the Maratha defence against Aurangzeb's army. She led the attacks from the front, travelling between forts, mobilizing resources and motivating her commanders. She also mastered Aurangzeb's technique of bribing commanders on both sides of the conflict.

Bhimsen, a Mughal officer, stated in his *Tarikh-i-Dilkusha* that Tarabai 'was a stronger ruler than her husband'. He also observed that Tarabai 'became all in all and regulated things so well that not a single Maratha leader acted without her order'.

Khafi Khan also concurs when he says of Tarabai: 'She won the hearts of her officers, and for all the struggles and schemes, the campaigns and sieges of Aurangzeb up to the end of his reign, the power of the Mahrattas increased day by day.'

Meanwhile, sick of the corruption among his officers, Aurangzeb decided to personally handle the campaign – he dragged himself from fort to fort from 1701 to 1706, taking them over one by one.

To counter Aurangzeb, Tarabai made an ingenious move based on the old military maxim that offence is the best defence. Every year, she sent large forces of up to 50,000 troops beyond the Marathi-speaking Deccan deep into Mughal domains in the north, as far as Malwa and Gujarat, even while major forts of her own were falling into Aurangzeb's hands. These were more than just raids; her aim was to establish permanent collection centres in the Mughal territories, which had been denuded of troops by Aurangzeb for his Deccan campaign.

Her troops practically set up a parallel government to the Mughals in these areas. They divided the districts among themselves, and even appointed provincial governors and revenue and toll collectors. Khafi Khan states: 'they passed the years and months to their satisfaction, with their wives and children, tents and elephants. Their daring went beyond all bounds.'

Tarabai's clear vision and unerring judgement was visible both on the battlefield as well as in the council chamber.

Sick and dispirited, Aurangzeb died in 1707 at the age of 89 and was buried in Aurangabad. Before his death, he stated that after him only chaos would prevail, and it did, for the Maratha menace had still not been quelled. His sons fought among themselves for the kingdom under the classic Mughal tenet for princes – *takht ya takhta* (the throne or a bier). The victor of this internecine warfare, Bahadur Shah I, was crowned emperor in 1707.

Aurangzeb's death was not a relief for Tarabai; on the contrary, it was a disaster for her on the personal front. After Aurangzeb's death, Shahu was released by the Mughals mainly to counter Tarabai and to divide the Marathas under the well-enshrined political principle of *divide et impera*, divide and rule. Hearing of this, Tarabai immediately declared him an imposter. Then, realizing it would be difficult to sustain the lie, she declared that Shahu had become totally Mughal in character because of his long imprisonment of 18 years and was no longer suitable to be a Maratha king. Shahu gave some credence to her claims when he made a pilgrimage to his foster father Aurangzeb's tomb on foot to pay his last respects.

However, partly because of his greater claim to the throne, and partly because of his gender, chieftain after chieftain sent to fight against Shahu started defecting to his camp. He won a battle against Tarabai's troops at Khed, and finally entered Satara in triumph in 1708 and was crowned king with the full support of the Mughal emperor.

Tarabai retreated to Panhala and for the next few years, two distinct Maratha kingdoms prevailed, though they were constantly at war with each other. Over the next seven years, both these Maratha kingdoms tried to extract the maximum from the Mughal Empire, both claiming the *chauth* and *sardeshmukhi* – taxes originally instituted by Shivaji as revenue to be collected from enemy territory – from the Deccan, and taking it forcibly from the Mughal territories.

In 1713, Shahu made Balaji Vishwanath, a clever Konkani Brahmin, his peshwa, or chief minister. He managed to win over Tarabai's most powerful supporter, the naval commander Kanhoji Angre, and helped engineer a coup in 1714, whereby her husband Rajaram's third wife, Rajasbai, and her son Sambhaji II assumed power in the southern kingdom, now based out of nearby Kolhapur. Tarabai and her son Shivaji were thrown into prison at Panhala, where she spent 16 years and where her son eventually died after 12 years.

Tarabai mouldered in prison till 1730, when Shahu, who had entered into hostilities with Sambhaji II, finally freed her and, overcome with family feeling, generously invited her to stay in Satara, albeit under house arrest. When offered the option by Shahu, Tarabai is supposed to have said, 'Whether I go back or stay, I shall have to spend my life in prison anyway; let me therefore stay with you.' Some say that she realized that Shahu's kingdom was far more powerful and had much greater potential for her energies. She possibly also thought that Shahu would treat her better than her stepson Sambhaji II, whom she had previously imprisoned for so many years.

Sambhaji II continued to rule from Kolhapur, restricted by a treaty to a small area. The Kolhapur Bhonsle dynasty descended from Sambhaji II continued till Independence, with a descendent, Chhatrapati Shahuji Maharaj, greatly funding Dalit education, including that of Baba Saheb Ambedkar, and undertaking many pioneering reforms. He is revered as a Dalit icon.

Shahu's rule was a period of great expansion for the Maratha Empire. Power, however, had passed on to the peshwa, who paid lip service to the king in Satara. The peshwaship became hereditary. Under Balaji Vishwanath (1713–20 CE) and his warrior son Baji Rao I (1720–40 CE), the Marathas penetrated farther north, becoming the undisputed rulers of India.

Meanwhile, Tarabai continued living in Satara. In 1748, Shahu fell ill. With no blood descendants of Shivaji available as heir, Tarabai now pulled a rabbit out of a hat. Though 73 years old now, her lust for power had clearly not withered. She alleged that she had a grandson, Ramraja, who had been born after her son's death in prison at Panhala. Scared of what her rival, Rajasbai, would do if she found out, she had given him to a Brahmin couple in a village to rear and he had now grown up to be a young man of twenty-two – the hidden prince waiting for his destiny.

Shahu was inclined to believe the story and seriously considered adopting the youth, but he faced stiff resistance, particularly from his wife Sakwarbai, who hated Tarabai with a vengeance. An indecisive Shahu, apprehensive about the future of the empire, signed over a number of his powers to Peshwa Balaji Baji Rao in October 1749 effectively making the peshwa sovereign, and the king a titular head. Shahu died by the end of the year. Thereafter, a delegation found Ramraja, and crowned him king in 1750 as Rajaram II, with Peshwa Balaji Baji Rao and Tarabai as his guides.

Real power, though, had already passed into the hands of the peshwa. He moved his court away from Tarabai to Pune while she remained in Satara, mercilessly bullying the young Ramraja. When he had the temerity to show some independence of thought, she threw him in the dungeon and fed him coarse millet, announcing to a stunned court that he was actually *not* her grandson but a lowly peasant and that she had staged this elaborate charade to grab power.

At the same time, she openly opposed Balaji Baji Rao, exhorting the peshwa's enemies, including the Nizam of Hyderabad, to take up arms and remove him from power. She even tried to play the caste card, pitting herself as the champion of the Marathas against the dominance of Brahmins like the peshwa. None of her ploys worked, however, and she finally came to a compromise with the peshwa; they both swore to an accord in the temple of Jejuri in Pune that the peshwa would show his loyalty to her and Tarabai would acknowledge his right to govern the country.

By now none of the Maratha chieftains was willing to tangle with Tarabai – they cared little about control over Satara, and still less about the titular 'king'. The true court was in Pune, and the true ruler was the peshwa. Besides, it was rumoured that Tarabai had supernatural powers and nobody was prepared to put that to the test.

For the rest of her days Tarabai ruled as the dowager, maintaining a regular court, issuing *farmans* and building temples. The peshwa would make a show of sometimes seeking her advice; he once had her write letters to Maratha chieftains mobilizing them against an invasion. She kept abreast of the times; there is a record of a letter from the Portuguese governor of Goa written in April 1758 agreeing to sell her 2,000 guns – she was 83 at the time.

She was alive when the Marathas suffered at the hands of Ahmad Shah Abdali in Panipat in 1761 – considered the single bloodiest day of war in Indian history. She died six months later in 1761 at the age of 86, no doubt giving rise to a huge collective sigh of relief.

Rajaram II continued ruling from Satara. His descendants were finally deposed by the British in 1839.

Tarabai was witness to the rise and fall of the Marathas: from the early years of the independent kingdom founded by Chhatrapati Shivaji in 1674 just before her birth, to their near destruction by Aurangzeb in 1700, their rise to national power where they effectively controlled almost all of India by 1760, and their decimation by Ahmad Shah Abdali in the Third Battle of Panipat in 1761. The Marathas, however, rose again and were finally tamed by the British in a series of engagements in the 19th century, culminating in the uprising of 1857.

Had she not been there in 1701, it is quite likely that Aurangzeb would have snuffed out Maratha rule completely, and the history of India would have been quite different. As historian Jadunath Sarkar has commented, 'In that awful crisis her character and strength saved the nation.'

Shivaji, Aurangzeb's Nemesis

The Marathas were a thorn in the flesh of the Mughal Empire. Aurangzeb could never forgive himself for allowing Shivaji to escape from Agra in a fruit basket in 1666. He flayed himself mentally for the rest of his life for this lapse, to the extent that he wrote in his last words of wisdom to his son: 'Negligence for a single moment becomes the cause of disgrace for long years. The escape of the wretch Shiva took place through my carelessness and I have to labour hard against the Marathas to the end of my life as a result of it.'

The Deccan campaign over time cost the Mughals an estimated hundred thousand lives a year and an enormous amount of money. Historian Stanley Wolpert records that Aurangzeb's encampment was like a moving capital – a city of tents 30 miles in circumference, with some 250 bazaars, half a million camp followers, 50,000 camels and 30,000 elephants, all of whom had to be fed. The Deccan was stripped of its surplus grain and wealth, and the land was struck by famine and bubonic plague. Revenue from the Deccan fell to 10 per cent of its earlier level and dispossessed farmers rushed off to join the Maratha guerrilla forces.

Shivaji left no opportunity to needle Aurangzeb. Here are some excerpts from a letter he wrote when Aurangzeb reimposed the *jaziya* tax on non-Muslims, which Akbar had withdrawn a hundred years ago.

> This firm and constant well-wisher Shivaji, after rendering thanks for the grace of God and the favours of the

Emperor – which are clearer than the Sun – begs you to inform your Majesty that, although this well-wisher was led by his adverse Fate to come away from your august Presence without taking leave, yet he is ever ready to perform, to the fullest extent possible and proper, everything that duty as a servant and gratitude demand of him...

It has recently come to my ears that, on the ground of the war with me having exhausted your wealth and emptied your treasury, your Majesty has ordered that money under the name of *jaziya* should be collected from the Hindus and imperial needs supplied with it.

Akbar Padshah... the aim of his liberal heart was to cherish and protect all the people... Through the auspicious effect of this sublime disposition, wherever he [Akbar] bent the glance of his august wish, Victory and Success advanced to welcome him on the way...

But in *your* Majesty's reign, many of the forts and provinces have gone out of your possession, and the rest will soon do so too, because there will be no slackness on my part in ruining and devastating them. Your peasants are down-trodden; the yield of every village has declined – in the place of one lakh [of Rupees] only one thousand, and in the place of a thousand only ten are collected and that too with difficulty.

The Philosopher Queen

Ahilya Bai Holkar

This great ruler in Indore encouraged all within her realm to do their best. Merchants produced their finest cloths, trade flourished, the farmers were at peace and oppression ceased, for each case that came to the queen's notice was dealt with severely. She loved to see her people prosper, and to watch the fine cities grow, and to watch that her subjects were not afraid to display their wealth, lest the ruler should snatch it from them. Far and wide the roads were planted with shady trees, and wells were made, and rest-houses for travellers. The poor, the homeless, the orphaned were all helped according to their needs.

Annie Besant, *Children of the Motherland*

Ahilya Bai Holkar (r. 1767–95 CE) is one of India's most revered rulers. Often known as India's 'philosopher queen' (the philosopher king as described by Plato constitutes the Western ideal of kingship), she created an island of peace and prosperity in her beautifully governed state of Indore in the tumultuous 18th century.

After the death of Aurangzeb in 1707, the Mughal Empire was rife with warfare. The Marathas came up in this period as a significant power. From the 1720s, the Maratha king, Shahu, who was Shivaji's grandson, ruled from Satara, but the power was firmly in the hands of his chief minister, the peshwa, who held court in Pune. Peshwa Baji Rao I took the Maratha armies to every part of India from 1721 to 1740, and reduced Mughal rule to a shadow.

The Marathas had evolved an interesting structure for their expansion. Territories were conquered from the Mughals and assigned to important generals who would technically be *subedars*, or provincial governors, but actually function as rulers. They operated as a loose confederacy owing allegiance to the peshwa; a certain amount of revenue would have to be sent to the peshwa's treasury every year, and the *subedars* would have to be available to the peshwa for joint battles across the country. Major Maratha kingdoms thus created were the Scindias, Holkars, Gaikwads, Bhonsles and Pawars.

The relationship between these Maratha kingdoms and the Mughals was quite strange. While the Marathas preyed on Mughal territories, the Mughal emperor became dependent on them over time, and they were often called upon to fight battles on behalf of various factions of Mughals. They could potentially have deposed the Mughal king at various points, but they chose not to.

Malhar Rao Holkar was one of the chief generals of Baji Rao I. He belonged to the Dhangar or shepherd community, and had spent his youth grazing cattle before joining the Maratha army. There he rose rapidly until he became one of the peshwa's most trusted lieutenants. When Baji Rao first distributed territories among his chief generals Shinde (Scindia), Holkar and Pawar in 1732, Holkar, as the senior-most, received the best of the territories that remained after the peshwa had kept aside the crucial areas for himself. Two-fifths of Malwa was granted to Holkar as *saranjam*, or territory, for maintenance of his army. Holkar was later awarded more *saranjams* in western Khandesh, as well as revenue from other scattered conquests.

The story of Ahilya Bai begins thus. On his way back to his capital Indore in 1733, Malhar Rao spent the night in the village of Chaudi in his dominion. There he saw the eight-year-old daughter of the village chief, Manikji Shinde, and was struck by her intelligence and her regal bearing. He immediately decided to marry her to his only son, 10-year-old Khande Rao, and took her off to Indore. Ahilya Bai was Khande Rao's first wife.

This was a world where women were illiterate, to the extent that in Bengal, even a hundred years later, there existed a superstition that if a woman learnt to read, her husband would die (as quoted in the autobiography of Haimabati Sen, a 19th-century Bengali woman doctor). Malhar Rao, however, gave Ahilya Bai the education of a prince – not only in religious and secular texts, but also in the practice of arms, accounting, statecraft, strategy and administration. Ahilya Bai's son, Male Rao, was born in 1745, when she was 20, and her daughter, Muktabai, was born in 1748. These were Khande Rao's only children, although he married about ten more women over the next two decades.

Khande Rao was a pleasure-loving prince who did not involve himself much in administration, though he did go to war sometimes. While British chroniclers tend to dismiss him as a wastrel, the numerous Indian hagiographies of Ahilya Bai talk about Ahilya Bai's devotion, emphasizing how her influence and her Scheherazade-like recounting of inspiring stories from the epics turned Khande Rao away from his bad habits and made him more warrior-like. This is clearly to burnish Ahilya Bai's image.

Malhar Rao was seldom in Indore. The whole Maratha state machinery was geared to launching campaigns for fresh territorial acquisition and tribute collection, and he ranged far and wide raiding and conquering territories for the Marathas, even travelling beyond the Indus, the traditional limit of India, right up to Attock and Peshawar.

Malhar Rao relied heavily on Ahilya Bai for local administration, along with his long-time diwan, Gangadhar Yashwant Chandrachur, who had been sent along by Baji Rao I when Malhar Rao was first allotted Indore. Ahilya Bai was a workaholic, and soon gained a reputation for being extremely competent and fair. Malhar Rao's deputy in war was Tukoji Holkar, a young man who was a couple of years older than Ahilya Bai. Though he was not related to him, Malhar Rao had brought Tukoji up almost like an adopted son. As mentioned earlier, Khande Rao was more involved in his own personal life.

In 1754, two noblemen in Delhi were fighting to control the weak Mughal emperor Ahmad Shah Bahadur. One of them, Imad-ul-Mulk, asked Malhar Rao for help to capture Kumner, which belonged to Surajmal Jat, the ruler of Bharatpur.

Surajmal was supporting Safdarjung, the other nobleman.

Khande Rao was present at the siege of Kumner along with Malhar Rao, and was unfortunately killed by a shot from the fort. All his wives rushed there to commit sati. For a non-Kshatriya family this was unusual, as sati was typically a practice followed by higher castes, particularly Kshatriyas. The Dhangars, when following their traditional occupation as cattle herders, did not practice it; in fact, widows sometimes remarried. But once elevated to royalty, they adopted many practices from Kshatriya royal houses as a part of their exercise in upward mobility; one such practice was sati. The wives of the Dhangars committed sati with the zeal of the converted, treating their sacrifice as a point of honour. Ahilya Bai was, however, held back by her father-in-law, who implored her to live for an old man and her small children, who could not survive without her. The other 10 queens of Khande Rao perished in the flames. As per some records, one was Muslim.

Malhar Rao was already 60 by then and did not expect to live for very long. His heir, Ahilya Bai's son Male Rao, was just nine, and he realized that Ahilya Bai was his only hope to preserve the dynasty. She would have to rule as regent until Male Rao came of age.

As evinced by the letters he wrote Ahilya Bai, Malhar Rao continued to train her in administration. He kept her informed about political developments, and about his own movements. In a letter dated 16 March 1765, Malhar Rao writes, 'A messenger told us that you captured Gohadkars' fort with a cannon: You should now stay at Gwalior and manufacture gun – balls. The ruler of Gohad must, this year, be crushed.' In a letter relating to officials who had defaulted in their duty, Malhar Rao asks her to make them return what they had misappropriated or attach the *parganah* (tax collection territory).

In 1761, the Marathas lost the Third Battle of Panipat fought against the Afghan invader Ahmad Shah Abdali, with a death toll in the lakhs. Malhar Rao left with his troops during the battle, and had to live with many accusations levelled at him by other Maratha leaders till the day he died. The Marathas were pushed back to the south of the Narmada. Malhar Rao's Malwa, however, was north of the Narmada, and the Rajputs, Jats, Sikhs and Bundelas soon converged at the outer rim of the kingdom. Malhar Rao had to battle them incessantly until he died fighting in Alampur on his northern border in May 1766. On his deathbed, he apparently extracted a promise from Mahadji Scindia of Gwalior, the most powerful Maratha sardar, to protect the Holkar family. Mahadji remained a loyal ally of the Holkars all his life.

After Malhar Rao's death, Ahilya Bai's son Male Rao was invested by the peshwa as the *subedar*, 'with full powers and undiminished territory on the condition of rendering faithful service to the Peshwa just as Malharji had done'.

Male Rao, however, had been mentally disturbed since childhood. British general Sir John Malcolm, who had been involved in the Maratha wars and had also been the governor of Bombay, wrote a detailed account of Ahilya Bai's life in his book *A Memoir of Central India*. He said that Male Rao was

> considered of weak and unsettled intellect... His conduct was at first more marked by extremes of folly. Brahmins... became objects of Mallee Row's malicious ridicule. It was a common usage with him to place scorpions in clothes and slippers that he gave them; he also put these venomous reptiles in pots filled with rupees, which he invited the holy mendicants to take... his joy was as excessive, as the grief of the pious Ahalya Baee, who used to lament aloud her hard destiny, in having a perfect demon born to her as a son.

Male Rao died within a year of his coming to power, at the age of 22. The rumoured cause of death was that the spirit of a man whom he had killed unjustly had occupied his body. Male Rao fell ill and died raving while his tearful mother tried all medical options as well as exorcisms in an effort to save him. His wives committed sati. Male Rao had no children.

Thus after Male Rao's death, the issue of inheritance arose. The diwan, Gangadhar Yashwant Chandrachur, recommended that Ahilya Bai should adopt a likely boy and make him the heir. Ahilya Bai did not want to choose an untried boy in a hurry and saw no reason why she could not herself become the official ruler. Gangadhar, who had been a faithful and competent retainer for the Holkars for more than thirty years, was horrified. He wrote to Raghoba, the uncle of the young peshwa, and the de facto regent, inviting him to take back Malwa directly under the rule of the peshwa. He promised Raghoba a substantial gift as well.

Raghoba, known for his avarice, was delighted, and moved towards Indore with 50,000 of the peshwa's troops. He camped near Ujjain on the banks of the Shipra River.

Ahilya Bai, well informed by her network of spies, decided to fight back on many fronts. She wrote to all the major Maratha sardars, reminding them of the favours they owed Malhar Rao – Scindia, Dabhade, Bhonsle, Pawar and Gaikwad. She wrote to Peshwa Madhav Rao, saying she was perfectly competent to decide who should rule after her son's death. She called back Tukoji Holkar from his expeditions and asked him to prepare troops for the confrontation. She sent the troublesome Gangadhar off on pilgrimage.

Then she played a master stroke. To paint Raghoba as an oppressor of widows, she got together about five hundred women and formed a small army contingent, giving them some elementary battle training. These women were not warriors – most of them had not even sat on a horse before – but were willing to fight for their country. She herself had her favourite elephant publicly readied for battle, with quivers of arrows placed on all four corners of the howdah, and announced her intention of fighting Raghoba with her contingent of women.

She then wrote a letter to Raghoba, saying that he could only gain infamy battling with women; to win would be a dishonour, and to lose a still greater one.

Raghoba realized that he had bitten off more than he could chew. Instead of the cowed woman he had expected, who would meekly surrender to the peshwa's troops, he now had the Holkar troops and, horror of horrors, armed women, facing him across the Shipra. The other Maratha sardars were emphatically in support of Ahilya Bai, who had an image of unimpeachable virtue. In addition, his nephew, the young peshwa, sent him a letter asking him to leave Indore alone.

Raghoba, in an attempt to save face, sent a message to Tukoji that that he had only come to Indore to offer his condolences on the death of Male Rao. Tukoji then graciously invited him to Indore (sans his troops, of course). Raghoba was royally entertained for a month before he finally left for Pune. He was accompanied by Tukoji, who went for formal confirmation in the post of commander-in-chief of the Holkar army by the peshwa, as requested by Ahilya Bai.

Ahilya Bai was now the titular ruler of Indore. She divided the responsibilities of running the kingdom amicably with Tukoji over the next 30 years. Tukoji was seldom in the kingdom, roaming north and south in pursuit of Maratha aims. Ahilya Bai looked after the administration of the state. Surprisingly, Tukoji deferred to Ahilya Bai almost as a mother, although he was two years older than her.

Ahilya Bai's rule of 30 years was extraordinary and is considered one of the best reigns in the country, by man or woman. Her philosophy of governance was very modern. She believed in providing physical and institutional infrastructure, well-implemented, moderate taxation, enforcing diligently the rule of the law, rigorously defending individual rights to property, and attempting to solve all issues amicably, with force as a last resort.

John Malcolm writes about her, 40 years after her death:

> Her first principle of Government appears to have been moderate assessment and an almost sacred respect for the native rights of the village officers and proprietary land. She heard every complaint in person and although she continually referred cases to the courts of equity and arbitration... she was always accessible, patient and unwearied in the investigation of most insignificant cases when appeals were made to her for decision.

She saw herself as a trustee of the people and wanted prosperity for all. She was also a great believer in individual rights, to property and otherwise, and was not of the school which believed in sacrificing other people's rights to the 'greater good'. Indeed, in many cases where the state appropriated the properties of men who had died without sons, she had these properties returned to their widows. She made inheritance of properties by widows the norm, which was practically unheard of at the time. She also believed the state had no right to private property – when some women wanted to bequeath their property to the state to be used for public good, she refused to take it, advising them to carry out charitable works themselves.

Indore grew to be a great mercantile centre because of her well-implemented rule of law. Traditionally, there have always been jokes about the frugality, indeed the miserliness, of merchants across the world. They have typically lived well below the level their wealth would permit them. There was a logical reason for this. In most feudal communities, merchants had money, while power was in the hands of the ruler and noblemen. If a merchant had visible wealth, the ruling class would simply take it away from him through taxation, loans or extortion. Therefore, merchants would traditionally not invest much in land; most of their wealth would be in movable gold and gemstones, which were easy to flee with in case life became difficult. The safe haven Ahilya Bai created where earning money and living well did not automatically make one prey to extortion was a rarity in those days, and merchants poured into her kingdom from all around the country, setting up flourishing businesses, making Indore a major trading and financial centre.

Her good management increased the revenue of Indore from 73 lakh rupees when she took over to more than 1 crore rupees, even at a time of incessant warfare in India, when most states were losing income.

The other extremely unusual aspect of Ahilya Bai's rule was her pan-India perspective. Her efforts and spending were not restricted to her kingdom of Indore; she gave grants to build and restore buildings at hundreds of religious locations across India. Over the past few centuries of Muslim rule, many major Hindu pilgrimage sites had fallen into disrepair. Many of the major temples had been destroyed, particularly during the rule of Aurangzeb. Ahilya Bai took the crores of personal wealth accumulated by Malhar Rao, and formally dedicated it with a *sankalp*, or religious ritual, to the welfare of people across the country. She funded renovations, temples, ghats, dharmashalas and education centres at all the major Hindu pilgrimage sites, Shaivite and Vaishnavite, including the 12 *jyotirlingas*, the four *dhams*, the five *kedars* and the seven *puris*. She built a new Kashi Vishwanath temple in Varanasi, right next to the mosque which had been built by Aurangzeb on the remains of the original temple. She also had water from the Ganga regularly delivered to more than thirty temples in the south for their rituals. She would write letters to rulers across the country – the raja of Odisha, the nawab of Hyderabad, the nawab of Awadh – asking for permission to build in their kingdoms, which was gladly granted, as her reputation as a saint preceded her. Admittedly, there were some questions raised about whether it was wise on her part to 'waste' the funds of Indore and spend so extravagantly in building in other rulers' domains. However, the reputation as a saint that this garnered her prevented her kingdom being attacked by any other ruler, and saved her a fortune which would have otherwise been spent on armies and warfare.

Ahilya Bai was quite reluctant to administer the death penalty and would exclaim, when urged by her ministers to acts of extreme severity, 'Let us, mortals, beware how we destroy the works of the Almighty.' However, she did have a temper. It was said that when really in anger, her countenance struck terror into the boldest of people.

She seems to have had no major or minor vices, not even that of susceptibility to praise; when a Brahmin wrote a book on her great deeds, she had it thrown in the Narmada as an exercise in modesty. Naturally, biographers such as Malcolm were a little suspicious about the praise heaped on the queen, and her apparent infallibility. Yet, even he had to admit:

> but, although enquiries have been made among all ranks and classes, nothing has been discovered to diminish the eulogiums, or rather blessings, which are poured forth whenever her name is mentioned. The more, indeed, enquiry is pursued, the more admiration is excited: but it appears above all extraordinary, how she had mental and bodily powers to go through with the labours she imposed upon herself.

The spirit of charity pervaded Ahilya Bai's life. Malcolm says:

> The beasts of the field, the birds of the air, and the fish of the river shared in her compassion; portions of food were allotted to them, and the peasant near Mhysir used in hot days to see his yoke of oxen stopped during their labour to be refreshed with water brought by a servant of Ahalya Baee; while fields she had purchased were covered with flocks of birds.

Early in her reign, Ahilya Bai shifted her capital from the established luxury of Indore to Maheshwar, on the banks of the Narmada, where she lived as a *rajyogi*, leading the frugal and disciplined life of a yogi despite being a royal. She rose at the Brahmamuhurt, one hour before dawn, said her prayers and distributed food to Brahmins. She sat in her court from two to six in the afternoon, and then again from nine to eleven in the evening. She ate a frugal vegetarian diet, having given up meat.

Ahilya Bai had superb relationships with her neighbours, though she was very suspicious of the British. In a prescient letter written to the peshwa in 1772, she warns:

> Other beasts, like tigers, can be killed by might or contrivance, but to kill a bear it is very difficult. It will die only if you kill it straight in the face. Or else, once caught in its powerful hold, the bear will kill its prey by tickling. Such is the way of the English. And in view of this, it is difficult to triumph over them...
>
> It behoves the Peshwa to enlist good number of Silehdars and increase the standing army and Nawab, Bhonsle and the rest should make a common cause and crush the English.

However, her advice was little heeded.

Ahilya Bai often solved problems in novel ways. For instance, the areas surrounding Indore were beset with dacoits who made travel unsafe. In a quixotic gesture straight out of a folk tale, Ahilya Bai declared that she would give in marriage the hand of her daughter, the princess Muktabai, to the brave young man who would rid her kingdom of the menace of dacoits. As in all folk tales, a poor but brave young man, Yashwantrao Phanse, took up the challenge, and with troops and funds offered by her, made the kingdom safe. With her characteristic magnanimity, Ahilya Bai made the dacoits guardians of the highway, instead of executing them, and gave them the right to collect a highway toll!

She duly married off her daughter to Yashwantrao Phanse. They soon had a son – Nathyba.

By the time she was 65, things were going well for Ahilya Bai. Her kingdom was prosperous. She enjoyed an unparalleled reputation all over the country and her subjects loved her. She had a capable daughter and son-in-law, and a grandson grown to maturity who already had two wives.

However, in 1789, her grandson Nathyba, her only blood heir, died of disease, and his two wives committed sati. Barely a year later, her son-in-law died of cholera. To her horror, her daughter, Muktabai, wanted to commit sati.

According to Malcolm, Ahilya Bai

> humbled herself to the dust before her, and entreated her, as she revered her God, not to leave her desolate and alone upon earth. Muchta Baee, although affectionate, was calm and resolved. You are old, mother, (she said) and a few years will end your pious life. My only child and husband are gone, and when you follow, life, I feel, will be insupportable; but the opportunity of terminating it with honour will then have passed.

Ahilya Bai somehow managed to hold herself 'till the first blaze of the flame made her lose all self-command'. In a rare public loss of control, she screamed with agony and gnawed at the hands of her retainers restraining her. After the immolation was over, she locked herself away for three days. She then stoically retained to her tasks.

Ahilya Bai died five years later in 1795. Tukoji ruled after her for two years and thereafter, the kingdom passed on to his sons, from whom the current rulers are descended.

Jawaharlal Nehru said of her in his *The Discovery of India*:

> The reign of Ahilya has become almost legendary as a period during which perfect order and good government prevailed... She was... highly respected during her lifetime, and considered as a saint by a grateful people after her death.

The Bloodiest Battle in Indian History

By the 1750s, the Marathas were regularly confronting the forces of Ahmad Shah Abdali, the king of Afghanistan, who came to India for annual raids. The Marathas planned a major face-off, and in 1760 moved north to occupy Delhi with a splendid army of about 1,00,000 combatants under the leadership of Sadashiv Rao Bhau, the peshwa Madhav Rao's brother. However, in a classic case of overconfidence, they also had 2,00,000 non-combatants with them – women, children – who thought this was a good opportunity to go on a pilgrimage to northern sites like Kurukshetra. This, needless to say, ended up having disastrous results for the Marathas.

A series of bad decisions, mostly attributed to the arrogance of the young Sadashiv Rao, and his refusal to listen to sager and more experienced campaigners like Malhar Rao Holkar and Mahadji Scindia, led to the Maratha army being surrounded by Abdali in Panipat. They were unable to slip away in the classic agile Maratha style because of the non-combatants accompanying them. Rations soon ran short, and the Marathas starved for over two months, before finally attacking on Makar Sankranti, 14 January 1761.

It is impossible to overestimate the carnage. More than 50,000 men – an entire generation of Maratha fighting men – supposedly died at war, while 40,000 Maratha prisoners were killed in cold blood the day after they lost the battle. Many of the non-combatants were slaughtered and several women enslaved and carried away to Afghanistan. The total number of Maratha dead is estimated to be 1–2 lakh.

A coded message sent to the peshwa after the debacle said that two pearls, 27 gold mohurs, and innumerable silver and copper coins were lost – conveying the deaths of two members of the peshwa's family (Vishwas Rao, the heir, and Sadashiv Rao, the supreme commander), 27 from the main Maratha sardar families, and many, many soldiers.

The Queen Who Bested the British

Velu Nachiyar

Everything was taken from her
save her self-respect
She spent every waking moment strategizing best
ways to sever the beast
defeat the British East
to avenge deceased

From a hip-hop song 'Our Queen'
in the album *Tamilmatic* by Professor A.L.I.

Veeramangai (brave woman) Velu Nachiyar (r. 1780–90 CE), queen of Sivaganga in Tamil Nadu, is a much-feted Tamil heroine. She has been hailed as the first woman freedom fighter against the British in the 1770s, predating the Kannadiga Chennamma of Kittur in the 1820s and the much-celebrated Rani of Jhansi. Velu Nachiyar is a symbol of Tamil pride, with postage stamps, commemorative buildings, annual parades, dance dramas and even a big-budget movie being planned around her.

The 18th century in south India was a time of great turmoil, with continuously shifting alliances; there were many players engaged in the game of war and peace with each other. There were the newly independent Mughal governors, the Nizam of Hyderabad and the nawab of Arcot in the Carnatic region; the Marathas; a resurgent Mysore under Haider Ali and Tipu Sultan; and the European powers, most significantly the British and the French alongside the Dutch, Danes and Portuguese, jostling for pre-eminence. Along with these forces were the many Naiks and Poligars (zamindars), hereditary feudatories of the Vijayanagara Empire until its decimation in 1565, who had not yet learnt to bend the knee to the Mughals or the British. Matters were further complicated by incessant wars within these factions as well as internal wars of succession.

The story of Velu Nachiyar is quite hard to reconstruct. There are very brief British accounts, legends recounted by her family and by the priests in temples she built, and *kummis* (folk songs) sung in villages. A host of tall tales has also grown around her persona, and it is quite difficult to separate the wheat from the chaff. However, from all this chaos emerges the picture of an exceptional woman.

Velu Nachiyar was born in 1730, in the Ramnad royal family, to Raja Chellamuthu Sethupathy and Rani Sakandhimuthal. The family held the royal title of Sethupathy because as feudatories of Vijayanagara in the 16th century, traditionally, they were the protectors of the Hindu pilgrimage site of Rameswaram – from where Rama is said to have launched his attack on Ravana's Lanka and whence began the *sethu*, or bridge, to Sri Lanka purportedly built by Rama. In 1725, shortly before Velu Nachiyar's birth, the kingdom of Ramnad had been divided into two parts. The smaller part was given to Sasivarma Thevar, a former feudatory and son-in-law, who now became the ruler of a new kingdom called Sivaganga. He had helped the king of Ramnad recover his kingdom from a contender; this was his reward. When Sasivarma had defeated the false contender, he had been blessed by a saint near a sacred spring; he set up his new capital city there and called it Sivaganga. The kingdom was small – about 4,500 square kilometres – and paid a tribute of 1.75 lakh rupees annually to Ramnad.

By all accounts, Velu was given an exceptional education. She spoke ten languages, including English, French, Urdu and Persian. She was taught many martial arts including sword fighting and archery; she was an expert at Tamil techniques like the *Silambam*, or fighting with bamboo sticks, and the *valari*, a boomerang-like weapon. Her community, the Thevars, a warrior clan, was also known for their unarmed combat techniques like *adi murai* and *varma kalai*. There are the usual folk tales of her riding untameable horses and winning *Silambam* contests against everyone else. In a rare tale of the princess saving the prince, she goes roaming in the beautiful forests of Courtallam as a bride, where a tiger attacks her husband. Velu, as the story goes, catches hold of its tail, jumps on its back and strangles it with her bare hands!

Velu was married to Muthu Vaduganatha Periyavudaya Thevar, the prince of Sivaganga, in 1746, at the age of 16. She had only one child, born after nearly two decades of marriage.

Muthu Vaduganatha Thevar became king in 1750, coming to power at a time when the Deccan was in turmoil. As Sivaganga was a small border kingdom, its overlords continuously changed. It was a tributary to the nawab of Arcot in 1725, the Marathas in 1741, the Nizam in 1744, and then again the nawab of Arcot. The first Anglo-Mysore war had concluded in 1769, and the British were now free to subdue the fractious feudatories of their dependent, the nawab of Arcot. The nawab of Arcot had written to the Madras Council the previous year, alleging that the Sivaganga king had ascended the throne without his approval and had evaded paying tribute to the tune of 1 lakh rupees. A British invasion of the kingdom took place on 25 June 1772 under Colonel Joseph Smith and Major Abraham Bonjour. The king, Muthu, was caught unawares at the temple of Kalayar Kovil and killed, along with another wife, Gowri Nachiyar. Sivaganga was thereafter occupied by the nawab of Arcot. He made his son the king and renamed it Hussainnagar. Velu, who was in another town, Kollangudi, swore revenge. Popular representations compare her to the Sangam heroine Kannagi, who revenged herself on the Pandya kingdom for the death of her husband.

She decided to take shelter along with her daughter in the neighbouring kingdom of Mysore, so that she could regroup her forces. According to legend, as she fled through the forest, she was closely followed by the British. They questioned Udaiyal, a girl grazing her cattle, and when she refused to divulge the queen's whereabouts they tortured and killed her.

Meanwhile, Velu reached Virupakshi Palayar, a border fort in Mysore, where the hereditary poligar Gopal Naicker immediately gave her shelter, as a fellow Nayak. She was accompanied by her chief minister, Thandavarayan Pillai, an old retainer since the time of her father-in-law, and her advisors, the Maruthu brothers, who would go on to become the ultimate symbol of resistance to the British.

Periya (elder) and Chinna (younger) Maruthu were the sons of a general in the Ramnad state military. As children, the brothers worked in the palace as aides to the king – apparently as betel bearer and dog keeper, respectively. They soon grew to be feared and important warriors. Popular representations of the brothers show them as the archetypal Indian heroes – tall and muscular, brandishing swords, with turbans and fierce moustaches and eyes filled with rage. Periya Maruthu was considered a great hunter and expert with the *valari*, while Chinna was the administrator.

Thandavarayan Pillai, Velu's chief minister, wrote to Haider Ali asking for 5,000 soldiers to win back the kingdom. When Haider Ali visited the nearby fortress of Dindigul, Velu went to meet him. It is said that when Haider Ali entered the meeting hall, he saw only men; when he asked for Velu, she revealed herself by pulling off her turban. Velu then spoke to him in excellent Urdu. Impressed, he made her an allowance of 400 gold coins, and asked her to live on in Dindigul. He promised military aid to reconquer Sivaganga when the time was right; he had signed a peace treaty with the British at the end of the first Anglo-Mysore war in 1769, just a few years ago, and was biding his time.

The elderly Thandavarayan Pillai died soon after. Velu, now living in Dindigul, became more directly involved with political affairs. The Maruthu brothers soon became her most important advisors. They worked at creating spy networks in Sivaganga and setting up support among the people for the day they returned. Velu, unusually, started training and creating an army of women, which she called 'Udaiyal padai' in memory of the brave girl who had given up her life. Her *dalavai*, or commander, was Kuyili, a Dalit.

The relationship between Haider Ali and the British was worsening and Haider now allied himself with the French, who declared war against the British in 1778, pursuant to the American War of Independence. The British quickly captured the remaining French outposts in India; their capture of Mahe in 1779 particularly inconvenienced Haider Ali, as he used to import French arms through this port on the Malabar Coast. Haider managed to convince the Marathas and the Nizam to join him, and he invaded the Carnatic in July 1780, crossing over the Eastern Ghats and descending on the nawab of Arcot's territories on the east coast with 80,000 soldiers, engaging the British on many fronts.

After eight years of exile, this was Velu's opportunity. With a small force they got from Syed Sahib, the governor of Dindigul, and her women's troops, Velu and the Maruthu brothers started their march to Sivaganga. In Sivaganga, the locals joined her; many had been preparing themselves for this day.

They were intercepted by both the nawab's troops and British troops at various points such as Madurai, but eventually overcame them. They reached the outskirts of Sivaganga on the night before the festival of Vijayadashami.

Sivaganga, however, was well-fortified so Velu had to come up with a plan. On Vijayadashami, the local women would gather for a special puja at the temple of Rajarajeshwari, next to the palace. Velu and her women warriors mingled with the throngs going to the temple. As soon as they got into the palace complex, they tried to capture it. Popular depictions of this scene always show the women pulling out their hidden swords, and attacking the soldiers shouting '*Vetrivel, Veeravel*', the ancient Tamil battle cry. Vel is the divine spear used by the god Murugan – the war cry translates to 'Victorious Vel, Courageous Vel.' But their weapons were no match for the British guns. Velu quickly realized that the room that stored British ammunition had to be destroyed. Kuyili, her commander, fought her way to the room. As she neared the entrance, she doused herself with oil from the burning lamps, set herself on fire and hurled herself into the room, blowing up all the ammunition. Kuyili is now considered the first 'human bomb'. She is also lauded as a Dalit icon. The women took control after that, rang the temple bells to signal their forces outside, and Sivaganga was conquered. The Hanuman flag of the dynasty flew again on the fort – particularly significant to the kingdom, as the monkey god had crossed over to Lanka from Rameswaram.

After Velu finally regained her kingdom, one of the first things she did was build a temple enshrining Udaiyal, the shepherd girl who had given up her life for her, representing her as Kali; she then donated her *thaali* (mangalsutra) as the first offering in the temple. Even today, one can visit the temple in Ariyakuruchi village, 13 kilometres from Sivaganga, where they tell this tale. The goddess is particularly popular with pilgrims suffering injustice at the hands of the government, and those seeking revenge. Supplicants pray to Udaiyal Kali for redress and cut a coin in two with a chisel and mallet, perhaps symbolizing an attack on the king whose head was normally depicted on the coin.

Elsewhere, Haider Ali was quite successful in his campaigns against the British, besieging and conquering Arcot itself. After his death in 1782, his son Tipu Sultan carried on the war. The Treaty of Mangalore brought an end to the Second Anglo-Mysore war in 1784, restoring the status quo ante bellum. This was the last time the British made a treaty with an Indian ruler on equal terms.

Since the British were more amenable after their lack of success, Velu managed to come to an arrangement with the nawab of Arcot, who was then completely engaged with the Mysore forces. She was allowed to retain Sivaganga on payment of an annual tribute to him.

She now ruled, essentially on behalf of her minor daughter Vellachi. She made Periya Maruthu the commander of the army, and Chinna Maruthu the chief minister. But this was not the end of her travails. Neighbours like Ramnad (her relatives!) and Pudukkottai attacked. The nawab would also periodically send troops to exact dues from the reluctant Maruthus.

Soon, Velu became involved in a power struggle with the Maruthus. The king of Ramnad was keen to marry Vellachi and unite the two kingdoms. When Vellachi refused, he started hostilities, raiding the borders of Sivaganga. Velu wanted to marry Vellachi to Pommathur Gowri Vallabha Deva, a relative of her husband, who also had a reasonably good claim to be the king of Sivaganga. The Maruthu brothers, however, favoured another of her relatives, Vengam Peria Udaya Thevar. They imprisoned Gowri in the Kalayar Kovil temple, but he managed to escape with the help of the temple dancer Karuppayee and took shelter with the poligar of Pudukkottai. Vellachi, meanwhile, was married off to Udaya Thevar.

Things finally came to a head in 1789. Velu even asked the nawab of Arcot and the British to intervene in her favour; they sent troops under Colonel Stuart to cow the Maruthus, along with troops from Pudukkottai, Madura, Tanjore and Tiruchirappalli. The Maruthus lost some battles, particularly after their French general Du Pre joined the British, and finally fled to Tipu. They returned with troops to conquer the fort of Tirupatthur. The British realized that they could possibly lose Sivaganga to Tipu and bowed to realpolitik. They made an agreement with Udaya Thevar, Vellachi's husband. Vellachi now became the official ruler in 1790; Velu was abandoned and put out to pasture. The Maruthus returned to rule.

Family annals say that Velu became unwell, apparently with a heart problem; she was now 60. She handed over the kingdom to Vellachi and went off to France for medical treatment in 1791. This was France in the throes of the revolution; one wonders what her experience might have been. She is supposed to have returned in 1793. Her daughter Vellachi had died, along with her infant daughter, and Vellachi's husband

Udaya Thevar was now crowned king. The Maruthu brothers were well in control; they had even married off a daughter to the king. Velu retired to the fort of Virupakshi Palayar once again, and finally died there in 1796. According to East India Company documents, the queen died under somewhat suspicious circumstances.

In 1799, after the death of Tipu Sultan in the battle of Seringapatam, and the conquest of Mysore by the British, there was a revolt by the Poligars of the south against British exactions. They lost. Ramnad was downgraded from a kingdom to a zamindari and given over to the ruler's sister Mangaleswari to rule. The Company decided very craftily in favour of her 'as she was an aged woman and not likely to have children'.

After the Poligar wars, Udaya Thevar, the king of Sivaganga, was banished in 1802 for aiding the Maruthu brothers. Gowri, Vellachi's erstwhile suitor who had escaped the Maruthus with a devadasi, had already been proclaimed the zamindar of Sivaganga by the British in 1801 prior to the capture of the Maruthus, to divide the loyalty of Sivaganga residents. His descendants ruled until India's independence, when zamindari was abolished.

Velu lives on in folk memory. Her legacy, and those of the other brave women like Kuyili who fought with her, is only now being celebrated. On 18 July 2014, the then chief minister of Tamil Nadu J. Jayalalithaa inaugurated the Veeramangai Velu Nachiyar Memorial in Sivaganga and also declared that 3 January would be celebrated every year as her birth anniversary.

Poligar Wars

Velu's rebellion was the precursor to the Poligar wars. The Palayakkars or Poligars were the feudal noblemen in the region.

The Poligar wars (1799–1801) can be considered the first true people's rebellion against British rule; it is, however, unwept, unhonoured and unsung on the greater Indian stage.

In 1792, the nawab of Arcot transferred the revenue he received from the Poligars to the Company, which then became their overlords. In 1799, after the death of Tipu Sultan in the battle of Seringapatam, and the conquest of Mysore by the British, there was a revolt of the Poligars of the south against British exactions; they fought the British in an early edition of the great uprising of 1857. The Maruthu brothers were at the heart of it, along with Veerapandiya Kattabomman, and Gopal Naicker of Virupakshi. The Maruthus, who called themselves 'the implacable enemy of the European low wretches', issued a famous proclamation in 1801, which called upon all the people of India to band together and extirpate the foreigners.

> ...in the Island of Jamboo in the Peninsula of Jamboo Dweepa this notice is given... The Europeans violating their faith have deceitfully made the kingdom their own and considering the inhabitants as dogs, accordingly exercise authority over them... In these countries now governed by these low wretches, the Inhabitants have become poor...

There existing no unity and friendship amongst you the above castes… therefore you Brahmins, Kshetriyas, Vysyas, Sudras and Musselmen, all who wear whiskers, whether civil or military, serving in the field or elsewhere, and you subedars, jamedars, havildars, nayaks and sepoys in the service of the low wretches and all capable of bearing arms, let them in the first place display their bravery as follows.

Wherever you find any of the low wretches destroy them and continue to do so until they are extirpated…

The Poligar wars had some unique features. Different communities like the Maravars, Nadars, Totiens, Kallars, Parawas, Gounders and Muslims flocked to voluntarily join the rebellion. The *killah*, a leaf pierced with a nail, was used as summons to bring out the village to fight. The Poligars trained Rajapalayam dogs, also called the Poligar hound, to attack their enemies in the battlefield, particularly to bite the knees of the horses of the cavalry. The Maruthu brothers employed trained Combai dogs to protect the fort at Kalayar Kovil.

Ultimately, however, British military strength prevailed. The Poligars were suppressed brutally, the leaders of the rebellion captured. Gopal Naicker was betrayed for a reward of 20,000 rupees and the Maruthu brothers were publicly hanged in 1801 along with their sons and grandsons. A raging Chinna Maruthu was apparently carried in a cage to the hanging.

The populace was slaughtered; rebels were hanged from trees, mutilated bodies paraded through the streets, and heads set on pikes through the highways. These horrors have been captured in the ballads and folk songs composed during that period, and still haunt folk memory. The Maruthu brothers, who fought to the finish, have become great folk heroes, with temples still dedicated to their worship.

The Dealmaker

Begum Samru

> By means of her uncommon ability and discretion, united to a masculine firmness and intrepidity... she managed to preserve her country nearly unmolested, and her authority generally unimpaired, during a period of surrounding storm and tempest, which shook several great powers from their thrones...
>
> James Skinner, *Military Memoirs of Lieut.-Col. James Skinner*

A four-and-a-half-foot girl, picked up from a Chawri Bazar brothel by a European adventurer, went on to rule the prosperous kingdom of Sardhana for 55 years, at a time when the largest of empires were crumbling and no man was safe. With her diplomatic abilities and her commanding presence, Begum Joanna Nobilis Samru (r. 1776–1836 CE) is an unlikely feminist icon of that age.

It was the end of the 18th century, otherwise known as *gardi ka waqt*, or a time of trouble. The Mughal Empire, which had been at its greatest geographical spread at the time of Emperor Aurangzeb's death in 1707, was now in a shambles, weakened by years of internecine warfare and plunder by external raiders like Nadir Shah and Ahmad Shah Abdali. It is said that by the end of the 18th century, the Mughal ruler Shah Alam II's rule only extended from Delhi to Palam in the suburbs of Delhi, leading to the saying: *Badshahat e Shah Alam, az Dilli ta Palam*. He barely had 5,000 troops: a sad comedown from the lakhs commanded by his ancestors.

With no strong central power, *Matsya Nyaya* (the law of the jungle) prevailed, with everyone scrambling for a piece of the pie. Erstwhile Mughal governors had declared themselves rulers of their own provinces; native groups like the Rajputs, Marathas and Sikhs, long suppressed, were trying to create their own empires; and the British, French and other European powers began to morph from traders to the far more profitable role of rulers, inspired by the singular success of Robert Clive in Bengal. The British had gained control of Bengal after the Battle of Plassey in 1757 and forced the Mughal emperor Shah Alam to grant them the *diwani* of Bengal, the right to collect taxes, when they captured him after the Battle of Buxar in 1764.

Indeed, anyone with a brave heart and a few soldiers at his disposal began to dream of carving out his own kingdom. Unsurprisingly, therefore, it was also the heyday for European mercenaries, who led troops of a few thousand men trained in European technology and organization, and offered their services to the highest bidder. Many of these mercenaries were French, like the legendary Benoît de Boigne, who made his fortune in India with the Marathas.

Into this thick soup of intrigue entered Walter Reinhardt Sombre in 1750, an Austrian mercenary who had been part of the French army in India. In his account of Sombre, James

Skinner, a military adventurer in the East India Company, who later came to be known as Sikandar Sahib, says that Sombre had originally been a carpenter. In 1760, Sombre offered his services to Mir Qasim, the nawab of Bengal – then chafing under British dominance – to aid him in his efforts to reoccupy Patna. Sombre's troops carried out the massacre of about 150 Englishmen, which earned him the soubriquet 'The Butcher of Patna'. Soon afterwards, Sombre fled from British retribution to Oudh (in western Uttar Pradesh), where he continued his career as a mercenary.

In 1765, at the age of 45, Sombre dropped into Khanum Jan's *kotha* (brothel) in Chawri Bazar in Delhi for an evening of entertainment. There he encountered the charming 15-year-old Kashmiri dancer, Farzana. Her origins are uncertain; she is variously considered to be the offspring of a Mughal nobleman, or even a child picked up by the *kotha*'s owner from the street. Enchanted by Farzana, Sombre soon moved her to his zenana, or harem. He already had children from a previous concubine, Barri Bibi, but this was not unusual. Many Europeans at the time maintained large harems. Sir David Ochterlony, the British resident in Delhi in the early 19th century, for instance, had 13 *bibis*, or concubines, whom he would promenade every evening down the main thoroughfare of Chandni Chowk, seated on elephants! The quick-witted and astute Farzana became Sombre's companion and comrade in arms as he offered his military services to various nobles, including the Jat rulers of Deeg, who were then occupying Agra. Surajmal Jat had grown very powerful in the aftermath of the Third Battle of Panipat in 1761. In 1773 the Mughal forces under Najaf Khan, a vizier in the court of Shah Alam II, fought the Jats and expelled them from Agra. Even though the Jats had lost this battle, Najaf Khan was so impressed by the fighting prowess of Sombre's troops that he invited him to join the Mughals.

In those fickle times, Sombre had already changed 14 masters. He and his troops gladly joined the Mughals. Over the next three years, while living in Delhi, Sombre and Farzana, now called Begum Samru (from Sombre), entrenched themselves in the affairs of the Mughal court, becoming favourites of both Shah Alam II and Najaf Khan. This was often attributed to the begum's ability to make friends and influence people.

The couple became so influential that not only did they manage to escape being handed over to the vengeful British, but were also granted the rights to the rich *jagir* (territory) of Sardhana, which yielded around 6 lakh rupees in revenue per annum (equivalent to about 30 crore rupees today) in 1776, with a royal *sanad*, or deed, from Shah Alam II. And so, these penniless adventurers became rulers. Sombre was also made the civil and military governor of Agra.

However, Sombre did not live long to enjoy his good fortune; he died just two years later, in 1778. Skinner is not very flattering in his assessment of Sombre.

> Sumroo appears to have been a man whose evil propensities far outweighed the good; he was stern and bloody-minded, in no degree remarkable for fidelity or devotion to his

> employers... hard, unscrupulous, and reckless, though bold, military adventurer. He is said to have despised show, dressing in the plain Moghul garb, and never disowning his low origin: one of his most marked traits is a cautious prudence, which at length amounted to a suspicious jealousy that rendered his life entirely a burthen.

As per norm, his son from Barri Bibi, Zafaryab Khan, though considered feeble-minded, was next in line to inherit the *jagir*. But Begum Samru was not about to give up her rule without a fight. She managed to get Sombre's troops to support her and used her influence with Najaf Khan, her patron, to get Sardhana allotted to her. Zafaryab continued to live in luxury in Delhi, leading a life immersed in poetry and the arts, funded by Begum Samru.

The begum began her career as the supreme commander of about 4,000 troops which she had inherited from Sombre, which included 100-odd European officers and soldiers. She held court in Sardhana, wearing a masculine turban and smoking a hookah. Inexplicably, she converted to Catholicism in 1781 and took the name of Joanna, though she maintained Mughal dress and etiquette. Occasionally, however, she would shed purdah and dine with her European officers.

She would lead her troops in battle, even coming to the rescue of the hapless Mughal emperor Shah Alam many a time. He started calling her his 'beloved daughter' and gave her the title *zebunnisa*, or ornament among women. She was a skilled diplomat and negotiated many deals for the emperor. One instance of this was in 1783, when the Sikh military general,

Baghel Singh, occupied Delhi, and camped with 30,000 Sikh soldiers in an area which henceforth came to be called 'Tis Hazari' (or 30,000 in Hindi). A petrified Shah Alam II, who thought he would lose his throne, asked Begum Samru to negotiate. She managed to get rid of them relatively cheaply, in exchange for the right to build eight gurdwaras in Delhi and a percentage of the revenue collected for just that year.

In another instance, the Rohilla chieftain Ghulam Qadir occupied Delhi in 1788. The Rohillas were a powerful Afghan clan and they controlled a substantial region in Uttar Pradesh, later called Rohillakhand. The story goes that Ghulam Qadir had been captured and abused by the Mughals as a child. Widely considered a psychopath, Ghulam Qadir tortured the Mughal royal family to get them to reveal the whereabouts of their treasures and, in a fit of rage, blinded his erstwhile tormentor, the emperor Shah Alam II, by personally gouging out his eyes. The begum meanwhile came to the emperor's rescue, 'rejecting contemptuously that powerful miscreant's [Ghulam Qadir's] offer of marriage and equality of power', in the words of Skinner. Faced with her artillery and troops, Ghulam Qadir fled Delhi. He was later captured by Mahadji Scindia at the behest of the emperor and tortured to death. It is said that his eyeballs were sent in a box to the now blind Shah Alam II to feel with his fingers.

Though the begum was known for her judgement and forethought, there is an instance where she let her heart rule her head, and paid a high price for her actions. This tale of high drama and romance begins with George Thomas, an Irish dockworker turned Indian mercenary, who joined her troops in 1787 after her husband's death. A bold fighter, he was the head of her troops and, by many accounts, her lover. He was known as 'Jahazi Sahib', a corruption of the name 'George'.

Their partnership flourished and the begum and Thomas won many a battle together, but things changed. A dashing and sophisticated French adventurer, Armand Le Vassoult, joined the begum's troops in 1790 and the 40-year-old begum fell madly in love with him. She secretly married the Frenchman, and a furiously jealous George Thomas left with some soldiers loyal to him and joined a Maratha adventurer. Le Vassoult was very high-handed and wanted to maintain a court in the grand 'roi soleil' style. He managed to alienate the begum's previously loyal troops, who now, under a discontented Belgian, called upon her stepson Zafaryab Khan to lead a revolt against her.

The lovers fled, chased by the begum's soldiers. They had made a suicide pact and just as they were about to be captured, the Begum, in her palanquin, stabbed herself. Seeing her blood-soaked clothes, in a scene reminiscent of *Romeo and Juliet*, Le Vassoult shot himself, though he could possibly have escaped on his horse. The begum, however, did not die, and her soldiers dragged her and tied her to a cannon. George Thomas, the begum's former lover, had meanwhile heard about the revolt, and came to her rescue post-haste. He restored her to power. Begum Samru, thereafter, placed her stepson under house arrest in Delhi, where he continued with his poetic endeavours and died ten years later in 1803. She rewarded George Thomas by marrying him off to a lady-in-waiting and he left again on his adventures. Between 1798 and 1801 Thomas briefly ruled the small kingdom of Hansi, in modern Haryana, and was that rarest of things in India, a white 'raja'. He built the Jahaz Kothi in Hisar, which is still standing. The grateful begum looked after his wife and children after he died.

The British were becoming more powerful under their new viceroy, Lord Wellesley, and his brother Arthur, who later became the celebrated Duke of Wellington. The duo had conquered Mysore in 1799, killing Tipu Sultan, and were now taking on the Marathas. The decisive Battle of Assaye was fought between the British and the Marathas in 1803. The begum, as part of her Mughal allegiance, had to send five battalions to the Maratha side. In this hard-fought battle, which Wellington rated as his finest victory (he rated it even higher than the famed Battle of Waterloo, where he defeated Napoleon!), the begum's troops, under her covert instructions, managed to preserve themselves and return safe and sound. As Skinner put it, 'They were charged by our cavalry towards the close of the day, but without effect... The people in the Dekhan, who knew the Begum by reputation, believed her to be a witch, who destroyed her enemies by throwing her *chadir* at them; the word *chadir* meaning "chain-shot" as well as a woman's veil.'

Meanwhile, the Marathas had lost the battle for Delhi at Patparganj to the British troops led by Lord Lake, and the latter entered Delhi.

The British now wanted to take away the begum's *jagir*, given her husband Sombre's massacre of Englishmen in Patna and her participation in battle against them at the Battle of Assaye, but the begum had survived many sticky situations before this. She helped negotiate the release of a British official held hostage by the Sikhs, and charmed Lord Lake with her wit and diplomacy. She went to meet him at his encampment, and as she emerged from her palanquin, according to Skinner,

> his lordship came out to meet and receive her. As the adhesion of every petty chieftain was, in those days, of consequence, Lord Lake was not a little pleased at the early demonstration of the Begum's loyalty; and being a little elevated by the wine which had just been drunk, he forgot the novel circumstance of its being a native female he was about to receive, instead of some well-bearded chief, so he gallantly advanced, and, to the utter dismay of her attendants, took her in his arms and kissed her.

This could have been quite awkward, but with great presence of mind the begum explained the situation to her horrified troops by saying that this was the way a padre greeted his daughter, even though, at the time, she was about fifty years old and he was just about five years older than her!

The negotiations between the begum and the British went on for a couple of years, and the British were finally convinced that the begum would be a useful and faithful ally. The new viceroy, Lord Cornwallis, confirmed her rights over her *jagir*. Half her troops were let out to the British at her expense, and her mercenary days now came to an end under the new Pax Britannica. She spent the next 30 years tending to Sardhana and its people. She worked on agriculture and rural indebtedness, and managed to increase the revenue from her *jagir* manifold. A contemporary historian William Francklin writes, 'An unremitting attention to the cultivation of the lands, a mild and upright administration, and for the welfare of the inhabitants, has enabled this small tract to yield a revenue of ten lakhs of rupees per annum (up from six...).'

Begum Samru was also a patron of art, especially if it glorified her. Not only did she support several artists and poets but was also fond of gifting lifelike portraits of herself to dignitaries. A poet, Gokul Chand, wrote a panegyric to her called *Zebul Tawarikh*.

She had an Italian-style basilica built in Sardhana, based on St. Peter's in Rome, and also a grand palace. The architect of the basilica was Antonio Reghelini, an Italian from the city of Vicenza. The highlight of the structure was an 18-foot monument showing the begum holding her court, surrounded by European and Indian courtiers, including her minister, Diwan Rae Singh, who was an ancestor of Jawaharlal Nehru. This tableau was carved in Italy by Adamo Tadolini, and was transported from Italy to Calcutta, then by water up the Ganga, and finally by bullock cart to Sardhana. The basilica is still a site for pilgrimage today.

The begum lived on friendly terms with the British, dining often with the resident. The British looked upon her with fascinated horror, describing her as 'a very little queer-looking old woman, with brilliant, wicked-looking eyes.' Skinner writes,

> She was cruel, unforgiving, relentless, deceitful, liberal only where self-interest required it, and courteous too often merely to hide enmity. One anecdote – it is given by Bishop Heber, and we believe is in the main correct – will serve to show something of her ruthless and implacable nature. A slave girl had offended her – an affair, we believe, of jealousy. The poor creature was brought before her – a hole dug in the earth under the floor of the room, in which she was buried alive – and, as if it had been trifling occurrence, her mistress smoked her hookah unconcernedly on this living grave.

Begum Samru died an immensely wealthy woman in 1836. She had a beautiful residence in Delhi in Chandni Chowk, just opposite the fort, gifted to her by the Mughal emperor. The Italian-style palace she built is now a wholesale market called Bhagirath Palace. During her lifetime, she had adopted and brought up her stepson Zafaryab Khan's grandson, David Ochterlony Dyce Sombre, as her heir. But, after her death, the British would not accept him as the ruler of Sardhana because of the doctrine of lapse they promulgated – without a direct blood heir, the state would lapse to the British Raj.

Whose Money Is It Anyway?

David Ochterlony Dyce Sombre, Begum Samru's heir, had a very colourful life, and deserves to be better known as the first Indian- and Asian-origin Member of the British Parliament – no it was not Dadabhai Naoroji! David Sombre did not inherit Sardhana; he did, however, inherit the begum's personal wealth, and travelled to England to fight cases against the government for the restoration of his territories. There he became the first Asian Member of the British Parliament from Sudbury (in 1841) and married a British aristocrat. When he objected to her adulteries, his wife managed to get him declared a lunatic and all his inheritance passed to her. She, however, died childless, and the estate reverted to the British government, which undertook to turn it over to its proper heirs.

Remarkably, nearly two centuries later, the battle for Begum Samru's inheritance still continues, with many putative heirs trying to get the British government to hand over her fortune. Hundreds of descendants and relatives of Reinhardt Sombre from all over the world have banded together, attempting to prove their claim to this fortune, now worth perhaps a billion dollars!

The Queen Who Would Not Yield

Kittur Chennamma

'Kappa? Nimageke kodabeku kappa? Neevenu nammavarondige uthira, bithira, nati nettira, danidavarige ammali. Kappa...'

[Tribute? You want us to pay tribute? Why should we pay you tribute? Did you till the land with our people? Did you sow, transplant the seedlings, heat or feed gruel for those working the field?]

Saroja Devi as Chennamma
in the film *Kittur Chennamma* (1961)

Chennamma was the queen of Kittur, a small principality in north Karnataka, who refused to let the British annex her state in 1824 in an early exercise of their ill-conceived doctrine of lapse, and fought them with great courage, albeit unsuccessfully. She is often called the first woman freedom fighter, predating the more famous Rani of Jhansi by a quarter of a century, and is a great folk heroine in Karnataka; there are innumerable folk songs like Lavanis, Kaifiyats and Bakhars and scores of books written about her; stadiums, airports and ships are named after her; and statues of her dot the landscape, including one in the Indian Parliament in Delhi.

Chennamma was born in the village of Kakati in the Desrut (area controlled by a Desai) of Kittur in 1778. She was the daughter of Dhulappagowda Desai and Padmavati. Kakati, a *jagir* of 29 villages, had been given by the Adil Shahis of Bijapur to her ancestor Mariamma, who had migrated there from Bijapur. This *jagir* was now held by her uncle Kannagowda. Chennamma was well educated. She was trained in Persian, Kannada, Marathi and Urdu, and was able to read books in all four languages. She was knowledgeable about the arts and music and had, surprisingly, trained in martial arts like horse riding, fencing, swimming and spear throwing and was also known to be a good hunter. She was beautiful, very fair, and later would often be called 'Chennagowri' by her husband.

Folk songs of Karnataka speak of Chennamma's romantic meeting with Mallasarja Desai, the ruler of Kittur. Mallasarja was hunting near Kakati when he shot an arrow at a tiger, killing it instantly. As he went towards it, a beautiful girl stepped forward from the trees saying that the tiger belonged to her as *she* had shot it. He then noticed two arrows in the tiger. Struck by love, he asked to call on her father the next day and instructed his retainers to carry the tiger to her house. Mallasarja duly called on Chennamma's father and asked for her hand in marriage. They were married in Kakati in 1793. Chennamma was 15 at the time.

Kittur was a small principality of 280 villages near Dharwad in north Karnataka. It had been founded by the two warriors, Hiremallasetty and Chikkamallasetty, when they were allotted the area by the Adil Shahis of Bijapur in 1585. They were Veershaiva, or Lingayats. Kittur's rulers continued as feudatories of Bijapur for many years till Aurangzeb conquered Bijapur in 1686, and the area came under Mughal dominion. After Aurangzeb's death in 1707, both the Nizam of Hyderabad and the Marathas fought over the area, and the Desai of Kittur, as the feudal ruler was now known, would pay tribute to whoever the hegemon was. In 1746, the Desai Rudragouda started paying tribute to the Marathas.

With the rise of Haider Ali in Mysore, a third major power became important in the politics of the Deccan, along with the Marathas and the Nizam of Hyderabad. Caught between the three, Kittur became a battleground. Virappa Desai died in a Maratha prison in 1782, and was succeeded by Mallasarja, his 17-year-old adopted son. Three years later, in 1785, Kittur was captured by Haider's son, Tipu Sultan of Mysore, who imprisoned Mallasarja in the Kapaladurga Fort. He escaped after three years and, by assuming various disguises, reached the pilgrimage spot of Babaleshwar, where he was sheltered by some relatives of his first wife, Rudramma. By then, in 1787, Kittur had been handed over to the Marathas by Tipu. Maratha suzerainty over this area was formalized by the treaty of 1792.

Chennamma lived in amity with Rudramma in Kittur. Rudramma was from a local Desai family and is said to have personally taken part in the fight against Tipu Sultan in the Battle of Desnur. She was well educated, knew Urdu and Persian, and helped Mallasarja in his official correspondence. In fact, most of the letters exchanged between Mallasarja and Tipu Sultan are said to have been drafted by her.

Over time, Rudramma had two sons born to her, Shivalingarudrasarja (Bapu Saheb) and Veerarudrasarja (Baba

Saheb). Chennamma herself had a son Shivabasavaraj (Bala Saheb) and she concerned herself with the education of all three. Mallasarja was a connoisseur of beautiful things. He patronized the theatre, dance, art and literature, and a new style of folk poetry, Dumdumi, was born in his time. The poet Amriteshvara wrote the *prashasti* (laudatory poem) *Mallendra Manasollasa Mantarangini* in 1810 in this style. Mallasarja was fond of clothes – he had robes from all over the country – and good food; the Kittur kitchens were famous. He was also an avid collector of plants of varying kinds and invested in creating botanical gardens. Chennamma was involved in the administration of the state, accompanying Mallasarja on expeditions, and sitting with him in court. She greatly cared for the people. There is an extant tale about how she funded Saidansab of Amatur to help rebuild a mosque in his village from her personal wealth, and another about her allowing African slaves who had escaped from the Portuguese to settle down in her kingdom.

In 1799, with the help of the Marathas and the Nizam, the British finally defeated Tipu Sultan of Mysore; he died fighting in the siege of Seringapatam. The British then turned their attention to the Marathas. In 1802, they signed the Treaty of Bassein with the last peshwa of the Marathas, Baji Rao II, who agreed to come under British protection because of the rising power of other Maratha nobles such as the Holkars and the Scindias.

Peshwa Baji Rao II was a suspicious and not very honourable man, whose character has been reviled by historians later as the reason behind the conflict within the Marathas, which eventually led to their defeat at the hands of the British. The peshwa did not look kindly on Mallasarja. The reasons attributed are various: he was apprehensive of the strength of Kittur; he was covetous of Kittur's wealth; even that he had been dreadfully insulted when Mallasarja had once refused to attend a dinner at Shaniwar Wada in Pune as, for an orthodox Lingayat like Mallasarja, it was unthinkable to eat with a Bhavi, a non-Lingayat.

In 1813, the peshwa came to the region to visit the Kumaraswamy temple at Sandur. Mallasarja was tardy in waiting on him. Meanwhile, neighbouring rulers such as Allappagowda Desai used the opportunity to complain to the peshwa about Mallasarja's exactions. By the time Mallasarja showed up to meet Baji Rao II, an insulted peshwa had moved on, leaving instructions for him to come to Pune. In Pune, Mallasarja was unceremoniously thrown into prison. He was fed poor food like millet mixed with ashes and, as a result, his health started deteriorating. His ministers kept negotiating for his release and finally the peshwa let him go three years later, when Mallasarja was at death's door.

Thus, in 1816, Mallasarja finally made his way back to Kittur, but he was unconscious by the time he reached, and died there. Shivalingarudrasarja was now crowned the ruler; his brothers had died by then. He was passionate about literature and wrote three books in Kannada. The chief minister was Gurusiddhappa, a legacy from his father's days, who was loyal to Chennamma. Shivalingarudrasarja was, however, overtly influenced by a faction of nobles led by Venkatarao and Malappa Shetty.

Kittur chose to help the British with troops in the Third Anglo-Maratha war of 1818 since Shivalingarudrasarja hated the peshwa, holding him responsible for his father's death. The British won the war and took over the peshwa's territories. They were now the overlords of Kittur. They signed an agreement with Shivalingarudrasarja, and he was to now pay an annual tribute to the British. The British promised not to interfere with the internal workings of the kingdom and guaranteed the inheritance of Kittur by Shivalingarudrasarja's sons and grandsons. He however had to hand over the Khanpur taluk to the British.

Chennamma was involved in the governance of Kittur for the next few years alongside her stepson. She was known for taking quick and accurate decisions in court. She kept the army in good fighting condition, and maintained a deep relationship with her people, building up incredible loyalty. The country flourished. The British political agent and collector for the region, St. John Thackeray, would come and meet Shivalingarudrasarja periodically.

In 1824, after ruling for eight years, Shivalingarudrasarja fell ill. He had been diagnosed with tuberculosis and had little hope for survival. Since Shivalingarudrasarja had no children (his wife Viramma was only 11 years old), it was decided that an heir would be adopted. In July 1824, ministers went out to meet members of his extended family in the kingdom, and finally a boy was selected.

Shivalingarudrasarja wrote to the boy's father, Balappagowda of Mastmaradi, about his intention to adopt the boy. The boy was brought to Kittur for training. The king still hoped to get better, and someday have a son of his own. He kept postponing the adoption of the boy. He also did not talk of his intention to adopt to Thackeray, although he met him during this period.

In September he became gravely ill, and finally realized that he was not going to survive. He wrote a letter to Thackeray saying that he was ill and was adopting Shivalingappa as his heir. A public ceremony of adoption was conducted. On the morning of 12 September, his confidant Malappa Shetty was sent with the letter to Thackeray. Thackeray immediately sent the British civil surgeon Dr Bell to Kittur, but the king had already died. Dr Bell was of the opinion that the king had died some time ago.

This is where the conflict began.

Thackeray argued that the adoption was not valid; as the only members of the royal family left alive were three widows – Chennamma, Jankiamma, the 16-year-old widow of her son Shivabasavaraj, and Viramma, 11, the widow of the deceased king – the state should lapse to the British. He took the stand that the king had had no intention of adopting anyone and that the signature on the letter sent to him was a forgery. The adoption, according to Thackeray, was carried out by the coterie of nobles *after* the king had died in order to retain power. He refused to believe all evidence to the contrary, including eyewitness accounts and letters, insisting they were all part of a grand conspiracy.

It is not difficult to understand Thackeray's motivation. His employer, the East India Company, was in India to make a profit, not to provide fair and just governance, though they often maintained a facade of 'doing the right thing'. Kittur was a prosperous kingdom, known to have a large treasury full of gold. The share of the prize money for the officer involved in any acquisition by the Company could be as much as one-eighth. It was often retirement money for the decision maker.

Unsurprisingly, Thackeray was very keen on acquiring control over Kittur, and wrote to his seniors to say that he thought that the adoption was a fraud and suggested that he take over the governance of Kittur until the matter was resolved.

There was a slew of correspondence between the commissioner of the Deccan at Pune, William Chaplin, the chief secretary, William Newnham, and the governor of Bombay, Mountstuart Elphinstone, from which it is quite evident that the British were looking for arguments to take over Kittur. These ranged from the boy being too distantly related, the nobles stealing from the treasury (in fact, 1,50,000 rupees having already been stolen), as only women were left in the family it was only right that the fief which had been granted to the family should be resumed, to simply saying the British would do a much better job at governance.

They finally decided to take over the treasury and governance, and conduct an inquiry into whether the adoption was valid. Thackeray immediately took steps to secure the treasury by setting his own seal on to it and posting his own guards in front of it.

Chennamma and her nobles were horrified at Thackeray's stance. There was nothing in their covenant which required the king to seek permission from the East India Company for adoption. Under Hindu law, a widow could and often did adopt after her husband's death. She immediately sent Rachappa, the vakil of Kittur, to Elphinstone on 8 October 1824. But the appeal did not evoke a favourable response.

Thackeray, now in control, behaved obnoxiously, not even allowing the usual expenditure on religious donations and festivals from the royal treasury, and ignoring all protests from Chennamma.

Chennamma wrote repeatedly to senior British officers, including Chaplin, complaining about Thackeray. A letter sent by her to Chaplin on the 11 October gives a good idea of what was going on in Kittur at the time.

'Unmindful, however, of the respect to which we are entitled... Sahib is taking an account of the stables, palkhanas, Siledar, sebundies, etc., every minute thing is subject to scrutiny; we can have nothing that we wish for.'

Unfortunately, Chennamma got no reply from Chaplin. She finally lost hope and called a meeting of her nobles on 18 October 1824. She gave a rousing speech, preferring to fight to death rather than submit the kingdom to the tyrannies of an outsider. 'These Britishers... do not know that the people of Kittur love freedom more than life... Kittur will fight to the last man on its soil. They would die rather than be slaves of the British.'

The Kittur garrison in those days consisted of 7,000 army men, 2,000 horses, 1,000 camels, 50 elephants and 16 cannons. Additionally, there were about 6,000 *shetsanadies*, or trained fighters, whose services could be requisitioned in times of war. A statewide muster took place, and the army was put on alert. Gurusidappa was Chennamma's chief advisor, and Virappa was the head of the army.

Chennamma also wrote to neighbours like the raja of Kolhapur for help.

Thackeray did not have much of an opinion on the Kittur rulers and thought to cow the Kittur populace with a show of arms. He asked British troops en route from Kaldhagi to Belgaum to take a detour through Kittur for some shock and awe; there were 500 infantry and a 100-horse artillery. The British officers also had their wives and children with them. They reached Kittur on 20 October.

On 21 October, Stevenson and Elliot, Thackeray's assistants, went into the Kittur Fort to ask the nobles to sign a bond guaranteeing the treasury, but they refused, saying no documents were to be signed without the orders of Chennamma.

Enraged, Thackeray asked the horse artillery to storm into the fort and capture the commanders. However, they were chased out by the Kittur troops, and about forty soldiers, and some women and children, were captured and brought to Chennamma. The soldiers were imprisoned, but Chennamma reassured the women and children that they would not be harmed and had them put up in the guest rooms of the palace.

Thackeray sent a message saying he was willing to give Chennamma 11 villages for herself if she surrendered. He then came to meet her the following day, but she refused to meet him on grounds of ill health.

The next day, 23 October 1824, when British soldiers went to the fort to relieve the treasury guards, they found the gates of the fort closed. There were now upwards of 5,000 troops inside the fort.

Thackeray asked the artillery to train their guns on the gate and gave Kittur a *'gharee'*, or 24 minutes, to open the gates, before blowing them open. After that time elapsed, the British guns demolished the gates and immediately a battalion of waiting Kittur troops poured out and attacked them. Chennamma, it is said, could be seen on the ramparts, astride a horse, wearing a helmet and a golden sword belt, the sword held aloft. This image of her riding into battle has been immortalized by countless statues.

Nearly a hundred British soldiers were cut down, and the rest fled. Chennamma's bodyguard, Amatur Syed Bala Saheb, shot down Thackeray as he stood near his palanquin; and the Englishman was then hacked to death by Kittur soldiers. Elliot and Stevenson were captured.

It was the day of Dussehra, and elaborate celebrations were arranged in the fort in the euphoria of this victory.

Meanwhile, the fleeing British soldiers reached Dharwad, where Thackeray had been stationed, and gave the news of the ignominious defeat to Fullerton, the assistant collector.

He immediately wrote to all the nearby British troops with an eloquent note: 'for God's sake send a force immediately without delay to Kittur. The artillery is cut to pieces.'

Elliot and Stevenson, still Chennamma's prisoners, were allowed to write to Chaplin on 24 October. They wrote that Kittur had no intention of surrendering. The nobles of Kittur wanted an immediate approval of the adoption, else they would do something in the nature of a *jauhar*. '[T]hey would first kill both of them; and then kill their own women, including Rani Chennamma whose honour they valued most, and then each one of them would die fighting on the sacred soil of Kittur rather than submit to the British rule in Kittur.'

The muster continued – there were now more than 10,000 men in the fort, and more were gathering at important points in the countryside. The British now feared a general insurgency in the region, along with an attack on Dharwad.

An immediate requisition of British troops was set up, and more than 25,000 well-equipped troops started marching to Kittur from all around the Deccan, from places as far away as Hyderabad and Madras. The British had no intention of giving in to Chennamma's demands, even though one of the hostages, Elliot, was Elphinstone's nephew!

Elphinstone was convinced that the fracas had happened because of the stupidity of Thackeray and his obnoxious behaviour. The people of Kittur had been pushed into this situation; he was not inclined to blame them or even Chennamma.

He then issued a proclamation, which said that the adoption was not valid, and that the Company would take over the governance of Kittur and look for an heir; if no valid heir could be found, the Company would 'resume' the lands.

He would, however, pardon all except for Gurusidappa. He generously said:

> A suitable allowance shall be made for the widow of the late Desai and such provision as the Government on enquiry may judge proper shall be granted to the other females of the family. The treasure and private property of the late Desai will still be considered as belonging to his widow and if any part of it has escaped plunder it will be restored to her.

He thought this would effectively quell the rebellion. This proclamation was spread far and wide in the land of Kittur.

To the great astonishment of the British, no one surrendered, even to these favourable terms. They cleaved to Chennamma, who kept up her correspondence, reiterating that she only wanted the restoration of the *samsthan* (kingdom), and that her countrymen were not willing to surrender under any circumstance their freedom to the British. As a gesture of goodwill, she let all prisoners except Elliot and Stevenson go.

The British, meanwhile, invited the neighbouring *jagirdar*s (small rulers) to join the attack against Kittur. The raja of Kolhapur, who had moved 5,000 of his troops to the border close to Kittur to help Chennamma, was firmly warned and ultimately could not gather the courage to take on the British. Kolhapur was later annexed under the same pretext by the British.

By 25 November, 25,000 British troops had surrounded Kittur. In the course of the British negotiations to free the prisoners, Chaplin, who had come down from Pune, supposedly assured Chennamma's vakil that if the remaining two British prisoners were freed, he would stop the war. The prisoners were freed on the night of 2 December. They talked of their gracious treatment by Chennamma and urged Chaplin to consider Kittur's demands.

However, Chaplin now said that he could not make any changes in the conditions of the proclamation, and gave a deadline of 10 a.m. the next morning for surrender.

This then was the choice. If Chennamma wanted, she could have surrendered and led a reasonably prosperous and comfortable life. Practically none of the people in the fort would have suffered materially if they surrendered; they would have continued living their usual lives, albeit under British rulers. However, they consciously decided that it was better to die than surrender, even though the choice facing the populace of Kittur was not dire.

And so, the final battle began. The Kittur troops engaged the British at various locations but were defeated. British guns started shelling the fort. The shelling from Kittur was weak; it is said that traitors had adulterated the gunpowder with millet and cow dung.

Finally, the British broke through on the night of 4 December. Virappa managed to escape with some soldiers. However, the three widows and most of the nobles were captured. Many were hanged, including Gurusidappa.

The treasury was gleefully counted. There was cash of 16 lakh rupees, and jewellery estimated at 4 lakh rupees. There were 3,000 horses, 200 camels and 100 elephants. The royal belongings were auctioned, and a prize amount of 12,60,000 rupees was determined for distribution, of which Colonel Deacon, who had taken command of the troops only three days before the final battle, got 1.5 lakh rupees! This loot of about 30 lakh rupees, at an exchange rate of 10 rupees to the British pound was about 300,000 pounds; the overall profit of East India Company from its *worldwide* operations that year was 450,000 pounds!

The fort and palace were demolished by Chaplin. He announced that anyone could buy the debris at 5 rupees per cartload. Many of the beautifully carved columns and doors of the fort and palace ended up being used in buildings in neighbouring towns.

Chennamma and her daughters-in-law were made to sign a document conceding Kittur to the British. They were then sent to the impregnable fort of Bailhongal for imprisonment. The ladies were given a pension of 40,000 rupees per annum. Chennamma died four years later in 1829, spending the interim years in prison engaged in religious pursuits. She was buried in Bailhongal with full military honours. Within a few months both her daughters-in-law died as well.

Chennamma's fierce spirit of independence is still celebrated by thousands of girls across the country, who drape themselves in classic Lingayat-style saris and recite her lines immortalized in the movies for countless school functions.

Kittur's Fighting Spirit

The British involved in Kittur had interesting backgrounds.

The Thackeray family were old hands in India; John Thackeray's nephew William Makepeace Thackeray, born in India, would go on to become one of the most celebrated Victorian authors.

Mountstuart Elphinstone, the governor of Bombay, was a most unusual man. An Indophile and educationist, he founded several educational institutions in India and wrote many books, including a history of India in many volumes; he actually later refused the post of Governor General of India twice because he wanted to finish writing his book! He was a Fellow of the Royal Society.

One of the prisoners who had been released by Chennamma, the 21-year-old Elliot, went on to have a very distinguished career. He was an Indologist and archaeologist who translated a number of Kannada epigraphs. He was a friend of Darwin and sent exotic birds to him from India. He eventually became a Fellow of the Royal Society for his contributions.

Kittur continued the struggle. Chennamma's lieutenant, Sangolli Rayanna, kept up guerrilla warfare to restore Shivalingappa, the adopted heir, to the throne, raiding British treasuries and strongholds, making it practically impossible for the British to establish themselves in Kittur. Folk tales say that he had sneaked into Bailhongal disguised as a sadhu, and Chennamma secretly gave him her jewellery before she died. He managed to keep up the rebellion till 1831, when he was betrayed while bathing, and hanged publicly. In his last breath, Rayanna said, 'My last wish is to be born again in this land to fight against the British and drive them away from this sacred land.'

Kittur sporadically revolted, in 1833, and again in 1836. In 1837, 1845 and 1857 Shivalingappa led unsuccessful revolts.

The fighting spirit of the people of Kittur was much admired by the British. Chaplin himself says of the Kittur rebels: 'They have drawn the sword and thrown away the scabbard.' Stevenson, political agent to Chaplin, talks about 'the ungovernable spirit and fury' of the Kittur troops. The finest tribute, however, was paid by Chaplin while reporting the final victory over Kittur; he recorded that 'the strong fort of Kittur were defended by a garrison of an unusually determined character for its spirit and energy.'

In 1831, Mr Nisbet, collector of Dharwar, says in his reports:

> Every day brings to light, some fresh disclosure to confirm the belief that the whole province is united in one common cause and the people have, by some means, been inspired with the idea that it may be possible to recover their independence.

India's Iconic Queen

Lakshmibai, Rani of Jhansi

> The Ranee was remarkable for her bravery, cleverness and perseverance; her generosity to her subordinates was unbounded. These qualities, combined with her rank, rendered her the most dangerous of the rebel leaders.
>
> General Sir Hugh Rose, officer commanding the force that took Jhansi and Gwalior, in his report on the action

Jhansi was a prosperous kingdom, with an annual revenue of about 25 lakh rupees. It was part of the Bundela ruler Chhatrasal's territories, who had set up an independent kingdom in Bundelkhand. When Peshwa Baji Rao I saved Chhatrasal from the Mughals in 1730, Chhatrasal famously presented his daughter, Mastani, to him as a bride, and handed over one-third of his territory to the Marathas, which included the Jhansi region. He also called Baji Rao I his third son. The peshwa appointed a subedar. *In 1804, after the defeat of the Marathas in the second Anglo-Maratha wars, the then* subedar *of Jhansi, Shivram Bhau, signed a treaty with the British, where he was acknowledged as an independent ruler under British protection. His descendant, Gangadhar Rao, became king in 1838.*

This is where the rani enters the scene. Manikarnika, as she was named, was probably born in 1828 (her year of birth is not certain) in Assi Ghat in Varanasi. Her father, Moropant Tambe, was a Brahmin, part of the small court of the exiled peshwa Baji Rao II in Bithoor. Her mother had died and 'Manu' would spend all her time with her father. Unusually for the time, she was educated along with her father's royal students. Like any well-educated Marathi boy (and unlike well-brought-up Marathi girls), she learnt to wrestle and ride and shoot and wield the sword as well as the scriptures, administration, strategy and war. She spoke Marathi, Hindi, Sanskrit and Persian. She loved the epics and the heroic tales of Shivaji. She was a pet of the peshwa, who called her *chhabili* (pretty girl), and a companion of Nana Saheb, his adopted son, who was about four years older than her. There is a legend that Nana would not take her riding on his elephant, and she swore she would one day own ten elephants of her own. It is said that a condition she placed at the time of her marriage was that Nana should be presented an elephant!

Given how exceptional she was, her father was reluctant to marry her off to an indigent Brahmin like himself, which would normally have been her lot. In 1842, when she was 14, priests searching for a suitable Karhera Brahmin bride for the middle-aged, widowed and childless king of Jhansi, Gangadhar Rao, chanced upon her, and found her appropriate; the horoscopes also aligned favourably. Gangadhar Rao was known to have a fearsome temper, and also rumoured to have liked dressing up in women's clothes periodically, as recounted in *Majha Pravas*, the memoirs of Vishnubhat Godse, a contemporary chronicler. However, the chance to be a queen was a rare one, and so the proposal was accepted. She was married in Jhansi, and given a new name: Lakshmibai. Her father also moved to Jhansi, where he was given a suitable post, and finally remarried, now that he could afford it.

Lakshmibai, after all the unusual freedom she had enjoyed growing up, suddenly found herself living the life of a traditional royal woman. She could no longer wear boy's clothes and gallop across the land, arguing about war strategy. She was not at all interested in the theatre, a ruling passion of Gangadhar Rao. She was now confined to the women's quarters by a strict Gangadhar Rao, dressed demurely and richly in women's clothes, and expected to engage herself in womanly pursuits. How she chafed at her confinement!

In 1851, she had a son, Damodar Rao, but the infant died within three months of his birth. In November 1853, Gangadhar Rao fell ill, and adopted a distant relation, five-year-old Anand Rao, and renamed him Damodar Rao, in the presence of the British resident, Robert Ellis. Gangadhar Rao died the next day. The rani wrote to Dalhousie, the then governor general, asking for Damodar Rao to be recognized as the new ruler of Jhansi. The British resident supported her request. His senior, Malcolm, also recommended her: '[The rani] is a woman highly respected and esteemed, and I believe fully capable of doing justice to the charge [of governing Jhansi].'

The doctrine of lapse was not universally implemented; adoptions by the kingdoms of Datia, Orchha and Jalaun had been sanctioned. The rani expected that her existing treaty with the British would be renewed, because of her excellent relations with them. Dalhousie, the British governor general, however, wanted Jhansi, and was not prepared to listen to any requests, even after strong support for the rani by the British officers of the Central Provinces. Jhansi was particularly important to the British, because acquiring it would create a corridor connecting the northern territories of the British with the southern ones, which were separated by a contiguous swathe of princely states in central India. Jhansi would provide a passage right in the middle. In later times, Jhansi became an important railway junction because of this.

So, in February 1854, Dalhousie and his council signed an order acquiring Jhansi. The rani was pensioned off with the measly amount of 5,000 rupees a month. Even this was withheld, being set off against some old debts owed by Gangadhar Rao to the British, which as state debts should have been rightly set off against the state revenues of Jhansi. Sir John Kaye, the famed British historian of the mutiny, called it 'the worst of Dalhousie's annexations' and said it was 'so ungenerous, and being so ungenerous, so unwise' and of 'extraordinary meanness'.

Though the enraged rani famously said, '*Meri Jhansi nahin doongi*' ('I will not give up my Jhansi') when she was informed about the annexation, she really had few options. She used the legal route, sending representations to the court in Calcutta, and later hiring a British lawyer, John Lang, and sending him to London to appeal to the Privy Council.

John Lang came to Jhansi to meet her. He describes her as

> a woman of about middle size... [Her face] must have been very handsome when she was younger and even now it had many charms... The expression also was... very intelligent... [H]er dress was plain white muslin, so fine in texture and drawn about her in such a way that the outline of her figure was plainly discernible – and a remarkably fine figure she had.

She also reportedly had a tattoo of a crescent moon and star on her forehead.

After the annexation, the British disbanded the Jhansi army, and stationed 400 infantry and 200 cavalry of the Bengal army in Jhansi. Captain Alexander Skene was appointed the administrator of Jhansi.

The rani was now forced to live as a private citizen. She had moved out to a smaller fort and was allowed to retain her personal jewellery. She no longer had any administrative powers. She maintained a good relationship with the British stationed there, while pursuing legal options, and writing extensively to all who could help her case. She also kept up her relationships with the other neighbouring Maratha nobles like Nana Saheb, Tantia Tope and the nawab of Banda (a descendent of Baji Rao I and Mastani, brought up as a Muslim). She was short of funds and had to borrow 1 lakh rupees from the British to do the *yagnopavit*, or sacred thread ceremony, of her adopted son in 1856, where she invited many guests from the Maratha fraternity.

Unsurprisingly, the British administration was unpopular. The new administration stopped funding the Mahalakshmi temple and many of the other religious and social activities the rulers had sponsored earlier. They also set up butcheries where cows were killed. By 1857, the British were sitting on a powder keg of dissatisfaction across the northern plains, from displaced rulers and soldiers who felt their religion was under threat.

As is well chronicled, the introduction of the ill-conceived greased cartridges provided the trigger for the soldiers' mutiny. The cartridges had to be torn open for loading with the teeth, and it was rumoured that beef and pork fat had been used for greasing them, meats that were taboo for Hindus and Muslims, respectively.

The mutiny sparked off in Meerut on 10 May 1857, where the Indian troops shot their British officers and took control. The mutineers moved on to Delhi and declared the aged, and highly reluctant, Bahadur Shah Zafar as their leader. The news spread like wildfire, and in many towns where the garrisons were stationed, the troops mutinied and killed all the British they could find, men, women and children. Their battle cry was '*Deen*', or religion. The slogan of '*Khalk Khuda ka, Mulk Badshah ka, Amal Deen ka*' ('The Universe is God's, the country the emperor's, governed by religion') would be chanted in the streets of every town that the mutineers captured. The dispossessed erstwhile ruler of that region would usually join them. This was primarily restricted to the Indo-Gangetic plain and central India; Bengal, the south, Punjab and

Rajasthan were not affected, and indeed supplied troops to the British.

When the news reached Jhansi, there were 65 British stationed there, including women and children. In daily expectation of a mutiny by the native troops stationed in Jhansi, the rani wanted the women and children sent to Datia – a princely state loyal to the British with enough soldiers of its own to be a safe haven – as she personally had no soldiers except 40 palace guards and would be unable to protect the British. The British administrator, Skene, however, would not listen. Instead, he moved all British officers from the cantonment to inside the fort, which was situated three kilometres away. The men would ride out to the cantonment every day.

The British army's native infantry stationed in Jhansi was a Muslim troop from Ayodhya. Led by Havaldar Gurbakhsh, they took control of the cantonment on 4 June 1857. A few British officers outside were attacked and killed on 6 June. The British inside the fort got nervous and killed all their Indian servants. Thereafter, Englishmen who ventured into the city were attacked and killed by the relatives of those servants. On 7 June, Skene surrendered to the mutineers on the condition that the British be allowed to proceed unharmed to Sagar, 200 kilometres away. However, as the British walked out in a sorry procession on foot, they were set upon and murdered by the mutinous troops.

The only white man to escape the massacre was a Lieutenant Reives. A few other men and women who had Indian blood were able to escape, as they were indistinguishable in looks from the local populace.

The murderous mutineers now went to the rani and asked her to give them 3 lakh rupees to go away. She had no money, and finally gave them her personal jewellery worth 1 lakh rupees. They left for Delhi, after drumming their war cry – *Khalk Khuda ka, Mulk Badshah ka, Amal Rani ka* – through the town.

The rani was now in a troublesome place. A massacre of the British had been committed in Jhansi by foreign soldiers from Ayodhya over whom she had no control, and who had then left after looting the Bengalis in the city, whom they saw as British collaborators. Jhansi was totally unprotected as she had no troops, and was vulnerable to attack from its traditional enemies, Orchha and Datia.

She wrote to Major Erskine, the commissioner at Sagar and the British administrator for the region, detailing the situation, and asking for help. Erskine wrote to her on 2 July, asking her to take charge of Jhansi until he was able to send British troops.

The rani did so, hoping that this would help in the restoration of the rights of Damodar Rao by creating goodwill with the British. Little did she know that the governor general, Lord Canning, had decided that she was complicit in the massacre, and had condemned her and the whole city of Jhansi to death, to be implemented as soon as the British were able to send off troops to Bundelkhand.

The rani took control of the administration. This was the first time she was ruling, and she turned out to be an inspirational ruler. She tried to implement her vision in this brief moment of relative peace, surrounded as she was by the maelstrom of the mutiny. All she had thought of and dreamt of, when she was unable to act, either sequestered in the women's quarters, or fighting to regain Jhansi – her vision of a fair and just society, inclusive and participatory at all levels – could now be implemented. The people responded, performing far beyond what anyone expected of them, and were ready to die for her; this included the foreign mercenaries. There is a saying prevalent in Bundelkhand even today that the rani would touch a lump of mud and it would become gold. Another saying goes '*Patthar mitti se fauj banai*' ('She created an army from stones and soil').

But her incredible vision of an inclusive state had no opportunity to survive.

She needed an army, and the one she created was unprecedentedly inclusive. There were a few Marathas. She re-enlisted some of the old Jhansi troops: Rajputs, Bundelas, Baghelas. She started enlisting people from lower castes such as the Kumhars and Kunbis. She also bolstered her troops with about 3,000 Muslim Vilayatis – non-Indian troops from beyond Afghanistan, typically of Iranian and Central Asian origin – and Afghan mercenary troops.

She decided to create a women's troop, which was unheard of at the time. Though there have been other women rulers in India in the past, some of whom were warriors, few of them had chosen to involve other women in the administration, let alone create an actual fighting corps of women and structurally integrate them into the army.

These were more than a thousand women, from all castes and religions. She had a set of personal companions, who have also become heroines in their own right: Kashibai, Sundar, Mandar, Heera Korin and Juhi. Jhalkari Korin, now a Dalit icon, later impersonated the rani to allow her to escape. Moti Natakwali, a dancer in Gangadhar Rao's theatre troupe whom he was inordinately fond of, became a gunner in charge of the cannon Bhavani Shankar, and had a fabled romance with the soldier Khudabaksh. They died fighting the British, and are buried together in Jhansi. The rani would train these women personally on the palace grounds. They would train at the Malkhambh, wrestling, pistol shooting, sword fighting, riding and artillery. The Malkhambh was an interesting Indian sport where gymnastic exercises would be performed on a tall pole. The rani, astride her favourite mare Sarangi, and dressed in a Pathan-style outfit, would ride all over the fort, encouraging her people.

The rani had resumed her regimen of daily exercise at dawn, after the death of her husband removed the restrictions imposed on her. She would exercise like a warrior with wrestling, weightlifting and riding her horse hell for leather.

She was fond of long luxurious baths in perfumed water. The run-off would be gathered in a tank outside, and women in the fort would carry it away for their own baths.

After her prayers, she would be attended by her courtiers; even if one of the 150-odd men was missing, he would be called to account the next day. After lunch she held public court; sometimes dressed in a white Chanderi sari, and sometimes in male clothes: pyjamas, a waistcoat and a fanned turban.

The only jewellery she wore was a string of pearls and gold bangles. She gave quick and clever judgements on civil and criminal cases, often punishing the miscreant herself with a stick.

Vishnubhat laments in his *Majha Pravas* that he would never again see the grand spectacle of the rani visiting the temple of Mahalakshmi. She would go in a chariot in great procession. Beautiful young maids would run alongside dressed in gold ornaments and red velvet shoes, waving fly-whisks or golden parasols. Musicians and drummers would lead the procession, ministers would accompany the queen on horseback, along with hundreds from the Velayati cavalry. Sometimes, however, she would dress as a man and just ride to the temple with a few companions.

The rani respected learned men, scholars, artists and musicians. She was a collector of rare books.

However, this halcyon existence was but a moment in time. Even during her brief rule of nine months before the British arrived, she had to contend with war. An attempt to overthrow her was made by Sadashiv Rao, a cousin of Gangadhar Rao, who declared himself king. Her troops chased him and captured him in Orchha. He was then imprisoned by the rani in Jhansi, and later hanged by the British. The rani also personally went after dacoits operating in Barwa Sagar and defeated the dacoit chief Sagar Singh in a quixotic personal duel. He then joined her retinue.

The neighbouring kingdom of Orchha, ruled by the aptly named dowager Ladai Rani, sent an army against her, which besieged Jhansi in September 1857. Lakshmibai wrote to the British asking for help but got no response (she still wasn't aware that they held her responsible for the massacre!). She got her people together, and they defeated the invaders and chased them back to Orchha. She also captured a number of cannons which she later used during the siege of Jhansi. She is supposed to have rewarded the gunner Ghulam Ghaus with her anklets.

The British, meanwhile, had called for their troops from all over the world, and had quelled the uprising in the north. Kanpur was taken on 16 July, and Lucknow and Delhi in September. By November, the rani finally realized that the British held her responsible for the Jhansi massacre. She wrote to them trying to explain that she had no part in the killings, but her explanations were rejected. They were now calling her the Jezebel of India, and comparing her to Boudica, the British queen who had brutally killed the occupying Romans.

The rani finally declared open rebellion. She introduced currency in her own name, and hoisted the red Jhansi flag. She lit up Jhansi as if it were Diwali, and constituted her council of ministers. She was not without hope. Bundelkhand still held out, with Tantia Tope as the commander of the forces of the new peshwa, Baji Rao II, Nana Saheb's brother, since Nana Saheb had disappeared somewhere in the Terai after the initial rebellion. Tantia controlled Kalpi, a hundred miles away. Many of the rulers of the region had also joined the uprising against the British, like the raja of Banpur and the nawab of Banda.

A specially constituted British force to quell central India, under the command of Sir Hugh Rose, reached Bundelkhand in January 1858 and moved towards Jhansi. They were offered resistance every inch of the way, not only from the many forts, but also at every mountain defile, and every village on the way. Tantia defeated a British army at Charkhari, capturing 3 lakh rupees and many guns. The British took nearly three months to reach Jhansi, finally arriving there on 20 March 1858. Besides the British troops, there were contingents lent by the begum of Bhopal, the queen of Orchha and the Nizam of Hyderabad, eager to show their loyalty to the British, and partake of the loot. Sir Hugh Rose asked Rani Lakshmibai to meet him unarmed, but she refused. She also refused to surrender, quoting a Marathi poet, Moropant: 'Heroes prefer death to infamy.' The British shelling of Jhansi started immediately after.

The rani held off the British for 10 days while waiting for relief as promised by Tantia Tope. The Jhansi cannons under gunners like Khudabaksh, Ghulam Ghaus, Lallabhau and Motibai kept up their cannonade of the British. There were sorties against the British, in which both men and women participated. Breaches were swiftly repaired, and defended to the death.

Tantia was delayed, as he had suffered a defeat at the hands of Sir Colin Campbell near Kanpur. He managed to regroup and reach Jhansi with 20,000 men. He engaged with the British in the Battle of Betwa on 1 April. However, under the anguished eyes of the rani watching from the fort, his contingent was soundly defeated, and had to retreat.

The rani was losing hope. A huge crack opened up on the south wall on 2 April. Jhansi defenders, including the rani, held off the British for as long as they could, but on 4 April, the rani left the fort, Damodar tied to her back, accompanied by some of her women warriors, companions and ministers, and about two hundred Afghan troops.

She encountered the British at Bhander, and escaped after hand-to-hand combat. She then rode continuously for 160 kilometres and reached Kalpi, joining the peshwa and Tantia, where she offered her sword, Shatrusanharini, at the feet of the peshwa. She was devastated and riven with guilt at having to abandon her beloved people to certain destruction, and her only objective now was to defeat the British.

The British announced rewards of 20,000 rupees for the rani and 10,000 rupees for the nawab of Banda. Sir Hugh Rose rested for three weeks in Jhansi and left for Kalpi on 26 April. They engaged with the peshwa's troops in the Battle of Kunch on 5 May. The rani commanded the Indian forces but they lost badly. The rani's companion, Ganga, was killed, and the British briefly hoped it was the rani. They regrouped, and fought a pitched battle at Kalpi on 22 May. It was close, but the British won once again. The kings of Banpur and Shahgarh vanished after the battle. With the capture of the peshwa's stronghold, the British thought that Bundelkhand had finally been won.

However, the Indian troops rose like the phoenix. The rani, the peshwa, Tantia and the nawab of Banda met with the tattered remains of their army at Gopalpur to decide future strategy. The peshwa wanted to escape to the Deccan. The rani, however, thought they needed an unconquerable fort and proposed the idea of conquering Gwalior.

On the face of it, it was a ridiculous idea. Jayajirao, the Scindia ruler of Gwalior, was extremely powerful and rich, and completely loyal to the British. However, with great bravado, the peshwa showed up in Gwalior, and asked for money and a safe passage to the Deccan.

The Scindias refused to help them, and on 1 June came out with an army of 8,000 to face the peshwa in Morar. As the standard account goes, there was an engagement, the Scindia fled, and the rani and her allies captured Gwalior.

Vishnubhat's hearsay account, however, is much more detailed and quite fascinating. He says that at Morar, the Scindia's troops were reluctant to fight the peshwa, since he was their nominal overlord. For many hours, the Scindia kept unsuccessfully exhorting his troops to fight. Meanwhile, many soldiers from both sides were busy eating watermelons together, which were growing on the nearby riverbed, since it was the peak of summer and they were thirsty! When the soldiers in the peshwa's army took up the rebel cry '*Deen*', it was echoed by the some of the Scindia's troops. A frustrated Jayajirao tried to fire the cannon himself, but apparently the mouths had been stuffed with millet by disaffected soldiers!

The Scindia gave up and fled to Agra. The peshwa's forces occupied Gwalior, and the Scindia family's fabulous personal effects were auctioned off for a pittance. Largesse was distributed all around, Brahmins were fed and prayers commissioned for victory.

Even before they could finish celebrating their victory at Kalpi, the British heard of the unexpected fall of Gwalior. They quickly marched there and besieged it. On 16 June, the rani defeated a British troop at the head of 10,000 riders at the Battle of Kota ki Serai. However, on 19 June, she was trapped by the British, apparently when her new horse refused to jump a small stream, Sonrekha, and she was fatally injured by a sabre cut. She managed to reach a small temple near Phoolbagh, and died there, after distributing the pearls from her necklace to her companions and committing Damodar to their protection. She was cremated there; a small memorial was built later. With her death, the people lost heart; the Gwalior Fort fell two days later and this was the effective end of the uprising.

The rani was gone, after blazing a brief trail in the sky. The rani's father, Moropant Tambe, was turned in by the *talukdar* of Akola, and hanged on 19 April.

Damodar Rao was awarded a pension of 200 rupees by the British and settled in Indore. He took up the new art of photography as a pastime. His son Lakshman Rao Jhansiwale and grandson Krishna Rao went on to work as freelance typists in front of the court at Indore. Their descendants live on.

The British crown took over the administration of India from the East India Company, and stopped all further acquisitions of the princely states.

Whatever the outcome of her valiant struggle, the rani is still remembered today as a national heroine, celebrated not only for her valour, but also because of her dream of establishing a fair, just and inclusive society, far ahead of its time.

Khub ladi mardani voh to Jhansi wali rani thi.
Bundele harbolo ke munh hamne suni kahani thi.

Poem by Subhadra Kumari Chauhan

Jhansi in the Aftermath

Vishnubhat describes the fate of Jhansi after the massacre in a masterpiece of black comedy. Jhansi, after the rani left, was given up to destruction with a *katl-i-aam*, a command to kill all adult men to avenge the massacre of the British, in which the citizens of Jhansi had actually had no hand! For three days, bloodthirsty British soldiers killed all men in sight. When the killing was officially announced as over, the survivors, who had managed to escape by hiding, were allowed to burn the dead, lying in the thousands.

A formal period of loot was then declared, which began at sunrise and ceased at sunset and was signalled by trumpets. The plundered goods were auctioned by the British, and the proceeds divided systematically. In a marvel of British organization and hierarchy, first, the white troops looted gold, silver, gemstones and precious fabrics. The books in the rani's famed library were torn apart to remove the silk binding on them. The next day, the Madras contingent systematically looted brass, copper and other metals. As per Vishnubhat, there were now no cooking vessels, or latches and hinges on doors left. The Hyderabad contingent then looted cloth, and all the residents were reduced to roaming about in scanty rags. Finally a mixed loot was allowed to the soldiers lowest in the hierarchy, where grain and any other sellable material was carried away.

When it was all over, Vishnubhat left Jhansi, penniless and starving, clad in a small towel. His hosts bid him a shamefaced farewell, profusely apologizing for having failed in their *atithi satkar*, their hospitality to a guest, although undoubtedly he could not have had a more memorable visit! After the fall of Gwalior, Tantia and the peshwa fled to Rajputana. Tantia amazingly managed to harry the British for over a year, all over Rajputana, Gujarat and Madhya Pradesh. In April 1859, he was betrayed to the British by Man Singh, raja of Narwar, and hanged. The peshwa disguised himself as a sadhu in January 1859. He managed to escape for four years before he was captured in Jammu and hanged in Bithoor. The nawab of Banda accepted amnesty in November 1858 and was awarded a pension of 400 rupees a month.

The Scindias, of course, continue to be wealthy, and politically prominent.

The Hundred-Year Rule

The Begums of Bhopal

> The writer, from a study of the histories of the world and from her knowledge of her own dynasty, has come to the conclusion that administrative capacity is more inherent in women than in men, and that nature specially intended them for rulers. Men are given bodily strength to earn their living and to enable them to fight in battles. Women have been granted the qualities of mercy, sympathy, toleration, fidelity and firmness. These render them specially suitable as rulers of kingdoms though no doubt education and careful upbringing are necessary for both sexes. Given these, women are superior to men.
>
> Sultan Jahan, Nawab Begum of Bhopal,
> *An Account of My Life*

The principality of Bhopal is truly an outlier in the history of India, and perhaps in the world. It is the only kingdom which was ruled by four women rulers in succession, for more than a century. This rule of women started with Qudsia Begum, who set the pattern: they were not just titular rulers, but hands-on administrators and decision makers. Most women rulers in India have had short reigns, eventually overwhelmed by the internal and external forces acting against them, but the nawab begums managed to navigate their kingdoms successfully through the prevailing storms which destroyed so many dynasties around them. Their enlightened and inclusive rule saw efforts to better the lives of the people, creating an early prototype of a welfare state.

The city of Bhopal was founded by the legendary Paramara king Bhoj as Bhojpal in the 11th century. The area around Bhopal was part of the kingdom of Malwa in the middle ages, which was conquered by Akbar in the 16th century. At the beginning of the 18th century, it had a classic feudal structure, ruled by petty Rajput and Gond chieftains who owed fealty to the local Mughal governor. After the death of Aurangzeb in 1707, with no central authority left to restrain them, local chieftains were busy raiding and occupying each other's territories.

Around this time, an impecunious young man from Afghanistan, Dost Mohammad Khan (1657–1728), came to India to make his fortune. He joined Aurangzeb's army, and after a while was posted to the Deccan. Cleverly offering his mercenary services, he managed to conquer many of the small fiefdoms, and created the kingdom of Bhopal. The kingdom waxed and waned according to the abilities of his successors and was under threat from the powerful Marathas.

In 1797, a long-lost descendant of Dost Mohammad, Wazir Mohammad Khan, showed up at the gates of Bhopal. His part of the family had been shunted aside decades ago, and hearing of Bhopal's troubles, he had come to offer his services to the beleaguered and ineffectual nawab.

He was warmly welcomed, and made the diwan and commander of forces. Thus began the revival of the fortunes of Bhopal, as he successfully held off Maratha attacks, suppressed local dissension and recovered lost territory. He made sure his son, Nazar Khan, was married to the then nawab of Bhopal Ghaus Mohammad's 15-year-old daughter, Qudsia, and designated as the heir, setting aside Ghaus Mohammad's 56 other children, which included sons, legitimate and otherwise.

Wazir Mohammad died in 1816, and Nazar Khan became the new nawab; Ghaus Mohammad had retired earlier. Nazar Khan managed to sign an agreement with the British in 1818 that guaranteed him and his descendants the rule of Bhopal. He was also rewarded with territory for his help to the British against the Marathas. Nazar was an efficient ruler, and particularly devoted to Qudsia. In 1818, a daughter, Sikandar, was born to Nazar Khan and Qudsia Begum. In 1819, a calamity befell the happy family. Nazar Khan was killed in a mosque in his palace while playing with his daughter, by a shot from his own pistol. The only other person present was Qudsia's eight-year-old-brother Faujdar, who said that the gun had gone off by mistake while he was playing with it. There were suspicions that Qudsia's dispossessed and aggrieved elder brothers, who had been set aside in favour of Nazar Khan, had coached their younger brother to shoot Nazar. A British report said that the gun had been fired so close to the face that there were singe marks on Nazar's body. However, it was publicly accepted as an accident.

The succession was now thrown wide open. Contenders included Qudsia's brothers, and Nazar Khan's elder brother

Amir Mohammad, who had been passed over by his father because of his debauchery.

On the third day after the death, the family and nobles got together for the Fatiha ceremony. To everyone's shock, the 19-year-old Qudsia made an unanticipated and surprising move. She produced a will ostensibly written by Nazar Khan, in which he declared as heir the future husband of his 15-month-old daughter, Sikandar, with Qudsia to act as the regent until she came of age. Qudsia was also carrying opinions by senior Islamic clerics saying that Islam permitted women to rule.

Everyone was horrified at the thought of a woman ruling, when there were so many able-bodied men in the family, especially in such turbulent times of constant war with the neighbouring Marathas. But Qudsia had primed her husband's chief advisors, the 'loyal quartet' of Shahzad Masih, Raja Khushwakht Rai, Mian Karam Muhammad Khan and Bakshi Bahadur Muhammad Khan, and they convinced the nobles present to accept Sikandar as the candidate who unified all contending factions, and to sign a declaration supporting her.

The document was sent to the British for approval, as Bhopal was now under their aegis. They were not very happy because they wanted a strong ruler as an ally against the Marathas. However, they agreed, influenced by their friends, the loyal quartet.

To further reduce dissension, Qudsia gave a generous *jagir* to her brother, Moiz, where he happily drowned himself in sensual pleasures. Her husband's elder brother, Amir, was tougher to dismiss. She finally struck a deal, betrothing her daughter to his son Munir, promising she would step aside in his favour after Munir came of age and married Sikandar.

This was quite a coup for Qudsia. She had kept a cool head and managed to orchestrate this in just three days after her husband's death, in the midst of mind-numbing grief as well as advanced pregnancy. The strain, however, was too much, and she miscarried.

Although Amir Mohammad had been temporarily appeased by a betrothal, he nonetheless tried to convince the British to rule in his favour as the true claimant to the throne. However, he got no support from them and bided his time. He kept pressing for an early marriage between Sikandar and Munir and encouraged Munir to keep trying to seize power. The 15-year-old Munir surrounded himself with rascally adventurers, and tried to capture small forts in the kingdom.

Qudsia complained to the British political agent for Bhopal, Mr Thomas Maddock, writing that Munir was leading a 'revolt against my authority', and that his advisor Jamal Mahommed Khan had embezzled six or seven thousand rupees from the Bhopal exchequer. Mr Maddock wrote to Munir admonishing him and warning that 'any one interfering in State affairs is the enemy of the British Government'.

These warnings, unfortunately, had no effect on Munir Khan, who made a plan to covertly attack the homes of all of Qudsia's principal ministers. Shahzad Masih and Bakshi Bahadur got wind of this, and after much fighting managed to capture Munir. Munir fell at Qudsia's feet and begged pardon. She ostensibly forgave him but exiled his father.

Qudsia realized that Munir would simply never be an appropriate nawab, and in 1827, she successfully had him declared impotent, based on the testimony of a courtesan, and refused to marry her daughter to him. (This was patently not true, as he had many children later.)

Qudsia then betrothed her daughter to Munir's brother Jahangir, who was eight years old at the time. She thus bought herself 10 more years of regency. She also took charge of Jahangir's upbringing and Amir Muhammad relinquished his claim in a letter. 'I have surrendered my rights as his parent. He should accept Qudsia Begum as his real mother and he should make it the object of his life to fulfill his duties to her. She is his master.' The British governor general sanctioned the new arrangements.

Both Sikandar and Jahangir were given the same royal education. They learnt combat, riding, leadership, administration, the arts, Farsi and the Quran. Sikandar excelled. She was strong and an excellent shot. Jahangir 'was indolent and unwilling to learn', and started causing Qudsia trouble.

But this was not Qudsia's only problem. Her supporters among the British officials posted to the region, Mr Maddock and Major Evans, had been transferred, and Major Henley was dead. Shahzad Masih, of the loyal quartet, had also died in 1829, presumably poisoned by Qudsia's detractors. The misogynistic Lancelot Wilkinson was appointed the British agent in 1830. He was revolted at the reversal of the 'natural order' of things. Qudsia's great-granddaughter Sultan

Jahan, the fourth begum of Bhopal, says in her biography of Qudsia:

> Mr Wilkinson... once declared to Qudsia Begum that history did not support the contention that women could be satisfactory rulers. When reminded by Qudsia Begum that a great lady had just ascended the throne of England he gave the astonishing reply that female rule was not allowed in Islam. His argument being that Fatima did not succeed to the Caliphate on the death of the Prophet (may peace and God's blessing be upon him).

Jahangir's family, unsurprisingly, cultivated Wilkinson assiduously, and started pressing for an early marriage. Wilkinson also supported them in their never-ending demands like change of tutors and higher allowances. A few years later, when the then governor general, William Bentinck, was passing by, Jahangir called on him in state and requested him to arrange an early marriage. Bentinck agreed.

Qudsia received a blunt letter from Wilkinson: 'Surely it is time for the Begum to accomplish it [the marriage] in order to allay any suspicion which may exist as to her motives for postponing matters.'

A formal consent to the marriage had to be taken from Sikandar. She was unwilling, anticipating trouble, but finally consented on the condition that Jahangir executed an agreement with her defining her position, and that the document be attested by Wilkinson. Wilkinson refused to do this as this was opposed to official custom.

Finally matters came to a head, and Wilkinson proceeded to Bhopal and informed Qudsia Begum that he would not return to his residence in Sehore till he had heard the sound of the drums proclaiming the nawab's marriage. He threatened the reluctant mother and daughter with the displeasure of the governor general, and warned them that they ran the risk of being confined to the fort and even losing the state. Sikandar then drew out an agreement between the nawab and herself and requested Qudsia to sign and attest it, which Qudsia agreed to.

Eventually, Nawab Jahangir Mahommed Khan signed the bond, unheard of previously, which read: 'I will not take any other woman to wife when I have married her daughter... I will try to carry out all her orders and wishes and I will not permit anyone to oppose her... I take the Begum as my mother... I will give her my hearty obedience always.'

The wedding took place in April 1835, and Jahangir became the nawab, though Qudsia still ruled as regent since he was underage. His family now plotted to kill both the begums and seize total control. Armed men were introduced into the city, but they were apprehended by Qudsia. All her complaints were dismissed by Wilkinson, who thought Jahangir was simply a high-spirited youth well within his rights. Wilkinson even mocked Qudsia's rages:

'But the Begum now begins to manifest frequent symptoms of furious passion approaching to insanity. At times she becomes quite frantic; and as one of the soldiers observed, more terrible to approach than a tigress.'

Qudsia's complaints to Lord Auckland, now the governor general, were also fruitless.

In 1837, Jahangir's family combined their forces and captured some forts. Qudsia sent an army under Raja Khushwakht Rai to win back the territories. They were successful, and finally besieged Jahangir in the fort of Ashta.

However, on Mr Wilkinson's advice, the governor general intervened. Jahangir was now of age, and Wilkinson had painted a picture of a family quarrel caused by a jealous mother-in-law unwilling to give up power to an able young man who was only asking for his rights.

Wilkinson showed up with troops stipulating that Qudsia had to hand over the reins of the government to Jahangir. She was given a *jagir* and asked to move away. The British government would guarantee her income and safety – if 'Qudsia Begum will not interfere in matters of State whatever action the Nawab may take, and will not conspire against the Nawab's life or the safety of the State'! Sikandar, unwillingly, returned to Jahangir as a dutiful wife.

Jahangir now started ruling as nawab. His family looted the country while he indulged himself. He was forever in conflict with Sikandar and she was forced to observe purdah. As a British official put it, Jahangir resented Sikandar since 'in Sikandar Begum the Nawab had a wife with abilities far greater than his own, an ambition as lofty, and a mind more even and more resolute.'

Sikandar soon became pregnant. As per the book *The Begums of Bhopal* written by a descendant, Shaharyar Khan,

Jahangir's family decided to kill Sikandar in 1838, so that they would have total control over the throne. She was five months pregnant at the time, lying in bed, when she heard Jahangir come up to her room. She was suspicious, but could not escape as there was no other exit from the room. She took a large *gao takiya* (round pillow) placed it on herself and covered it with a sheet. A drunk Jahangir came in and struck her with his sword. The blow was mostly absorbed by the pillow, but Sikandar was injured on the arm. Seeing the blood gush out, Jahangir was satisfied that he had killed her and left.

Sikandar fled to her mother, who had moved away to the Islamnagar Fort. Outraged, she complained to Wilkinson, but he dismissed it as a spot of domestic violence.

In 1838, Sikandar gave birth to a daughter, Shah Jahan, and continued staying with her mother. She never forgave her husband. According to Sikandar's descendent, Abida Begum, Sikandar's favourite sport became terrorizing Jahangir with gunfire, arrows and cavalry charges. She even captured him once and locked him up in a fort. He was released on the intervention of the political agent. To add insult to injury, she went to release him personally and shook hands like a chivalrous warrior.

Jahangir's rule was terrible for the state. Tyranny and corruption were rampant everywhere. Old and reliable officials had been replaced by corrupt and dishonest men, many of the cultivators left the state owing to oppression, bankers were forced to give up sums of money, women were abused and murders were thought of slight account. The state started building up debt due to profligacy and mismanagement.

Even Wilkinson, who was essentially responsible for the transfer of power to Jahangir, ironically had to write a letter to Jahangir's chief minister where he stated:

> The people of Bhopal say that they lived in peace and comfort under the protection of the Nawab Qudsia Begum who was a widow, but under the present Nawab, who is a man, they live in terror and misery... it is surprising that singing and dancing continue in the palace of the Ruler while his subjects are oppressed and in misery.

In 1844, Jahangir died at the age of 24, after ruling for six years. Wilkinson had been succeeded by Henry Trevelyan as the British political agent. The British now acknowledged Sikandar's six-year-old daughter, Shah Jahan, as the ruler, with her uncle Faujdar Khan (who had shot Nazar Khan, Qudsia's husband!) as the regent, and Sikandar as advisor. Qudsia asked the British to make Sikandar the ruler, but the British disagreed, excluding her because they were punishing her for her armed uprising against Jahangir, whom the British supported.

There were conflicts inherent in this system of dual control, and within a year, Faujdar Khan resigned and Sikandar became the sole regent with British support. Qudsia had achieved her long-standing objective – the dream that her daughter, and her daughter after that, would rule independently as any male ruler would.

Qudsia was now allotted a *jagir* of 7 lakh rupees, which she administered like a small state. She remained in Bhopal in an advisory capacity, and spent most of her time on charitable works, and bringing up her granddaughter. She was treated with great respect by her daughter, who never sat in her presence.

It is important to note how Qudsia Begum set the tone for the sound governance of the kingdom by her daughters and granddaughters in the years to come. An excellent financial manager, upon assuming power in 1819, she gradually rid her kingdom of all its debt to the British. She lived an extremely frugal life, running a small cottage industry on the palace premises to support her personal expenses. An account from her later life shows the annual expense of her personal staff as 22 rupees. Her income from her personal *jagir* was 7 lakh rupees at the time!

She spent 2 lakh rupees a year on charity. As her biographer Sultan Jahan says, 'She bestowed jagirs from her own Estate to learned and godly persons and on old and loyal servants. These grants... were distributed almost equally between Mahommedans and Hindoos.'

Qudsia also looked after her cultivators, and granted remissions at the time of natural calamities. By all accounts, cultivators were generally happy and prosperous and the Begum would tour her estates from time to time to hear their grievances. She also set up a bell in her garden that anyone could ring for justice.

Abida Begum recounts a tale about her ancestors. Qudsia used to sit under a tree outside her palace every evening and meet her people. She and Sikandar would often go out at night in disguise to understand what the people thought. One night, she forgot the password to re-enter the palace, and the guard shooed her away, refusing to let her in. She sat on the porch all night and was recognized by other officials and finally let in in the morning. The guard feared for his life but was rewarded with a *jagir* instead for being so steadfast in his duty.

Much ahead of her time, Qudsia also built a system of pipes throughout the city to provide piped drinking water to Bhopal from an upper lake. She commissioned a Scots engineer David Cook, and spent between 5 and 6 lakh rupees to build the system. She then placed a sum of 3 lakh rupees with the British government to be a perpetual endowment for the upkeep of the waterworks, enjoining her heirs never to charge the common people for water. This supply of pure water stamped out cholera in the city, which used to be prevalent all over India at the time.

She also started the construction of a very fine mosque, Jama Masjid, in 1832, which was finally finished in 1857, at a very modest cost of 5.5 lakh rupees.

During the reign of Shah Jahan Begum, the British decided to build a railway connecting the north of India with Mumbai, and asked Gwalior, Indore and Bhopal to share the expenses as it would run through their territories. Seeing the great good it would bring the people, Qudsia contributed 15 lakh rupees from her private purse.

She was also extremely disciplined in her personal life. Sultan Jahan reminisces:

> Qudsia Begum was very fond of exercise and constantly walked for hours either in her Palace gardens or elsewhere, sometimes even she would enter the houses of poor people in the city and enquire about their condition and stay chatting with them. It was her custom only to eat two simple meals a day... took her dinners only after receiving the news every night that all her subjects had taken meals.

Qudsia was very devout. Though she was illiterate and could not even sign her name, she knew the whole Quran by heart. Besides the five prayers laid down in the Quran, she would often wake up at 2 a.m. and pray until 8 a.m. in a small room attached to her bedroom with nothing on the floor except stones.

She was, however, fond of a few good things. Sultan Jahan Begum recalls that 'She was very fond of giving parties and banquets both to European and Indian ladies, and on these occasions there was singing and music both by professional singers and by the Begum herself.' She would accompany herself on a dhol.

But despite her devotion, Qudsia was, in many ways, an iconoclast. She came out of purdah at the age of 34, after the death of Shahzad Masih. She had been carrying out conversations with officials and Europeans behind a curtain, but felt it was akin to governing in the dark. Anticipating an uproar over her decision, she planned the process with her usual degree of meticulousness. She first discussed the matter with her brothers, and enlisted their support, in case Jahangir or her husband's family raised any problems. They gathered many examples from history of Muslim women rulers who had held durbars.

She then carried out the process step by step over nearly twenty days, gradually exposing herself to more and more people. It must have caused great excitement at a time where there were very few unveiled women, and none in her kingdom. She then started riding lessons for the first time in her life. She excelled and conceived a lifelong passion for good horses.

She also made her daughter, Sikandar, abandon the purdah, though at that time it was understood that Sikandar's husband would rule the state, and not her.

Interestingly, Bhopal, under the begums, punched way above its weight with the British. It was not only well-governed, prosperous and progressive, but also the one state that never fought with the British and had offered their help to them on every possible occasion. This was a calculated move. Surrounded on all sides by the far more powerful Marathas, they could only look to the British for any hope of survival.

At Lord Lytton's great durbar in Delhi in 1876, Qudsia Begum was granted the order of the Crown of India, with the words 'token of Her Imperial Majesty's regard' for her loyalty and honour. Throughout the Bhopal State she is remembered with love and reverence for many generous deeds of charity. Those deeds and alms to the poor and needy were done for the sake of God and not from a desire for fame.

Qudsia Begum died in 1881, at the age of 81. She was buried in a grave which she had had dug some years previously. Before her death, the grave used to be filled with grain every year, which would be distributed along with an equal weight of silver to the poor.

This is some of the advice she left her daughter in her will:

> You should help the people although God helps everyone.
>
> Always keep to the union with the reigning power, that is the English Government, and consider their wishes prior to your own.
>
> You should personally hear the complaints of those who are oppressed and you should do them justice. Abstain from oppressing the people.
>
> You should dismiss cruel officers under you as you will be held responsible for their tyranny.
>
> Be moderate in everything.
>
> Trust more to old servants than new.
>
> Think of the result before commencing anything.
>
> You should take counsel in all matters and never depend on your own judgement.
>
> You must keep your expenses within your income and should never incur debt. You should always cut your coat according to your cloth.

The reign of Sikandar Begum (1844–68 CE) is considered the golden period of Bhopal. She paid off the kingdom's debt of 24 lakh rupees, accumulated by Jahangir. She implemented many administrative and structural reforms and soon Bhopal began to be considered one of the best managed states in the country.

During the uprising of 1857, Sikandar cannily bet on the British, and fully supported them. She prevented her own troops from mutinying by doubling their wages. Qudsia Begum worked very closely with her during this fraught time, digging into her savings for funds. The British garrison, which had mutinied in Sehore, was surrounded and neutralized by her troops. She suppressed maulvis who called for jihad against the British, banned the circulation of pamphlets, and even the mysterious chapatis, which became a symbol of resistance for the rebels. There was a rumour that rebels were circulating chapatis through the villages as a symbol of resistance. She lent troops to the British for the siege of Jhansi.

The British were very grateful to Bhopal and heaped Sikandar Begum with honours. In 1860, when Shah Jahan was 21, and came of age, she abdicated in favour of her mother, who then took on the title of nawab. Sikandar is supposed to have convinced the British to reopen Delhi's Jama Masjid to prayer, which they had shut down after the 1857 mutiny. She washed the courtyard with her own hands and was the first person to pray in it since the mutiny.

Sikandar Begum had a masculine physique, and was supposed to be as strong as an Amazon. She had a very powerful presence, her steely gaze, apparently, enough to frighten anyone. As French traveller Louis Rousselet puts it in his book *India and Its Native Princes*:

> Her thin face, lighted up by a pair of intelligent eyes, expresses such a singular amount of energy that one must be aware of it beforehand in order to realise the fact that a

> woman is before you. The costume itself aids the illusion... Her gestures and manners... reveal the sovereign and the autocrat accustomed to find everything yield to his all powerful will.

He also praises her administration. Many roads and dams were built. She worked 12 hours a day, travelling all over the kingdom on horseback, living in her tent. She forbade slavery, and established schools and orphanages in every centre of population. The English considered her administrative ability wonderful!

Sikandar Begum died in 1868 of a kidney ailment. She was succeeded by her daughter Shah Jahan Begum. Shah Jahan was quite different from her formidable mother, very petite and feminine, and interested in the arts. She had been reluctantly married off to the much older Baqi Mohammad Khan, the son of one of the loyal quartet. He was given the title of Umrao Doulah. In an interesting role reversal, the suffix *doulah*, meaning bridegroom, was used for all the male consorts after that. However, much to the horror of her mother, who had advised her to ignore her husband, Shah Jahan went into purdah at his insistence. Baqi Mohammad Khan was a simple man, obsessed with physical fitness, who worked out for three hours in the morning and then had six kilos of *rabri* for breakfast!

In 1858, Shah Jahan gave birth to a daughter, Sultan Begum, her only child. It was not a happy marriage, and Baqi died in 1867, leaving Shah Jahan a relieved widow. In 1871, Shah Jahan married her advisor, Siddiq Hassan, an extremely religious man. Qudsia was opposed to the marriage as she disliked Siddiq and viewed him as a parvenu. She refused to attend the wedding, or receive the groom, which created a permanent rift between her and her granddaughter.

Shah Jahan had a successful reign, conducted through purdah, though much of the rule was in the hands of her husband. She built many beautiful buildings, and was a great patron of art and culture. She funded the Aligarh Muslim University, and even built a mosque in Woking, England. She was very religious, however, and introduced separate laws for Hindus and Muslims. She was estranged from her daughter Sultan, which Sultan, in her autobiography, blames on the malign influence of Siddiq.

Sultan Begum became the nawab in 1901. She had been brought up in her early years by her tough grandmother, Sikandar. She had had a gruelling schedule since an early age, which Sikandar believed inculcated discipline. Her day began with open-air exercise at 5 a.m., and lessons continued nonstop till 6 p.m. on the Quran, calligraphy, English, Persian, arithmetic, Pashtun, fencing and riding. Later, as part of her training, she was sent official papers every day on which she had to issue orders as per her own discretion.

Sikandar Begum had brought in an eight-year-old boy, Ahmad Ali – from a branch of the royal family of Jalalabad in Afghanistan which had fallen on hard times – to be trained as Sultan Jahan's husband. In 1874, Sultan Jahan married him; at the time, they were both 16. She does not talk too much about her husband in her autobiography; an idea of their relationship can be had from her granddaughter Abida Sultan's memoirs – she remembers seeing scars on her grandmother Sultan's back from her husband's beatings 20 years after his death.

Under Sultan, Bhopal was run almost as a modern welfare state. She was a great educational reformer, especially for women, establishing free and compulsory primary education in 1918. From 1920 until her death, she was the chancellor of Aligarh Muslim University. She pioneered widespread inoculation and vaccination programmes and improved the water supply and standards of hygiene and sanitation.

Sultan had been brought up in purdah on her mother Shah Jahan's orders, and wrote tracts defending it. However, after her abdication in her sixties in favour of her son Hamidullah Khan, she gave up purdah at her son's behest, to enable her daughter-in-law and granddaughters to give it up as well, and in a volte-face insisted that the purdah was 'not prescribed either by God or the Prophet'.

She died in 1930 at the age of 71.

Bhopal became part of the Indian Union in 1949. The last nawab, Hamidullah Khan, had three daughters. The eldest, Abida Sultan, was the heir apparent and, in keeping with family tradition, shot, rode, played football and hockey, and was among the first women in India to get a pilot's licence. But she migrated to Pakistan, and after Hamidullah's death in 1960, his second daughter, Sajida Sultan, became the nawab. She was the wife of Iftikhar Ali Khan, the nawab of Pataudi, and the mother of Mansoor Ali Khan, both of whom were famous cricketers. After her death, Mansoor Ali Khan became the nawab of Bhopal, as well as the nawab of Pataudi. His son, Saif Ali Khan, the movie star, is the current nawab of Bhopal and Pataudi.

The begums of Bhopal were extraordinary in their uniqueness at a time when women hardly ever ruled in their own right. These amazing women dominated their environments, each in her own different way, and set up a dynasty that is unique to not just India but world history even today.

A Bourbon Prince and a Journey to Mecca

Qudsia's main advisor, Shahzad Masih (loosely translated as 'Christian prince'), had a truly romantic background. His real name was Balthazar de Bourbon; he was Catholic and claimed descent from the Bourbons, the French royal house.

He was descended from a Frenchman named Jean Philippe Bourbon, who had showed up in Akbar's court in 1560. Jean Phillippe said he was from the Bourbon royal family, and had been kidnapped and sold into slavery in Egypt. He had risen under the service of the Caliph of Egypt, until his successor had him thrown into prison. After many an adventure, including dalliances with Abyssinian princesses who fell in love with him, he had found his way to India. He served in Akbar's army, and married Juliana, the sister of Akbar's Christian wife. He was given a *jagir* and the important position of the head of the imperial harem, which was inherited by his descendants. Eventually their family fled from Delhi to Gwalior during Nadir Shah's invasion nearly two hundred years later. Shahzad's father eventually found his way to Bhopal in the 1780s. Shahzad Masih had become the senior-most political counsellor of Nazar Khan. He eventually married an Englishwoman called Isabel Stone who came to be called 'Sarkar Dulhan'. Other Bourbons also came and settled in Bhopal, and by the mid-19th century it was estimated that there were now 400 Bourbon families descended from Jean Phillippe, 300 of whom were in Bhopal. Many still live there today. A British Royal recently published a book claiming that one of the Bhopal Bourbons is the first in line to the lost French throne!

In 1863, Qudsia and Sikandar went on a visit to Mecca with a large entourage and gave much to charity, setting up permanent rest houses for pilgrims from Bhopal. They however found Mecca badly managed, dirty and unsafe. When Sikandar Begum, who justifiably prided herself on her management skills, heard that the Ottoman sultan spent as much as 30 lakh rupees a year on upkeep, she was horrified, and reportedly said that if that money was given to her, 'you would see what state of order and cleanliness I would keep the good city in... I, in a few days would effect a complete reformation.' Understandably, they were not popular with the local administrators. The local chief was already upset because they were not eating the food he sent them every day as a mark of respect, which they found bland and tasteless, much preferring their own Indian food.

Qudsia, to her lasting regret, could not travel to Medina, even though she remained in Mecca for four months, as her reputation for wealth meant she was in great danger of being kidnapped. There had already been a foiled attempt at kidnapping. When travelling on a camel to Mecca, some twenty Bedouin had tried to lead her camel away from the rest, evidently to rob her; however, a slave whom Qudsia had freed flung himself on the neck of the camel and shouted for help, with the result that her armed escort came up and drove off the Bedouin.

Acknowledgements

I would like to thank my mother, Chandra Garodia, for creating a beautiful world growing up where we could follow our inclinations and passions, without even an inkling that there were roles that we as women were supposed to play. My father, Balkrishna Garodia, for creating a home drowned in books where knowledge and reason were worshipped for their own sake. My husband, Manoj Gupta, for his warm support and for taking so many responsibilities off my back. My sisters, Aparna, Manjari, Meenakshi and Shruti, for their unstinting support and encouragement. My sister-in-law, Nidhi Gupta Williams, for her support.

At Hachette, Thomas Abraham, for making my dream of writing possible. Poulomi Chatterjee for her vote of confidence, and her team members Cibani Premkumar and Sohini Pal for patiently working with me line by line.

Sandipan Deb at *Swarajya*, who started me on this journey by publishing the first few of these stories, and the readers whose appreciation encouraged me to dare.

My nieces and nephews Justin Williams, Pia Geismar, Neil Saran, Soham Kapadia, Uma Geismar, Vedita Kapadia and Vihana Kapadia who have patiently put up with (and hopefully enjoyed) the innumerable tales from history I regale them with.

Further Reading

I am listing a few books I consulted, which would be good for further reading, though a very large number of other books, articles and reports were also used.

I must recommend Archive.org as an incredible resource for historical documents, especially British-era books and papers.

The Bhaumakara Queens

Binayak Misra, *Orissa under the Bhauma Kings*, 1934.

Biswarupa Das, 'The Bhaumakaras of Orissa', thesis, Utkal University.

Elin Sand, *Woman Ruler: Woman Rule*.

Didda

Sir Marc Aurel Stein, trans., *Kalhana's Rajatarangini: A Chronicle of the Kings of the Kashmir*.

Raziya Sultan

John Dowson, *The History of India: As Told by Its Own Historians, the Muhammadan Period, the Posthumous Papers of the Late Sir H.M. Elliot*, 2nd ed., 1952.

Minhaj-al-Siraj, *Tabaqat-i-Nasiri*.

Rudrama Devi

Cynthia Talbot, *Precolonial India in Practice: Society, Region, and Identity in Medieval Andhra*.

Richard M. Eaton, *A Social History of the Deccan, 1300–1761.*

The Heroines of Chittor

James Tod, *Annals and Antiquities of Rajasthan.*
Kaviraj Shyamaldas, *Vir Vinod.*
S.K. Banerji, *Humayun Badshah.*

Rani Durgavati

Alexander Cunningham, *Report of a Tour in the Central Provinces and Lower Gangetic Doab in 1881–82.*
Eyre Chatterton, *The Story of Gondwana.*
Vincent Smith, *The Oxford History of India.*

The Rani Abbakkas of Ullal

Frederick Charles Danvers, *The Portuguese in India.*
George Havers and Edward Grey, ed., *The Travels of Pietro Della Valle in India.*
Kailash Misra, *Abbakka Rani: The Unsung Warrior Queen.*
Sarojini Shintri and Kurukundi Raghavendra Rao, *Women Freedom Fighters in Karnataka.*

Chand Bibi

Abul Fazl, *Akbarnama.*
Mahomed Kasim Ferishta, *History of the Rise of the Mahomedan Power in India till the Year A.D. 1612*, trans. John Briggs.

Nur Jahan

Abraham Eraly, *Emperors of the Peacock Throne*, 2001.
Ellison Banks Findly, *Nur Jahan: Empress of Mughal India*, 1993.

Rani Karnavati of Garhwal

Ajay S. Rawat, *Garhwal Himalayas: A Study in Historical Perspective*.

Samsamud Daula Shah Nawaz Khan and Abdul Hai Khan, *Ma'asir al-Umara*, trans. Beni Prasad and H. Beveridge.

Rani Mangammal

R. Sathyanatha Aiyar, *History of the Nayaks of Madura*.

Velcheru Narayana Rao, David Dean Shulman and Sanjay Subrahmanyam, *Symbols of Substance: Court and State in Nāyaka Period Tamilnadu*.

Chennamma of Keladi

L.D. Barnett, *The Journal of the Royal Asiatic Society of Great Britain and Ireland*, 1910 [doi 10.2307_25189640].

Lennart Bes, 'Toddlers, Widows, and Bastards Enthroned: Dynastic Successions in Early-Modern South India as Observed by the Dutch', research paper, Leidschrift: Historisch Tijdschrift, 27 January 2012.

Stanley Lane-Poole, *Aurangzib and the Decay of the Mughal Empire*.

The Attingal Queens

Manu S. Pillai, *The Ivory Throne: Chronicles of the House of Travancore*, 2015.

P. Shungoonny Menon, *History of Travancore from the Earliest Times*.

T.K. Velu Pillai, *The Travancore State Manual*, rev. ed., vol. 2, 1996.

Rani Tarabai

John Dowson, *The History of India: As Told by Its Own Historians, the Muhammadan Period, the Posthumous Papers of the Late Sir H.M. Elliot*, 2nd ed., 1952.

Muhammad Hashim and Khafi Khan, *Muntakhabu-l Lubab*.

Richard M. Eaton, *A Social History of the Deccan, 1300–1761*.

Ahilya Bai Holkar

Charles A. Kincaid, *A History of the Maratha People*.

Jawaharlal Nehru, *The Discovery of India*.

John Malcolm, *A Memoir of Central India: Including Malwa and Adjoining Provinces*.

Velu Nachiyar

M. Geetha, *Velu Nachiyar Novelil Penniya Sinthanagal*.

Madhan Kumar, *Thamizh Is Not Just a Language: The Valour*.

Begum Samru

James Baillie Fraser, *Military Memoir of Lieut.-Col James Skinner, C.B.*, vol. 2.

Kittur Chennamma

Sadashiva S. Wodeyar, *Rani Chennamma*.

Lakshmibai, Rani of Jhansi

Amritlal Nagar, *Akhon Dekha Gadar*.

Mahasweta Devi, *The Queen of Jhansi*.

Vishnubhat Godse, *Majha Pravas*.

The Begums of Bhopal

Lieut.-Col. Willoughby-Osborne, *Historical Sketch of the Reigning Family of Bhopal*, trans. the Rev. William Wilkinson, 1870.

Nawab Sikandar Begum of Bhopal, *A Pilgrimage to Mecca*, trans. and ed. Mrs Willoughby-Osborne, 1870.

Nawab Sultan Jahan Begum of Bhopal, *An Account of My Life*, trans. C.H. Payne.

Nawab Sultan Jahan Begum of Bhopal, *Hayat-i-Qudsi: Life of the Nawab Gauhar Begum Alias the Nawa Begum Qudsia of Bhopal*, trans. W.S. Davis, 1918.

Shaharyar Khan, *The Begums of Bhopal: A Dynasty of Women Rulers in Raj India*.

Siobhan Lambert-Hurley, *Muslim Women, Reform and Princely Patronage: Nawab Sultan Jahan Begam of Bhopal*.

William Hough, *A Brief History of the Bhopal Principality in Central India*.